STAY
WOKE

optation colorblind racism colorism cross-cutting issue culture of poverty dehumaniza
versity dog whistle politics epistemology of ignorance false equivalence gaslight
plicit attitudes intersectionality meritocracy microaggression misogynoir nationa
oliberalism race racial euphemisms racialized social system racism respectability pol
erse discrimination transracial white fragility white privilege whitesplaining w
premacy affirmative action American dream antiracism Black girl magic capita
izenship co-optation colorblind racism colorism cross-cutting issue culture of pov
humanization diversity dog whistle politics epistemology of ignorance false equival
slighting implicit attitudes intersectionality meritocracy microaggression misogy
tionalism neoliberalism race racial euphemisms racialized social system rac
rectability politics reverse discrimination transracial white fragility white privi
itesplaining white supremacy affirmative action American dream antiracism B
l magic capitalism citizenship co-optation colorblind racism colorism cross-cut
ue culture of poverty dehumanization diversity dog whistle politics epistemolog
orance false equivalence gaslighting implicit attitudes intersectionality meritoc
croaggression misogynoir nationalism neoliberalism race racial euphemisms racial
ial system racism respectability politics reverse discrimination transracial w
gility white privilege whitesplaining white supremacy affirmative action Ameri
ram antiracism Black girl magic capitalism citizenship co-optation colorblind rac
orism cross-cutting issue culture of poverty dehumanization diversity dog whistle pol
stemology of ignorance false equivalence gaslighting implicit attitudes intersectiona
ritocracy microaggression misogynoir nationalism neoliberalism race ra
hemisms racialized social system racism respectability politics reverse discrimina
nsracial white fragility white privilege whitesplaining white supremacy affirma
tion American dream antiracism Black girl magic capitalism citizenship co-opta
orblind racism colorism cross-cutting issue culture of poverty dehumaniza
ersity dog whistle politics epistemology of ignorance false equivalence gaslight
plicit attitudes intersectionality meritocracy microaggression misogynoir national
oliberalism race racial euphemisms racialized social system racism respectability pol
erse discrimination transracial white fragility white privilege whitesplaining w
remacy affirmative action American dream antiracism Black girl magic capital
zenship co-optation colorblind racism colorism cross-cutting issue culture of pov
umanization diversity dog whistle politics epistemology of ignorance false equivale
lighting implicit attitudes intersectionality meritocracy microaggression misogyn
ionalism neoliberalism race racial euphemisms racialized social system rac
rectability politics reverse discrimination transracial white fragility white privi
itesplaining white supremacy affirmative action American dream antiracism Bl
l magic capitalism citizenship co-optation colorblind racism colorism cross-cutt
ue culture of poverty dehumanization diversity dog whistle politics epistemolog
orance false equivalence gaslighting implicit attitudes intersectionality meritoca

STAY WOKE

A PEOPLE'S GUIDE TO MAKING

ALL

BLACK LIVES

MATTER

TEHAMA LOPEZ BUNYASI
AND CANDIS WATTS SMITH

NEW YORK UNIVERSITY PRESS

New York

New York University Press
New York
www.nyupress.org

References to Internet websites (URLs) were accurate at the time of writing.
Neither the author nor New York University Press is responsible for URLs
that may have expired or changed since the manuscript was prepared.

Library of Congress Cataloging-in-Publication Data
Names: Lopez Bunyasi, Tehama, author. | Smith, Candis Watts, author.
Title: Stay woke : a people's guide to making all Black lives matter /
Tehama Lopez Bunyasi and Candis Watts Smith.
Description: New York : New York University Press, 2019. |
Includes bibliographical references and index.
Identifiers: LCCN 2018057315| ISBN 9781479874927 (cl : alk. paper) |
ISBN 9781479836482 (pb : alk. paper)
Subjects: LCSH: Black lives matter movement. | African Americans—
Social conditions—21st century. | African Americans—Race identity. |
United States—Race relations. | Race discrimination—United States.
Classification: LCC E185.615 .L66 2019 | DDC 305.896/073—dc23
LC record available at https://lccn.loc.gov/2018057315

New York University Press books are printed on acid-free paper,
and their binding materials are chosen for strength and durability.
We strive to use environmentally responsible suppliers and materials
to the greatest extent possible in publishing our books.

Manufactured in the United States of America

10 9 8 7 6 5 4 3 2 1

Also available as an ebook

For André and Ximena

Contents

Introduction

Everyone has heard of "Black Lives Matter." #BlackLivesMatter went viral in 2013. It is a seemingly innocuous slogan that has caused a great deal of rancor among some Americans. It is a social movement that expanded globally and has inspired millions of people but seems to have dissipated over the past couple of years. Many folks believe either that the Black Lives Matter movement is (or was) focused primarily on uprooting police brutality or, on the other end of the spectrum, that it is (or was) simply an anti-police rallying cry. Neither of these impressions captures its essence or its vision. Furthermore, the movement has not dissipated but instead has evolved, as social movements tend to do. In this book, we take a step back not only to debunk certain myths about this social movement but also to illuminate the lessons that this contemporary Movement for Black Lives provides to people who are interested in being effective racial justice advocates and antiracists.

Black Lives Matter—the hashtag, the slogan, the movement—is an effort to bring attention to the precarious nature of Black lives in the United States. It is concerned with the various ways that Black people across an array of identities—including those who are gay, lesbian, queer, transgender, poor, formerly incarcerated, undocumented, and/or differently abled—face special challenges that must *all* be attended to in order for *all* Black people to attain equality in the United States and in order for the United States to truly say that it is an egalitarian and free society.

In this book, we use our expertise as scholars and educators to get you thinking about why a movement called Black Lives Matter rose to prominence during the *first* self-identified Black president's *second* term in office. Relatedly, we'll get you thinking about how this moment in American political life relates to a deep history of structural racism. We'll have you critically examine many things that you probably take for granted or perhaps have never considered—including the ways in which you may participate in reproducing racial inequality—and do so in a way that brings otherwise-dry social science scholarship to life.

Who Should Read This Book?

Stay Woke participates in the public discussion about race in order to guide people through the structural and ideological systems of contemporary American racism. We aim to enrich our readers' understanding of the role that race and racism play in American society, treating the twenty-first-century Movement for Black Lives as a teachable moment. With that said, we know that not everyone will get on board with what we have to say, but that's not what we're looking for. Instead, we aim to convince enough people that until Black lives begin to matter, the United States of America will never be a liberal, egalitarian democracy. We know that not everyone will get on board with this book because they will not believe the information we share; the facts we provide will be new, shocking, and sometimes inconceivable to some. But, as they say, truth is stranger than fiction. We cannot make this stuff up, and we have not. We rely on accurate portrayals of US history and society. We rely on peer-reviewed books and articles, well-researched reports from reputable organizations, and data publicly provided by the US government. We integrate aspects of critical race theory with social science inquiry. We know that not everyone will get on board with this book because we are "academic elites with an agenda." Yes, we have an agenda, best characterized as an effort toward antiracism. The interpretations and perspectives are our own, and as Charles L. Edson, an affordable-housing attorney, wrote, "If any are controversial and serve to keep the reader awake, so much the better."[1]

——————

How Should You Use This Book?

Stay Woke is a little unorthodox, but the structure of this book is inspired by the many conversations we have had with our students, generational peers, colleagues, and college administrators, as well as folks from social justice organizations and antiracist trainings. Each chapter provides some insight into a contemporary or historical aspect of anti-Black racism in order to cultivate the reader's identity as an antiracist or "one who strives to change the norms and practices that allow racism to exist," as explained by the prominent sociologist Eduardo Bonilla-Silva.[2]

We begin in chapter 1, "On the Matter of Black Lives," by looking at why the Black Lives Matter movement is necessary. By illustrating how structural racism operates and detrimentally impacts the lives of Black people, we set the table for collectively thinking about how to enact change. We know that there are plenty of people who are looking to fight back, so throughout the book we provide tools and ideas about how to do so—especially for those of us who benefit from white privilege.

We have noticed that progressives and conservatives do a lot of talking past one another. They throw around all kinds of esoteric words and reference concepts that seem universally understood, but both groups often have different meanings in mind. To facilitate your way around the bumpy terrain of racial language, we have placed a glossary near the front of the book, in chapter 2, "All the Words People Throw Around" (as opposed to in the back of the book, where most glossaries are relegated) so that we can all be on the same page about some basic (and advanced) racial terminology. You can read each entry one by one as they appear or out of order; you can refer to them when they come up in the book (we boldface these concepts as they appear throughout the text) or when the pundits on the news bring them up; but ultimately, it is a toolkit we have built for folks who want to know more so they can do more.

There are also some commonsense notions that we aim to reexamine here. In chapter 3, "The Politics of Racial Progress," we evaluate the extent to which US society is on a steady march toward a postracial reality. We make clear that although Americans love the idea of racial progress, it is not inevitable. Racial progress is the product of resistance, demands, and vigilance. In chapter 4, "Are You Upholding White Supremacy?," we consider how difficult it is to see what is right in front of us: our own behavior. Here, we highlight how average Americans—progressives and conservatives across racial lines—talk *around* race. We bring attention to this issue in order to show how even well-meaning patterns of behavior can serve to the detriment of the most vulnerable people in society.

Afterward, in chapter 5, "It Doesn't Have to Be This Way," we elucidate the fact that the policies that cause the most problems are drawn up and implemented at the state and local levels of governance. What this means is that we don't need to have the ear of someone on Capitol Hill; instead, we each can take on leadership positions and advocate for the changes we need most in our own city halls and state legislatures. As the civil rights and human rights activist Ella Baker explained, we are better off with ten thousand candles rather than a single spotlight.[3] You'll find that in chapters 3 through 5, taken together, we cover what we believe are essential points of information for those who want to dig in to learn more as well as resources for political action.

At the time of this writing, justice-minded Americans are protesting a lot because there is a lot to protest—neo-Nazis and the so-called alt-right have been emboldened to come out of the shadows of the internet, migrant families are being separated, water rights and environmental regulations are being scaled back, and white citizens are calling the police on Black people for napping while Black, grilling in the park while Black, or waiting for their friends at Starbucks while Black. We want this book to inspire political novices to action and to reinvigorate those activists who are in the streets, so in chapter 6, "Twenty-One Affirmations for the Twenty-First Century," we provide bite-sized food for thought to nourish the racial egalitarian in us all.

One Last Thing

We are both mothers, wives, and daughters. We are both political scientists and experts in our fields. One of us was motivated to earn her PhD because she wanted other people to know that Black women are perfect . . . ly able to produce knowledge, inspire students, and interrogate some of society's most difficult questions. The other was motivated to receive her doctorate, in part, because Black mentors told her that was something she could and should do and modeled how to use that platform to advocate for social change. One of us is a Millennial. The other is a member of Generation X. Together, the two of us have a combined twenty years of classroom experience at seven universities and colleges in six states.

We have spoken to some unknown large number of students, faculty members, rooms full of college administrators, and social justice activists about matters of race and racism. And we have both noticed many of the same patterns of thinking and speaking about race, racism, and potential solutions to eradicate racial inequity. What we find is that an overwhelming proportion of people we talk to genuinely value the idea of a racially equitable society, but they are uneasy about talking about racism. Some have never had the opportunity to talk about racism, and they do not want to use the wrong words. Some are unsure about whether the United States is inches or miles from officially being declared a racism-free country. Some want to make sure that they are doing everything to not be a racist, but they are not yet aware that more is required of them if they actually want to work for racial justice.

We wrote this book because there are many people who want to help bring about racial equality and have been looking for help to take steps in the right direction; these people bring us hope. We wrote this book because we love Black people. We also wrote this book because we fear for the lives of our children, our husbands, our extended families, and our students who have a higher probability of being victims of state violence or of a vigilante who is suspicious of their presence and doubtful of their humanity. As mentioned, we hope to convince and encourage more people to live out their lives in a way that pushes us closer to living in a society where all Black lives matter. We use our expertise to do so, but we know that we are not above critique. We write from a posture of intellectual humility, which means that we are well aware that we don't know it all. In fact, sometimes we disagree with each other, but through our friendship and respect for each other, we are able to offer fresh perspectives, persuade each other, or teach the other something new. We invite our readers to challenge us, share their perspectives, and teach us.

1

On the Matter of
Black Lives

———

Let's imagine a street lined with high-rise buildings. One of them is burning. What do you do? All of the buildings matter, but the one on fire matters most at that moment.[1] The thing is, if you don't put out the fire in the burning building, you risk all of the surrounding buildings burning down as well. This is the message of the Black Lives Matter movement: Black lives are under attack, and we all ought to galvanize a sense of urgency to address the direct, structural, and cultural violence that Black people face.[2] It's not only the right thing to do, but the fate of the entire neighborhood depends on it. We, as a society, cannot say we are all free and equal until those who are at the bottom of various domains of our society—political, economic, social—are also free and equal.

Needless to say, this message of mattering sounds differently to different people. This is perhaps best illustrated by the competing hashtags in response to #BlackLivesMatter, such as #AllLivesMatter and #BlueLivesMatter. These rejoinders, or at least the motivation behind these alternative hashtags, we believe, can best be understood with the help of social science research, which tells us that Americans across different racial groups see the world differently. This is one of the few facts that social scientists actually agree on.[3]

On matters related to **race** and **racism**, white Americans and Black Americans, on the whole, have almost diametric perceptions about the way the world works. Latinx[4] and Asian American attitudes often fall somewhere in between these viewpoints, sometimes closer to Blacks', other times closer to whites'.[5]

There are many reasons for this divide, but one that strikes us as particularly noteworthy is the tendency for Americans to surround themselves with (or be surrounded by) people who are very similar to them. For example, one study showed that if the average Black American had one hundred friends, eighty-three of them would be Black, eight would be white, two would be Latinx, and the rest would be of some other race. If the average white person had the same number of friends, he or she would have one Black friend, one Latinx friend, one Asian American friend, a few friends of other races, and ninety-one white friends. Perhaps more striking is the finding that nearly 75 percent of whites do not have any nonwhite friends.[6]

Intuitively, this makes sense. We live in a racially segregated society. We tend to live in neighborhoods with people of similar racial, ethnic, and socioeconomic backgrounds. We go to schools with people who are demographically similar to us. And at eleven o'clock in the morning on Sundays, when many Americans go to church to worship, their communion with one another still initiates the most segregated hour of the week.[7] As we will explain, this reality is the outcome of historical and contemporary public policies, but it is also due to the choices of individuals, some of whom have more choices and greater latitude to pick and choose than others. Ubiquitous racial segregation across several domains of American life means that whites, Blacks, Latinxs, Asians, and American Indians live very different social, political, and economic realities.

People across racial groups also have different relationships with racial inequality and racial injustice. As such, when members of different racial groups hear "Black Lives Matter," some are likely to interpret the meaning of that message in different ways. Some folks may hear "White Lives Don't Matter" or "Black People Hate the Police," thus leading them to defensively declare, "All Lives Matter." We should like to note that these interpretations are quite

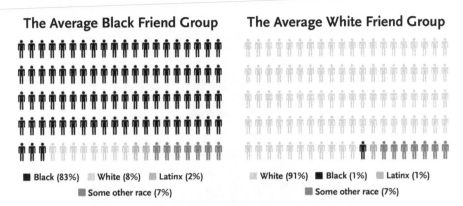

The Average Black Friend Group   The Average White Friend Group

Black (83%)   White (8%)   Latinx (2%)   White (91%)   Black (1%)   Latinx (1%)
Some other race (7%)   Some other race (7%)

The average Black friend group and the average white friend group. (Ingraham, "Three Quarters of Whites")

antithetical to what the participants of this social movement intend to communicate. Its supporters might be afraid, tepid, or even suspicious of some police officers, but they are not anti-police, mostly just anti–police brutality. They are not even anti-white, because that too would be antithetical to the purpose of the movement; although, to be clear, they are anti-**white supremacy**. While these alternative interpretations serve to undermine Black protestors' efforts to codetermine the narrative that explains ongoing racial inequality, they show us that some people are simply oriented toward inequality in a totally different way than others.[8]

For other people, the message of "Black Lives Matter" resonates clearly. In this slogan, they hear, "Yep. Black Lives *Don't* Really Matter" or "[Insert name of any Black person] Could Be Next," thus leading them to suggest that something needs to be done about **racism** in US society. Supporters and participants of this movement, like those of previous Black social movements, believe that "we must do what we can do, and fortify and save each other—we are not drowning in an apathetic self-contempt, we do feel ourselves sufficiently worthwhile to contend even with the inexorable forces in order to change our fate and the fate of our children and the condition of the world!"[9] Again, different life experiences lead to alternative perspectives of how the world works, what our roles are in it, and what we can do to change it for the better.

Photo by Mariah Warner.

The phrase "Black Lives Matter," generally speaking, is an odd thing to hear in the first place, particularly in the twenty-first century. If we could travel in time and report back to Frederick Douglass or Sojourner Truth, they might be surprised to learn that a major social movement that began nearly a century and a half after the ratification of the Thirteenth Amendment (which abolished slavery) and during the first self-identified African American president's *second* term in office is premised on the notion that Black people's lives are in a precarious position. Indeed, that is the point: "The brilliance of the slogan 'Black Lives Matter' is its ability to articulate the **dehumanizing** aspects of anti-Black **racism** in the United States."[10]

Many Americans often feel a sense of cognitive dissonance when they hear this slogan chanted in the street, printed on T-shirts, and debated by pundits on the evening news. On one hand, native-born Americans and immigrants alike have been taught that if people play by the rules and work hard, everybody has an equal opportunity to succeed. The path mapped out toward the **American dream** is indelibly imprinted on our brains; our shared language of individualism and value of **meritocracy** is practically learned through osmosis. We find comfort in knowing the formula to American-styled success like we know the back of our hand. On the other hand, a movement that suggests that some lives matter less/more than others has developed well past the historical era when Black Americans were first eligible for full **citizenship**. Something does not compute. Right?

These two dueling ideas existing at the same time is discombobulating. Martin Luther King Jr. predicted that this weird sensation might arise, noting that the thing about a Black political movement is that it "is much more than a struggle for the rights of Negroes. It is forcing America to face all its interrelated flaws—**racism**, poverty, militarism, and materialism. It is exposing the evils that are rooted deeply in the whole structure of our society. It reveals systemic rather than superficial flaws and suggests that radical reconstruction of society itself is the real issue to be faced."[11] His insights are as true now as when he was alive.

What are these flaws? Where did they come from? How do they evolve and persist? People in US society tend to have different answers to these questions because they have different historical narratives about these aforementioned flaws. And the truth of the matter is that most white Americans are simply not proximate to some of these problems, especially that of racism, or at least not in a way that disadvantages them. What this means is that despite the fact that anti-Black racism is pervasive in US society, there are many people who are shielded from even taking **race** into consideration. Racism is so embedded in our language and rhetoric, our political and economic institutions, and our social interactions (or lack thereof) that without any intention to do so, scores of people end up perpetuating racism by simply going about business as usual.

A NOTE ON THE STATUS OF BEING WOKE

Just so we're all on the same page, we should mention that having knowledge about the facts of racism and the mechanisms that (re)produce racial inequality doesn't necessarily make someone "woke." There are many people who know the facts and use them to insist on anti-Black narratives and pursue public policies that enhance inequity. Knowledge is a necessary but not sufficient component of being antiracist. You have to put your knowledge to use in order to eradicate the problems of racial injustice.

By moving beyond the dominant **colorblind** or postracial narrative of US society, we gain more leverage to answer those questions as well as a few others: How could we ameliorate these flaws? What could our society look like if these flaws did not exist altogether? The contemporary Movement for Black Lives has served to highlight many of the modern-day factors that prevent the United States from listening to its better angels, thus providing an illustrative teaching moment for those who are interested in working toward developing an **antiracist** society. We hope to provide readers the tools to partake in the debates around **race**, to navigate spaces of contestation on issues of **racism**, and to participate in antiracist movements in contemporary US society in a more fully informed way. We wrote this book for students of racial justice to critically engage and interrogate these factors. *Stay Woke* is for those who seek to engage in life in the United States from a different perspective.

We focus on Black lives, specifically, for three reasons. First, anti-Black racism is deeply embedded in the foundations of this country, including its founding documents, its institutions, and its policies, past and present. Second, from birth to death, Black people, on average, experience a very different United States than do members of other racial groups. When these experiences accumulate, layering one on top of the other, it becomes clear that there is a necessity for a social movement that reinvigorates calls for racial equality and racial justice in the twenty-first century. We do not mean to suggest that other groups do not matter, which brings us to the third reason: when we lump together the beautiful and the terrible histories and experiences of "people of color," we do all of them a disservice. The history of genocide and contemporary marginalization of Indigenous Americans, the history of slavery and contemporary mass incarceration of Black Americans, the history of exclusion and contemporary double standards set up for Asian Americans, and the history of colonization and contemporary demonization of Latinxs are inextricable intertwined, but they are not synonymous. Our intention is not to participate in an Oppression Olympics but instead to avoid universalizing the experiences of Americans across ethno-racial groups.

Coming back to the issue at hand—the matter of perspective—we use this chapter to outline some cold, hard, uncomfortable facts about the precariousness of Black life in the United States. Our aims are to make sure that we are all on the same page about the matter of Black lives and also to illustrate the axiom that "injustice anywhere is a threat to justice everywhere."

Some Uncomfortable Facts

The twenty-first-century Movement for Black Lives began to stir in 2013 after a jury acquitted George Zimmerman of the murder of Trayvon Martin. In reaction to the acquittal, Alicia Garza wrote a love letter to Black people, and she ended the letter by writing, "Black people. I love you. I love us. We matter. Our lives Matter." Patrisse Cullors, her friend, put a hashtag on it, and Opal Tometi helped to build a network of folks who wanted to unite under that message: #BlackLivesMatter.

The Black Lives Matter (BLM) movement has become known as one that is primarily concerned with police brutality, but it is actually one that is broadly concerned with raising awareness of ongoing racial disparities, developing empathy for Black life, and ending anti-Black **racism**. Since the development of the hashtag, many other organizations have joined to develop a united front under the moniker the Movement for Black Lives (M4BL)—which consists of about four dozen local and national organizations such as the Black Youth Project 100, Mothers Against Police Brutality, the National Conference of Black Lawyers, and BLM as well. While the focus of these organizations is on Black lives, the founders of the BLM movement assert, "when Black people get free, everybody gets free."[12]

AVERAGES, ANECDOTES, AND OUTLIERS

As social scientists, we aim to paint portraits of society that are not as detailed as Kehinde Wiley's but also not as interpretive as Jackson Pollock's. In order to find a happy medium, we rely on "averages," central tendencies, or what is "most common." We might use words like "many" or "most" almost synonymously with "on average." Average describes what you are most likely to see in this world.

Sometimes, you will read something, and think, "That cannot be true because I once knew a guy who . . ." This is an anecdote. An anecdote relies on one case, perhaps illustrative, but it does not carry the weight of an average. "Averages" rely on many, sometimes hundreds, thousands, or even millions of cases. We rely on data from large opinion polls, nationally representative surveys, peer-reviewed journals and books, and even the US Census Bureau to make claims throughout this book. We provide facts rooted in data.

Sometimes, you will read something and think, "This cannot be true because Obama was elected . . . twice!" Yes, Obama, Oprah, LeBron James, and Beyoncé are *phenomenal*. But they are what we call outliers. These people represent exceptions to the rule and do not represent the average, everyday person. Some people achieve beyond our wildest dreams, but many people do not or cannot because of compounding inequality. In other words, there are other people who can do what these people can do, but most of us cannot and do not because we are *average*.

Most Americans agree that **racism** still exists in the United States, but many people have a narrow understanding of what racism is. This makes sense. There are various interests involved in making a particular definition of racism dominant. For example, the leaders and participants of the civil rights movement made an effort to define racism as systemic and institutional, but the Nixon administration only a few years later was able to narrow this definition to one of overt intention to discriminate on the basis of **race**.[13] While there is some overlap between the two conceptualizations, two individuals each relying on a different definition of racism will probably never come to a shared conclusion about how to eradicate racism and its progeny. Being cognizant of the cacophony of definitions of racism with which Americans are faced helps us, as educators, to realize how difficult it is for students of **antiracism** to separate misinformation and disinformation from an otherwise-complex reality.

Typically, when people think of racism, they think of Jim Crow, lynchings, police with dogs, the N-word, and other overt behaviors and attitudes.[14] That is an accurate depiction of *a type* of racism, but racism also exists in other, more covert and enduring forms, which we call structural racism. Structural racism refers to the fact that political, economic, social, and even psychological benefits are disproportionately provided to some racial groups while disadvantages are doled out to other racial groups in a systematic way. In the United States, this has resulted in white Americans having greater political, economic, social, and psychological benefits, *on average*, while people of color have more political, economic, social, and psychological disadvantages, *on average*. Nobody needs to do anything with bad intentions for structural racism to persist, but people across racial groups can intentionally or unintentionally assist in perpetuating racial inequalities. The thing about structural racism is that it is embedded in our everyday affairs, making it difficult to see if you do not know what you are looking for. Consequently, it is unclear to some people why such a Movement for Black Lives needs to exist.

In the remainder of this chapter, we provide a slew of data that illuminates the ways in which Black citizens find themselves at risk in various domains of life in the United States. We start with the most contentious: policing and the criminal justice system. Then we move to highlight racial disparities in more mundane areas of our lives: housing, education, wealth, health, and employment. We hope that by presenting the evidence across various areas of society, the fact that Black lives are consistently marginalized becomes clearer.

——————

Police, Crime, and Justice

Many people, including a number of the movement's supporters, believe the Black Lives Matter movement is primarily focused on the police and police brutality. To be sure, it is the protests against such violence that made Black Lives Matter a household name. While this social movement is assuredly concerned with broader conceptions of the way that Black people are marginalized and contend with violence in US society, its attention to policing has been so impactful because it is a domain where people can point to individuals, policies, and patterns of behaviors across police departments to show that something is wrong and has been wrong for some time. An understandable ire arises from knowing that "there was [a] lynching every four days in the early decades of the twentieth century. [Over a century later, it's] been estimated that an African American is now killed by police every two to three days."[15]

The historian Russell Rickford explains,

> By confronting **racist** patterns of policing, Black Lives Matter is addressing a reality that touches the lives of a wide segment of people of color. Structural racism in the post-segregation era generally has lacked unambiguous symbols of apartheid around which a popular movement could cohere. Yet mass incarceration and the techniques of racialized policing on which it depends—"broken windows," stop-and-frisk, "predictive policing," and other extreme forms of surveillance—have exposed the refurbished, but no less ruthless, framework of **white supremacy**.[16]

Unlike overt racial bigotry and racially discriminatory Jim Crow–era laws, structural **racism**, as we see it play out today, has a "now-you-see-it, now-you-don't,"[17] elusive quality to it. Prior to the civil rights movement, folks could point to racial bigots in their legislature and racist laws in state constitutions; but today laws are written in a racially neutral way, and political leaders have become deft in their use of **dog whistle politics**, making it more difficult for many people to directly identify sources of racially disparate outcomes. However, when you see several videos of unarmed Black people shot by police

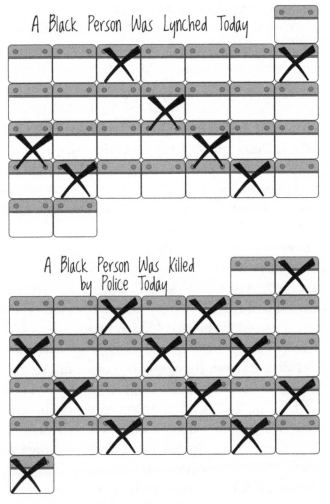

Timetables of injustice, one century apart.

officers across the country, in contrast to videos of police peacefully deescalating conflicts with armed white people, it is difficult to suggest that everything is kumbaya.

Although there are no comprehensive national data on police killings, there are a great deal of data about the ways in which Black (and Latinx and increasingly Muslim and Arab) people are treated differently not only by the police but by the criminal justice system more generally (and thus more pervasively). A lot of this begins with initial interactions with police. Policies such as "stop-and-frisk" increase the chances of Black and Brown people interacting with the police. At the most basic level, Terry stops, or stop-and-frisks, allow police to stop people on the basis of a reasonable suspicion of involvement with criminal activity. On its face, this policy is race-neutral, but the evidence shows that police use **race** in their execution of the policy. In 2011, New York City carried out nearly seven hundred thousand stop-and-frisk searches. The New York Civil Liberties Union (NYCLU) reported that only 11 percent of stops in New York City "were based on a description of a violent crime suspect. On the other hand, from 2002 to 2011, black and Latino residents made up close to 90 percent of people stopped." Of these stops, 88 percent were innocent civilians. The NYCLU also found that "even in neighborhoods that are predominantly white, black and Latino New Yorkers face the disproportionate brunt. For example, in 2011, black and Latino New Yorkers made up 24 percent of the population in Park Slope, but 79 percent of stops."[18] Overall, New York Police Department (NYPD) officers stopped and frisked more young Black men than the number who actually lived in the city![19] What this suggests is that police are more likely to believe that Black people (and men especially) are viewed as suspicious even though police often fail to produce evidence of wrongdoing during these stops.

Stop-and-frisk policies are not enforced everywhere, but traffic stops are ubiquitous. The political scientist Frank Baumgartner and a team of researchers have collected nearly *thirteen million* data points of police traffic stops in North Carolina. They find that young, Black and Latino men are not only more likely to be pulled over than are all other racial and gender groups for all sorts of reasons (e.g., seat belts, speed limit, stop lights/signs, vehicle regulation, and equipment issues) but are also more likely to be searched and arrested. Blacks are 80 percent more likely to be searched after a speed violation than are whites; Latinos are 174 percent more likely than whites are to be searched for the same purpose. For seat-belt violations, Blacks are 223 percent and Latinos are 106 percent more likely than whites are to be searched.[20] In a study of fifty-five million police stops for over six hundred police agencies across the nation—including North Carolina, Maryland, Connecticut, Vermont, Florida, and Texas—the team of researchers unveiled significant and clear patterns of racial profiling and racially discriminatory policing; they even found that police across states are more likely to stop Blacks than they are to stop other groups at the same time of day (around 5:00 p.m.)![21]

The Department of Justice (DOJ) has investigated police departments across the country. The DOJ's reports of the Ferguson Police Department (FPD), the Baltimore City Police Department (BCPD), and the Chicago Police Department (CPD) find that through different policies, these police departments have systematically discriminated against Black residents. In Ferguson, police targeted Blacks in order to increase revenue for the city.[22] In Baltimore, a "zero-tolerance" policy "prioritized officers making large number of stops, searches, and arrests—often resorting to force—with minimal training and insufficient oversight from supervisors or through other accountability structures"; this zero-tolerance policy was highly enforced in African American neighborhoods and less so in wealthier, whiter neighborhoods.[23] And in the majority-minority city of Chicago, the DOJ found that police were "insufficiently trained and supported to do their work effectively," thus fostering CPD's pattern or practice of "unreasonable force, [which] includes shooting at fleeing suspects who present no immediate threat," "firing at vehicles without justification," exhibiting "poor discipline in discharging weapons," and making "tactical decisions that unnecessarily increase the risk of deadly encounters."[24] Black lives are more at risk in their interactions with the police.

Michelle Alexander's *The New Jim Crow* reveals that at every step in the criminal justice system, Black people are treated differently than whites are, putting them at risk for harsher penalties. Scholars have found that Blacks are no more likely to do illegal drugs than whites are, but Blacks face greater penalties for doing so when caught. One major consequence of this is that people of color now make up 67 percent of the US prison population even though they only account for 37 percent of the population. Black men are six times as likely to be incarcerated as white men are, and Latinos are twice as likely.[25] Black women and Latinas are also overrepresented in prison populations, and nearly two-thirds of them are mothers of a minor child.[26] The journalist Matt Ford notes, "a brush with the criminal-justice system can hamstring a former inmate's employment and financial opportunities for life."[27] After individuals leave prison, they are likely to be treated as second-class citizens until the day they die.

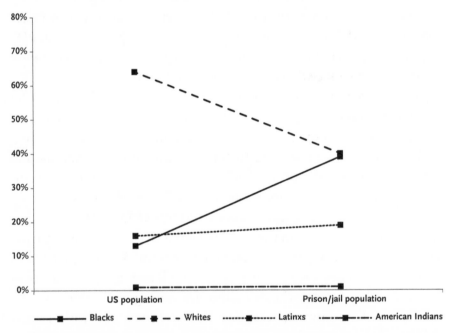

Racial representation in US jails and prisons. The United States imprisons a greater proportion of its residents than does any other country in the world. Currently, the nation's criminal justice system includes 1,719 state prisons, 102 federal prisons, 942 juvenile correctional facilities, 3,283 local jails, and 79 Indian Country jails. There are also military prisons, immigration detention facilities, prisons in the US territories, and civil commitment centers. There are about 2.3. million people in this system. (Prison Policy Initiative)

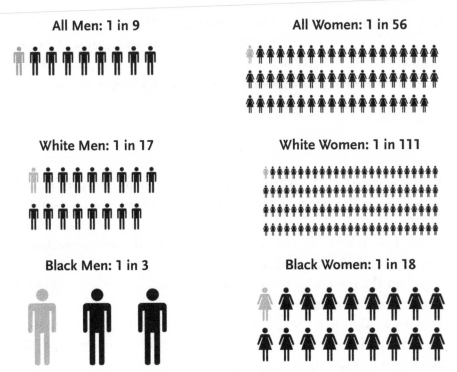

Lifetime likelihood of imprisonment for US residents born in 2001. (The Sentencing Project)

Moreover, research on the death penalty also shows that while Black men are the most likely victims of homicide, their perpetrators are least likely to receive the death penalty. That is to say, the **race** of the victim has a great deal to do with how the criminal justice system treats perpetrators. The death penalty is most likely to be handed down to those who murder whites.[28] Relatedly, among the cases of people who shot another person and claimed that they were "standing their ground," "individuals (i.e. defendants) in Florida were more likely to avoid charges if the victim was Black or Latino but not if the victim was White. Indeed, individuals are nearly two times more likely to be convicted in a case that involves White victims compared to those involving Black and Latino victims."[29] Putting aside the debates about the morality, necessity, or effectiveness of either the death penalty or "stand your ground" laws, outcomes of the judiciary reveal that Black lives don't matter, evidenced by the lack of penalization for the loss of Black life. The current Movement for Black Lives has encouraged people to protest against the most blatant forms of state violence and discrimination against Blacks, but this violence plays out in different, subtler ways across other domains of American life.

FAQ

Wait a second. . . . Aren't there a disproportionate number of Black people in prison because they commit a disproportionate amount of crime?

No. Let's take a step back. We focus here on the disproportionate amount of Black and Latinx people in prisons and jails in order to highlight the inequities rooted both in the law as written and in the way the law is implemented. But generally speaking, when a person asks a question like the one above, they are asking if Black people are simply more prone to criminal behavior than other groups. The answer to that question is also no.

When we think about issues of crime and **race**, we have to keep in mind that we do not live in a vacuum. We have to consider the context. For example, the War on Drugs has had a disproportionate impact on communities of color. More communities of color, especially poor communities, were surveilled, and thus more people of color were arrested. Another way of thinking about this is that whites are systematically underrepresented in prisons due to drug-related crimes. Whites report doing more illegal drugs than Blacks do, but Black people are more likely to be punished for doing so. Research shows that contexts matters a great deal, and when scholars control for things like income and wealth,[30] nearly all of the things that people believe are distinctly pathological for Blacks, such as "culture," go away. Or in other words, once we account for poverty and wealth, Blacks and whites behave about the same way, but there are simply a greater proportion of Blacks who are poor and lack wealth.

Second—let's just get this out of the way—it is true that a Black person who is murdered is most likely to be murdered by another Black person, but there is also such a thing as "white-on-white"

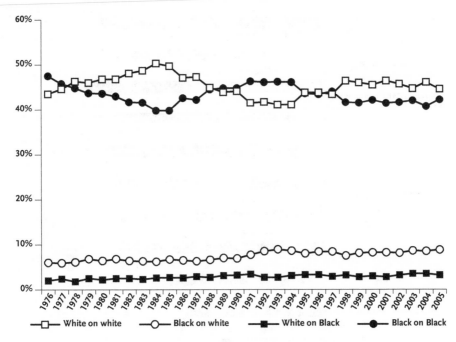

Inter- and intraracial homicides. (Baumgartner, Grigg, and Mastro, "#BlackLivesDon't Matter," 213)

crime. If someone is going to kill (or rape) you, he or she probably already knows you. Aside from being incredibly disturbing, this statistic is fascinating because what it really reveals is how segregated a society the United States is.

Third, according to the FBI, there were about 7.5 million people arrested for about three dozen crimes in 2015—ranging from violent crimes to vagrancy—so there are very few people, relatively speaking, who commit crimes. But we spend a lot of time thinking not just about crime but also about the supposed racial nature of crime. It's true that there are some crimes that Black people are disproportionately arrested for and also more likely to be victims of, such as homicides. But there are some crimes that white people are *most likely* to be arrested for. Driving while under the influence, for example, is a crime that is disproportionately committed by whites, usually men. But whites are also most likely to be arrested for rape, violent crimes, property crimes, arson, and drug crimes. In fact, whites are more likely to be arrested for crimes, generally speaking.

Arrests in Black and white. (Data compiled from FBI Uniform Crime Reporting, 2015)

All in all, we would like to encourage you to think about why some crimes (or crime, generally speaking) are racialized as "Black" and are erroneously linked with "Black culture." Furthermore, given that whites are more likely to be arrested, what are the factors that may prevent us from even considering the notion of *white criminality*? Why are crimes that are most likely to be committed by whites chalked up to the individual or seen as an aberration (e.g., mass school shootings, serial killing), rather than as a sign that there is something wrong with white people? Or, in other words, what are the implications of focusing on disproportionality by population size rather than probability of occurrence by people across age, gender, ethno-racial, or class groups?[31] How would our discussions and policy recommendations change if we did shift our focus?

Location, Location, Location

Racial disparities in one realm of US society are intricately related to disparities in other domains. But like the problem of the chicken and the egg, it's difficult to tell where it all starts. How do we best understand how privileges, advantages, burdens, and disadvantages that are systematically distributed across racial groups influence the ability or even the probability that any one person will attain the **American dream**? Let's consider housing, or where people live, because where one lives is inextricably linked to many other factors that allow people to access quality education, wealth building, and even good health outcomes. Why do people live where they live? Some of the reasons can be chalked up to personal preference, but it should be made crystal clear that personal preferences actually pale in comparison to the *huge* historical forces and accumulated public policies that help us to best understand why we live where we do.

Over time, residential segregation has been decreasing, but phrases like "other side of the tracks" and "rough neighborhoods" are popular **racial euphemisms** for poor, Black neighborhoods, or ghettos, "a word that accurately describes a neighborhood where government has not only concentrated a minority but established barriers to its exit."[32] Though it sometimes feels that racially homogeneous neighborhoods are natural—you know, because "birds of a feather flock together"—we should keep in mind that political leaders implemented policies in order to *intentionally* segregate US neighborhoods by **race**. Racial zoning, restrictive covenants, redlining, urban renewal, annexation, spot zoning, expulsive zoning, incorporation, and redevelopment represent some of the innovative policies developed at various levels of government to accomplish these goals. Scholars like Jessica Trounstine, Richard Rothstein, and

Ira Katznelson show not only that there were laws and policies put in place in the early twentieth century that explicitly allowed for the development of white neighborhoods and suburbs, purposefully excluding Black citizens in the process, but that this segregation inherently and systematically advantaged white Americans and disadvantaged Black Americans and other people of color, on average. It still does. Old policies stay alive through their legacy (e.g., white wealth accumulation, persistent racial segregation), and some race-neutral policies are still pursued in order to have a similar effect (e.g., zoning).

This is a long list of wrongdoing to cover in one book, so we'll just study one perverse housing policy to give you a sense of not only how the US government took the lead in providing additional benefits to some of its citizens while leaving out others but also how policy developed almost a century ago still influences contemporary patterns of residential segregation and thus racial inequality in housing (and education and employment and health and wealth): redlining.

The concept of "redlining" comes from a rubric developed by the Home Owners' Loan Corporation (HOLC), a government-sponsored corporation created in the early 1930s. The appraisers of this organization divided neighborhoods into categories based on the occupation, income, ethnicity, and **race** of the inhabitants in efforts to make determinations about where banks would be "safe" to provide home loans, including Federal Housing Administration (FHA)–backed loans. Green areas were pristine, racially homogeneous areas where "American Business and Professional Men" and their families lived; these areas were predicted to be in demand in good times and in bad. Blue areas were "still desirable," and though they "reached their peak," they were expected to remain stable for many years. Yellow neighborhoods were "definitely declining" with a "threat of infiltration of foreign-born, negro, or lower grade populations."[33] Finally, there were Red neighborhoods, which were considered the worst for lending: Black and low-income neighborhoods.[34]

In order to attain a high-quality, low-interest, government-backed loan, it helped (a) to be white and (b) to want to purchase a home in a neighborhood that the government deemed safe to invest in—Green or Blue (though a Yellow neighborhood's status could be upgraded by building a wall to clearly separate itself from a bordering Red neighborhood). Whites were able to purchase federally subsidized homes in neighborhoods that were exclusively white. Meanwhile, neighborhoods where Black people lived were not eligible for federally insured loans, and Black Americans were, for many decades, legally prevented from living in areas that weren't redlined. What this means is that Black people were not provided the opportunity to buy a home with the same federally backed resources as white Americans were, and furthermore, this policy meant that Black neighborhoods were not invested in as white neighborhoods were. If Blacks wanted to access home ownership, they were not only relegated to ghettos but also required to rely on predatory, high-interest, nonregulated loans or other black-market (no pun intended) systems of financing.

As mentioned, these HOLC categories were developed nearly eighty-five years ago, but their influence still reverberates today. We can think of neighborhoods and suburbs such as Levittown in New York and Pennsylvania (built by the same Levitt & Sons family business) that did not allow Blacks to buy for decades and today are still overwhelmingly white. While people were able to buy homes for about $7,000 in the early 1940s, today homes in Levittown, New York, are sold for upwards of $500,000. Meanwhile, in neighborhoods on the West Side of Chicago, where Blacks were segregated and made to rely on predatory financing, some homes twice the size of those in Levittown may be purchased now for around or even less than $150,000. This area is still predominantly Black.

Relatedly, in the case of Durham, North Carolina, the areas that were "redlined" in the 1930s, such as Wall Town, are still predominantly Black and low income today (although this area is undergoing gentrification). And the Green areas, such as Trinity Park, are still wealthy and white. These HOLC maps even influence the location of trees in the city! In the 1940s, the city of Durham planted trees in the Green neighborhoods. Now, the city cannot afford to plant trees in the Red areas, where low-income Blacks still live today, because they have to use money to maintain the trees in areas that were historically white and still are today. Research shows that trees influence levels of pollution in the air, which means that there may be more pollution in Black neighborhoods than in white neighborhoods.[35] This specific kind of inequality is referred to as *environmental racism*, but as we see here, this is business as usual. Nobody needs to do anything sinister for this kind of inequity to persist.

Thinking as a rational actor, one is likely to want to live in a "better" neighborhood—one that is, at base, safe, clean, and has good amenities, one where your home will accrue greater value and equity over time. Indeed, the **American dream** hinges on the notion of climbing up the social and economic hierarchies and purchasing a nice home for your family, but research shows that even attaining a loan to buy a home is much harder for Blacks and Latinxs. Furthermore, once a person of color attains that loan, she or he will probably pay higher fees and interest rates than a white person, even controlling for important factors like credit scores, loan-to-value ratios, subordinate liens, income, assets, expense ratios, and neighborhood characteristics.[36]

During the last housing boom, which led up to the 2008 financial crisis and the Great Recession, Latinxs and African Americans were more likely to be directed into high-cost, high-risk loans, loans that have been characterized as "financial time bombs." At the most basic level, this means they paid more for their homes. Some estimates project that Black borrowers will pay an excess of $14,904 over the course of a thirty-year mortgage, but this grows to $15,948 when we look at borrowers (Black or white) who borrowed in order to buy homes in Black neighborhoods. And the excess was still more for Black borrowers in white neighborhoods: $19,415. And it was even more for Black borrowers who made over $50,000 who wanted to live in predominantly white neighborhoods: $22,864.[37] But more importantly, the attempt to live the American dream "left them [Blacks and Latinxs] uniquely exposed to risks of default, foreclosure, repossession, and the loss of home equity, thus serving to exacerbate already skewed racial inequalities in the distribution of wealth."[38]

In many decades past, predatory contractors "targeted black people who had worked hard enough to save a down payment and dreamed of the emblem of American **citizenship**—homeownership";[39] in the past decade, the same was shown to be true. Middle-class Black homeowners were disproportionately affected by the housing crisis, nearly a quarter million people losing their homes. Much of their wealth, or the money people have after all their bills are paid, is in their homes, and a lot of people lost large swaths of their wealth after the Great Recession. American families' wealth was reduced by 28.5 percent, but for Black families, there was a loss of about 47.6 percent.[40] Getting foreclosed on your home is like getting evicted, and Black families were asked, sometimes forced, to vacate from their home at egregious rates. Systemic and often intentional **racism** increased the vulnerability of Blacks even in an era when they are supposedly protected by policies like the Fair Housing Act and an American ethos of working hard in order to attain the **American dream**.

Education

Where one lives often influences where one goes to school. Schools are racially segregated, in large part, because housing is racially segregated. Racial effects are further exacerbated by class inequities rooted in racial disparities. Put simply, there has never been an instance when Black people who were isolated from whites got the same positive benefits from public schools that white people did.[41] What makes the problem of the Black-white achievement gap in standardized testing scores such a fascinating problem to discuss is that anybody who knows anything about education policy knows that the problem can be largely fixed through racial integration. Needless to say, there is simply not enough political will to solve what seems to be a growing problem in the twenty-first century.

It's not so much that Black students need to sit next to white ones to do better. It's a matter of resources. Prior to the two *Brown v. Board of Education of Topeka* Supreme Court cases, "states spent very little on black schools relative to what they spent on white schools. Desegregation led to rapid increases in state spending on education, driven by white-controlled legislatures' desires to ensure that white students' school quality did not decline with integration."[42] With more resources, students have access to better teachers and materials and enjoy a lower student-to-teacher ratio. There are also indications that schools with more resources have a positive impact on both the students' and teachers' outlook on the educational process and learning environment.

The first *Brown* decision said that segregation was wrong and should be fixed. In the second *Brown* decision, the Supreme Court demanded that the states move faster to integrate schools. Northern and southern states alike moved slowly, but by the mid-1970s, several hundred school districts were under court-ordered desegregation plans. "Court-ordered desegregation was the single most important factor shaping the rapid declines in racial segregation in the 1960s and 1970s," so much so that the threat of being under one of these orders influenced nonsupervised districts to initiate and implement their own integration policies.[43] Once school districts began integrating through policies like busing, the achievement gap between Black and white students began to close. Voila!

At the peak of integration efforts around 1989, the achievement gap had closed significantly. Education scholars show that "from the early 1970s until the late 1980s, a very large narrowing of the [Black-white achievement] gap occurred in both reading and math. . . . For some cohorts, the gaps were cut by as much as half or more."[44] The effects of these policies have reverberated for two to three generations. Black students who desegregated schools between the 1960s and early 1980s were more likely to graduate from high school, to attend and graduate college, and to earn more money than those who attended segregated schools, and they were less likely to spend time in jail.[45] Those who were exposed to schools that were desegregated due to court orders were less likely to be victims of homicide, arrested, or incarcerated. There were improvements to adult health outcomes, too. By the way, white students' outcomes were not diminished in any way by school desegregation policies.[46] School desegregation policies widened the geography of opportunity for a greater number of people.

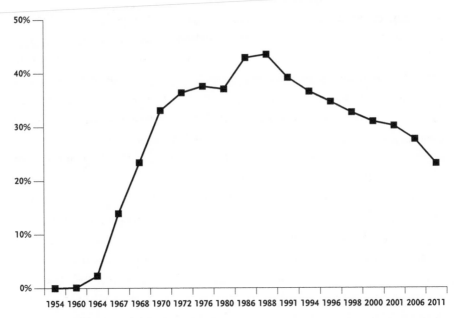

Percentage of Black students in majority-white schools, 1954–2011. (Orfield et al., "Brown at 60," 10)

What's the status of integration now? In 1972 (during strong desegregation enforcement), about 25 percent of Black students in the
South attended "intensely segregated schools in which nine out of 10
students were racial minorities," but between 1990 and 2011 (during
the decline in court orders), this number jumped up to 53 percent.[47]
This has occurred because of white flight, or the movement of white
families to predominantly white districts or to private schools. Court
orders primarily focus on within-district segregation, but they have
little direct effect on between-district dynamics. As such, parents
can move to racially homogeneous districts if they want their child to
go to racially homogeneous public schools. Moreover, some neighborhoods and towns have pushed for the creation of new school districts in order to legally segregate schools (and to hoard resources).
This is called *educational gerrymandering*.

Between 1990 and 2010, hundreds of school districts were released
from court supervision and thus are no longer required to implement
desegregation plans, which has hastened a new era of segregation.

As such, most white schoolchildren go to schools that are largely white, and most Black and Latinx students go to majority-minority schools. The proportion of Black students going to majority-white schools nowadays mimics the figures from 1968! Appropriately, the term "apartheid schools" has been adopted to describe severely segregated schools, ones in which only 1 percent or less of the school population is white. Perhaps counterintuitively, many of these schools are in the Northeast and Midwest, and about 12 percent of students in the South attend these schools.[48]

Scholars have found that racial inequality has widened since the end of race-based busing efforts. Some have found that since the dismissal of these court orders, there has been an uptick in dropout rates among Black and Latinx students.[49] Others show that both whites and students of color are likely to score lower on tests when they are assigned to predominantly minority schools and, further, that students are less likely to graduate high school or attend a four-year college.[50] Scholars have expected inequality to increase as more court orders are dismissed, and cursory statistics from the US government provide evidence for this prediction. As we have seen before, poor

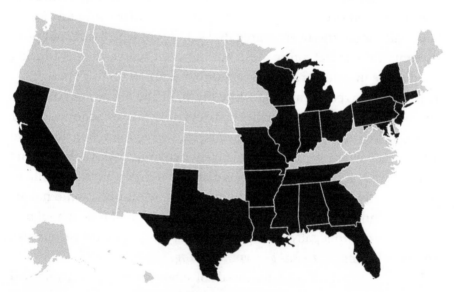

Top-twenty most segregated states for Black students, 2011–2012. (Orfield et al., "Brown at 60," 20)

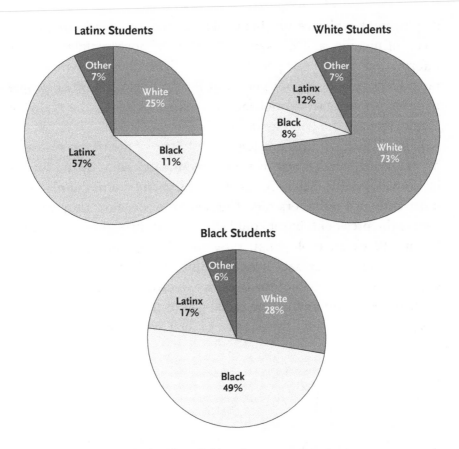

Who goes to school with whom? (Orfield et al., "Brown at 60," 12)

Black and Brown children in isolated schools have not received the same opportunities as everyone else, and there is a growing population of students in that very vulnerable position.

Employment

If you do not want to be poor, it is logical to believe that you should go to school and get a job. But layered on top of unequal access to high-quality education, Black people and other people of color, on average, are treated differently from whites in the realm of employment, which results in racial inequality in employment rates, levels of income, and consequently, rates of poverty. Just for your information, most poor people are not Black (they are white), and most Black people are not poor; but Black people and other people of color, on average, do not fare as well as whites in the realm of employment in the United States.

During the forty-fifth president's first State of the Union Address, he mentioned that Black unemployment rates were at the lowest in US history. The Black Congressional Caucus did not applaud, as most audience members did. This could be because they weren't feeling the president, but it could also be that throughout recent US history, Black unemployment rates have been, and still are, twice those of whites. Our data from the Bureau of Labor Statistics provide evidence of this fact for over five decades, and the economist William Darity notes that the racial gap in the unemployment rate has not improved since the passage of the Civil Rights Act of 1964.[51]

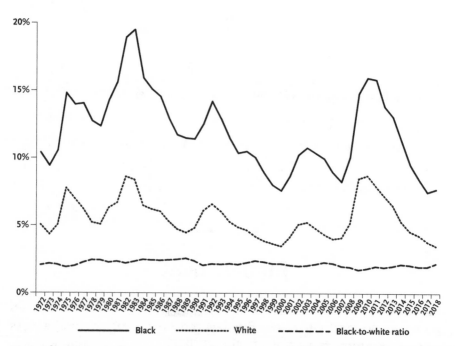

Unemployment rate by race, 1972–2018. (Data compiled from the Bureau of Labor Statistics, 2018)

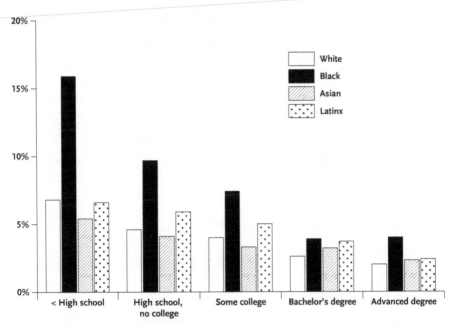

Unemployment by race and education. (Data compiled from the Bureau of Labor Statistics, 2015)

What's more, labor-force statistics from the US Census Bureau show that at every level of education, Black unemployment rates are about twice as high as white unemployment rates. Blacks with a college education or even an advanced degree have about the same rate of unemployment as whites without one, revealing that while more education does help to decrease chances of unemployment, the effects differ across racial groups. Blacks with a college education or even an advanced degree fare just about as well as whites with some college but no degree.

Why does this happen? Because discrimination still occurs in hiring and promotion practices: "[Discrimination] is not the only or even the most important factor shaping contemporary opportunities. Nevertheless, it is important to understand when and how discrimination does play a role in the allocation of resources and opportunities."[52] In an audit study, scholars sent out equivalent résumés with identifiably Black names (e.g., Jamal and Lakisha) and ones that are statistically white (e.g., Brad and Emily); they found that white names triggered 50 percent more callbacks than Black names.[53] In a similar study, the sociologist Devah Pager found that white men with a criminal record have about the same chances of getting called back for a job as Black men *without* a criminal record.[54] These differences in callback rates provide evidence of a barrier in employment due to **race**. Despite the fact that there have been policies put into place to prevent discrimination, these inequities still exist, and there is little recourse one can gain in this environment because proving that an employer intentionally discriminates is an incredibly difficult feat these days.

———

Income and Wealth

Income is the money that you bring in from your job. It is typically the case that as people get promoted within an organization, their income also increases. As we see more people of color in management, seated at the table of executive boards, and in administrative positions in institutions of higher education, many of us conclude that nonwhites must be doing better financially. Unfortunately, there is still plenty of wage inequality across racial groups. For instance, Pew Research shows that in 1980, Black men's median hourly wages accounted for about 83 percent of white men's hourly wages, and in 2015, Black men's median hourly wages accounted for about 83 percent of white men's hourly wages. The income gap between Black and white men has not changed in three and a half decades![55] When you add gender to the mix, researchers show that, with the exception of Asian men, all groups lag behind white men in terms of median hourly earnings.[56]

Some of this difference comes from the fact that Blacks and Latinxs do not attend college at the same rates as whites, but what happens when we account for these important differences? Researchers from the Economic Policy Institute reveal that in 2015, "relative to the average hourly wages of white men with the same education, experience, metro status, and region of residence, black men make 22.0 percent less, and black women make 34.2 percent less."[57] This gap

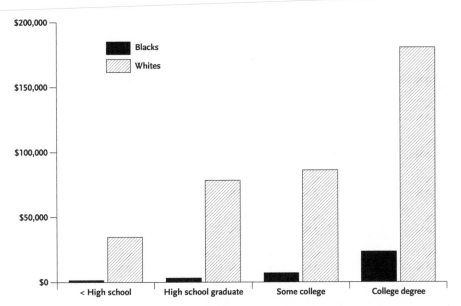

Family wealth, by race and education. (Hamilton et al., *Umbrellas Don't Make It Rain*, 5)

appears to increase as we move up the education ladder. Similarly, the *New York Times*' editorial board explained, "Last year [2016], black college graduates earned about 21 percent less per hour on average than white college graduates; in 1979, the gap was 13 percent. The racial disparity in earnings is even greater for men: Last year, the average hourly earnings of black college-educated men were about 25 percent less than of white college-educated men. The gaps widen up the economic ladder. The top 5 percent of black male earners make about 47 percent less than the top-earning white men."[58] That's a hard pill to swallow if you've been under the impression that education is the great equalizer. The thing is, income is actually a very superficial measure of financial well-being. Income pays your bills, but wealth is what you have left after all of your bills are paid. Examining wealth disparities is important because it reveals how being poor and Black is quite distinct from being poor and white. It also reveals that those high-income Black folks in management may be one or two pay checks from poverty. Even low-income white people have more wealth and more cushion to fall back on in really hard times than do well-paid and well-educated Black people, on average.

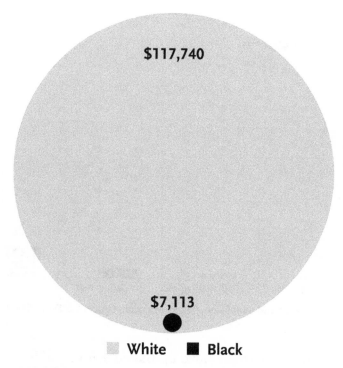

Median family wealth by race. (Hamilton et al., *Umbrellas Don't Make It Rain*, 4)

Currently, the median Black family's wealth is about $7,113, compared to $117,740 for the median white family. Here's the rub: it is generally difficult to attain wealth, and it is even more difficult for Black people. Blacks with an advanced degree have about $84,000 in wealth. Whites with the same level of education have about three and a half times that wealth, and whites who do not even have a college degree tend to have about $2,200 more in wealth. Black Americans with a college degree only have about 67 percent of the wealth that whites who never graduated from high school have.

Maybe all those Black people with doctoral degrees should just try to make more money? That doesn't do the trick. Blacks with high incomes ($93,000+) have lower levels of wealth than do whites making between $57,000 and $93,000. All in all, research shows that "racial wealth differences cannot be explained by education, employment, or income."[59] Experts have calculated that Black households would have to save 100 percent of their income *for three years* to close the wealth gap![60] And still, it is predicted that in 2053, the median wealth among Blacks will be $0.00.

How does this all work? Much of the wealth people have comes from their homes, but another source is one's family, especially one's parents and grandparents: wealth is often intergenerationally passed down.[61] Let's say your grandparents got a loan for a home in one of those Green neighborhoods we discussed earlier, and they passed it down to your parents. Your parents now live in a home with little or no payments, and their home is building equity (a house's value minus what is owed on it). When you go to college, they can borrow from the equity so that you do not have to take out loans. You're better off already.

Now let's imagine that they pass the house to you, but you have a low-paying job. You're still doing okay because you just have to pay utilities, upkeep, and taxes. Your kids can still go to the "good," well-resourced schools even though you make little money. This scenario looks much different for a person who is the descendant of people who bought a home in the Red neighborhood. There is no wealth on which to fall back on for college, and if you do live in that home, your children may go to a school that is underresourced. In all, we have to remember that some people were legally (and sometimes violently) excluded from amassing wealth through home ownership—the path that many white Americans have taken to weave a tightly knit social safety net for their families.

It's likely that you had very little to do with your inheritance—big or small—but the wealth gap that we see across groups is an outcome of historical, structural **racism** and racial terrorism. The wealth gap was fueled, in part, by the 1618 Headright System (which gave fifty acres of land in the "new colonies" to any European willing to travel across the Atlantic); exacerbated by the enactment of the Slave Codes in 1705 (which allowed whites to enslave and own Blacks, but not vice versa); ramped up by the 1785 Land Ordinance Act (which divvied up the ancestral lands of Indigenous Americans); deepened by the 1862 Homestead Act (which provided free land for citizens—note that Blacks were not eligible for **citizenship** until 1868); cemented by racially inequitable implementation of the 1944 Serviceman's Readjustment Act (better known as the GI Bill); intensified by redlining policies encouraged by the Federal Housing Administration through 1968; and further worsened by the Great Recession of 2008. The wealth gap is rooted in many hundreds of years and thousands of policies that might be best characterized as **affirmative action** for white people.[62]

The thing about wealth is that it helps when you need help most. Individuals and families with more wealth can more easily maneuver about the world than those without it can. If you need an attorney (after one of those "unlucky" police stops), you can rely on wealth. If you want to help your child pay for college or help him or her buy a new home, you can rely on wealth. If you want to run for public office, you can rely on wealth. You can attain more stuff with wealth: education, property, power, and more wealth. These disparities make Blacks vulnerable to the negative outcomes of economic shocks (like the Great Recession) and make the fall harder to bounce back from when they are knocked down by the loss of a job or a sudden decline in health.

Health

Basic indicators of quality of life measure how healthy people feel and how long they are expected to live. According to epidemiological research, Black people live shorter lives than whites do. Also shocking is the fact that the Black-white mortality gap did not close for the forty years between 1960 and 2000. Researchers project that if this gap had closed, nearly eighty-four thousand Black deaths *per year* could have been prevented.[63] Obviously, how healthy a person is has a lot to do with individual behavior (e.g., eating well, exercise), but there is so much more to it than that. To begin, "public health research increasingly recognizes that racial/ethnic disparities in health are rooted in social factors such as SES [socioeconomic status], discrimination, and residential segregation,"[64] things we have already discussed.

Again, where you live can have a tremendous influence on your life. Blacks are highly segregated, and Latinxs increasingly so, and thus are isolated from "high-opportunity neighborhoods," or neighborhoods marked by "sustainable employment, high-performing schools, healthy environments, access to high-quality health care, adequate transportation, high-quality child care, neighborhood safety, and institutions that facilitate civic engagement."[65] To a large extent, Blacks are excluded from the geography of opportunity, and their health outcomes are dampened as a consequence. Food deserts, or places where high-quality, affordable food is not easily accessible, are likely to form in low-income and Black neighborhoods.[66] When hospitals close, they are more likely to do so in low-income and Black neighborhoods.[67] When family-planning clinics are eliminated by state policies, Black and Latina women are the most negatively affected, as their access to reproductive health care services is substantially decreased.[68] If you thought we were being merely metaphorical by talking about the "geography of opportunity," guess again. Your zip code, as structural inequality would have it, is a helpful predictor of your life expectancy, such that five miles can make a twenty-year difference.[69] That's right, your zip code is a better predictor of your health than your genetic code is.

One thing that stands out to us is that even when Black people attain more education, there is not necessarily an increase in well-being (recall, for example, that even with more education, Blacks still fall behind in levels of wealth, and they pay even more for their homes). In the case of infant outcomes, research shows not only that Black babies are two to three times more likely to die than are white babies in their first year of life but also that even as Black women step into the middle class, infant-mortality rates do not decline. In fact, there is a larger disparity between Black and white women at the higher end of the socioeconomic spectrum than at the lower end. One emerging theory is that middle-class Black women have to contend with chronic stress, including stress that results from exposure to racial discrimination.[70] Black lives are literally more likely to be lost.

As mentioned, all of these domains of life we've discussed so far are interrelated. "Educational attainment and income provide psychosocial and material resources that protect against exposure to health risks in early and adult life"; meanwhile, "persons with low levels of education and income generally experience increased rates of mortality, morbidity, and risk-taking behaviors and decreased access to and quality of health care."[71] As we know, Blacks are less likely to have access to quality education and are shut out of job opportunities more so than whites. Keeping that in mind, it's important to note, "unemployed persons tend to have higher annual illness rates, lack health insurance and access to health care, and have an increased risk for death. Several studies indicate that employment status influences a person's health; however, poor health also affects a person's ability to obtain and retain employment."[72] Rinse. Repeat. The cycle continues.

When Black Lives Matter

James Baldwin wrote in a letter to Angela Davis, who was two decades his junior and imprisoned on false charges of murder, kidnapping, and criminal conspiracy,

> The enormous revolution in Black consciousness which has occurred in your generation, my dear sister, means the beginning or the end of America. Some of us, white and Black, know how great a price has already been paid to bring into existence a new consciousness, a new people, an unprecedented nation. If we know, and do nothing, we are worse than the murderers hired in our name. If we know, then we must fight for your life as though it were our own—which it is—and render impassable with our bodies the corridor to the gas chamber. For, if they take you in the morning, they will be coming for us that night.[73]

What's past is prologue, they say. Today, young Black people have again taken the United States to task, forcing it to face its greatest flaws, many of which are rooted in anti-Black **racism**. One of these problems is that many Americans have yet to come to the realization that though most of us value rugged individualism, this country thrives because it is upheld by the threads that weave together many interrelated—though segregated—communities. If we don't solve the problems that one community is facing, all Americans and the United States itself will suffer. If we do not protect the most vulnerable, we can be assured that we will find ourselves in that same undesirable position soon enough.

We see this dynamic playing out right now. For example, the War on Drugs served to punish people not only for the sale of drugs but also for drug use and addiction. When drugs such as crack cocaine ran rampant in highly segregated, poor, Black neighborhoods, African Americans bore the brunt of these policies, best evinced by the disproportionate number of Blacks who are incarcerated in the United States. As work disappeared from urban areas, Black unemployment rates skyrocketed, and all of the problems associated with highly unemployed areas developed: increased pessimism, drug use, homelessness, and crime. Behaviors that are stereotypically associated with poor Black people are neither unique to that group nor pathological. Instead, they are well predicted by structural factors, including the shape of the economy and the way that policy makers react to those who are most in need. Suffice it to say, policy makers tend to react negatively and with punitive policies to groups they see as undeserving.[74]

As a result of the Great Recession, many of these issues peaked again: unemployment, pessimism, drug use, homelessness. But this time, whites were affected as well, especially in the rural United States and in places where good-paying factory jobs left town. If we penalize whites who face similar challenges to what Blacks historically have in the same way, we will have an even bigger set of societal problems than we already do. What if whites were incarcerated at the same rate as Blacks? All things being equal (which they are not), then one in three white men would then have dealings with the criminal justice system. Let that sink in. US policy makers could have already prepared thoughtful, helpful, effective, cost-saving public policies to deal with the issues now faced by an even greater proportion of Americans decades ago when Blacks were the test case, for lack of better words.

Another thing: remember when we mentioned that if the gap between Black and white mortality closed, eighty-four thousand deaths could have been prevented? The assumption behind this projection is that Blacks' rate of mortality inches closer to whites', but what we're actually seeing is that whites', especially poor whites', well-being is declining. A lot of the reason why the United States does not have a better health care system and stronger safety-net policies is because of anti-Black **racism**—plainly and simply. The legal scholar Ian Haney López tracks the strategic use of anti-Black racism by white, conservative politicians across several decades and reveals a pattern of behavior; by suggesting, or even hinting, that "undeserving" Blacks are likely to benefit from a social policy, politicians are able to convince (poor) whites that we should constrain that policy.[75] Remember that fire we talked about? It's becoming clear that it is already starting to spread.

The thing about the contemporary Movement for Black Lives is that it provides an imaginative vision of society based on human flourishing. Such a realization requires not just a tweaking of the existing political, social, and economic systems but a major transformation of the way US society works. What would it take to accomplish this? *Stay Woke* provides a set of tools for its readers to begin to unpack the ways that anti-Black racism prevents the United States from living up to its fullest potential, and it guides them to envision what each of us can do to work toward a more vibrant and egalitarian society.

Questions and Debate

1 This chapter begins with an analogy of burning buildings. Is this analogy helpful? If so, what is the next building or buildings that may begin to burn if anti-Black **racism** isn't smothered? If not, what is your critique?

2 We've provided lots of facts, figures, and statistics about racial inequality in the United States. How would you measure racial progress? What metric would you use?

3 When people hear "Black Lives Matter," different people take this slogan to mean different things. Why do people interpret this slogan so differently? Why do people have such visceral reactions to this phrase—either positive or negative?

4 The term "postracial" gets bandied about quite a bit in the US news media. What does "postracial" mean? How do you know when the United States has become a "postracial" society? What would that look like? Is it possible? Why isn't there more talk about a "post-racist" society instead?

5 We discuss a variety of laws and policies that contributed to structural racism (e.g., Slave Codes, Homestead Act, redlining, GI Bill). How, if at all, have those policies shaped your life, your family members' lives, or those of your ancestors?

Additional Materials to Consider

BOOKS

Barrett, Dawson. *The Defiant: Protest Movements in Post-Liberal America.* New York: NYU Press, 2018.

Baumgartner, Frank, Derek A. Epp, and Kelsey Shoub. *Suspect Citizens: What 20 Million Traffic Stops Tell Us about Policing and Race.* New York: Cambridge University Press, 2018.

Khan-Cullors, Patrisse, and Asha Bandele. *When They Call You a Terrorist: A Black Lives Matter Memoir.* New York: St. Martin's, 2017.

Smith, Mychal Denzel. *Invisible Man, Got the Whole World Watching: A Young Black Man's Education.* New York: Nation Books, 2016.

Trounstine, Jessica. *Segregation by Design: Local Politics and Inequality in American Cities.* New York: Cambridge University Press, 2018.

FILMS

The Pruitt-Igoe Myth. Directed by Chad Freidrichs. First-Run Features, Films Media Group, 2011.

13th. Directed by Ava DuVernay. Netflix, 2016.

PODCASTS

Seeing White. Hosted by John Biewen and Chenjerai Kumanyika. Scene on Radio, Center for Documentary Studies, 2017. www.sceneonradio.org/seeing-white/.

Undisclosed. Hosted by Rabia Chaudry, Collin Miller, and Susan Simpson. http://undisclosed-podcast.com.

74 Seconds: The Death of Philando Castile and the Trial of Jeronimo Yanez. MPR News. www.mprnews.org/topic/philandocastile.

WEBSITES

Nelson, Robert K., LaDale Winling, Richard Marciano, Nathan Connolly, et al. "Mapping Inequality." *American Panorama,* edited by Robert K. Nelson and Edward L. Ayers. Accessed July 27, 2018, https://dsl.richmond.edu.

2

All the Words People Throw Around

One important step toward being an effective racial justice advocate is recognizing that many people bump heads over racial terminology. While it is the case that one person may fundamentally disagree with the argument another person is trying to make, it is also possible for people to simply talk past one another because they are uninformed of the meanings behind the words being used. Becoming conversant in racial terminology can empower you in either scenario. Here, we provide an entry point to the racial lexicon of the contemporary United States in hopes of better equipping you with the means to grapple with not only the semantics of a number of concepts but also why it is important. Given that language, like **race**, is ever evolving and responds to changing contexts, we do not claim to be exhaustive in our commentary, and we humbly advance that we are not the final word on the matter. There may even be places where you find yourself wanting to contest our analysis—this is your cue to step into the circle and be part of the conversation.

We selected words that showcase the contestation and emotional charge of racial politics. We chose concepts that represent phenomena that we think need addressing. We picked terms that many people have probably never heard of but nevertheless represent phenomena that you may have either seen, experienced, or thought about. Lastly, we discuss some words that get debated even among people who are politically allied with one another.

We order the terms alphabetically for two reasons: (1) to help make it more referential for you, the reader, and (2) because we believe it is more important for people to know that these concepts are connected and at times co-constitutive than to think about them as ranked in importance. We do, however, provide some organizational logic with the following categories:

* **Foundational concepts:** In order to best grasp what the Black Lives Matter movement and the Movement for Black Lives is all about, you would be well served to understand the weight of these words.

* **American mythology:** There are a few dominant narratives explaining why the United States is so special. We critically examine them.

* **Common sense revisited:** Some words get used so frequently in everyday language that we seldom stop to ask whether we are even using the same definition. Let's take some time to reflect.

* **Tools of liberation:** We spotlight ideas and instruments with which we can free ourselves and enhance the lives of others.

* **Tools of oppression:** We bring attention to ideas and instruments that are used to (a) control, exclude, exploit, ignore, and/or shame human beings on the basis of **race**, (b) excuse oneself from accountability or intervention, or (c) hinder the uplift of those who are working to get free.

* **Wisdom of popular culture:** We include some of the innovative concepts presented in various forms of media, including the genius of Black Twitter, that help us make sense of the world.

* **Extra credit:** The more you know, the more you grow.

You will find that some words fall under multiple categories. We also set in boldface words that are examined throughout the chapter to facilitate your consideration of their connection to one another. Interspersed in the chapter you will find activities and reflection pieces to complete alone or with others.

---

affirmative action

common sense revisited

1. Policies that aim to ameliorate disparities between structurally—and historically—contingent identity groups, such as marginalized racial groups and women, in the case of the United States

2. Predecessor to **diversity** programs and initiatives

   see also: diversity, reverse discrimination

In order to get beyond racism, we must first take account of race. There is no other way. And in order to treat some persons equally, we must treat them differently. We cannot—we dare not—let the Equal Protection Clause perpetuate racial supremacy.
—US Supreme Court Justice Harry Blackmun in
Regents of University of California v. Bakke (1978)

Historically, affirmative action programs were rooted in racial justice.[1] In a 1965 speech to the graduates of Howard University, President Lyndon B. Johnson explained that there was a need for programs aimed to dissolve racial inequality. Noting that the social, political, and economic differences seen historically between whites and Blacks "are not racial differences" but "are solely and simply the consequence of ancient brutality, past injustice, and present prejudice," Johnson was well aware that real policy change had to be made in order to close these gaps. He famously explained,

But freedom is not enough. You do not wipe away the scars of centuries by saying: Now you are free to go where you want, and do as you desire, and choose the leaders you please. You do not take a person who, for years, has been hobbled by chains and liberate him, bring him up to the starting line of a race and then say, "you are free to compete with all the others," and still justly believe that you have been completely fair. Thus it is not enough just to open the gates of opportunity. All our citizens must have the ability to walk through those gates. This is the next and the more profound stage of the battle for civil rights. We seek not just freedom but opportunity. We seek not just legal equity but human ability, not just equality as a right and a theory but equality as a fact and equality as a result.[2]

Assuming that talent is equally distributed across racial groups, we should expect equal outcomes, if indeed equal opportunity is a reality. Affirmative action policies seek to "level the playing field," or at least to loosen the purse strings of those who allocate jobs, college admissions, and other opportunities to a broader pool of applicants.

There is a lot that people get wrong about affirmative action. There are two things that we will address here. First is the idea that affirmative action is synonymous with racial quotas. This is false. Though there was a time when quotas were used, racial quotas were deemed unconstitutional in the 1978 *Bakke* Supreme Court decision.

Second is the notion that affirmative action is a form of **reverse discrimination**, whereby the **merits** of whites are discounted in efforts to attain a more **diverse** institution of higher education, corporation, or government workplace. There is actually a great deal of data that show that whites with mediocre qualifications have not had any major problems in accessing opportunities in any of these realms of life in the United States. But beyond that, we follow the sociologists Michael Omi and Howard Winant, who argue that a policy, program, idea, interaction, or the like is **racist** if "it creates or reproduces structures of domination based on racial significations and identities."[3] Policies like affirmative action are **antiracist** in that they have been used to change the structure of the racial hierarchy, aiming only to flatten it rather than to turn it upside down.

We should mention, though, there has been a shift in the rationale of affirmative action policies over time. We have gone from considering **race** as a means of rectifying historical injustices to pursuing a more **neoliberal** and profit-driven enterprise: **diversity**. This shift largely came out of the Supreme Court cases like *Grutter v. Bollinger* (2003) and *Gratz v. Bollinger* (2003), whereby the majority opinion rationalized that it is important to consider race and ethnicity not because of historical and present-day structural **racism** but because diversity is a compelling state interest (though it has been argued elsewhere that diversity's greatest benefit is actually for white people).[4] This shift is an important one because these policies, as they exist today, can be helpful, but they can also be implemented in a pernicious way.

Justice Sandra Day O'Connor suggested in *Grutter* that in twenty-five years' time, the necessity of considering structurally contingent identities should completely dissipate given the alleged progress we've seen thus far.[5] Whether former Justice O'Connor was naïve or not, someone on the current Supreme Court is surely watching the clock . . . tick tock.

American dream

American mythology, common sense revisited

1. A spouse, house with a white picket fence, 2.5 kids, and a dog

2. The mythological notion that through sheer hard work and perseverance alone, one will attain economic upward mobility in US society

   see also: meritocracy

Dreams—like hopes—can be motivational. However, implicit in the dominant logic of the American dream is the belief that those who move upward do so ruggedly on their own, and those who do not transform from rags to riches lack ingenuity and grit. Both notions are cause for concern. Let's consider the following caveats.

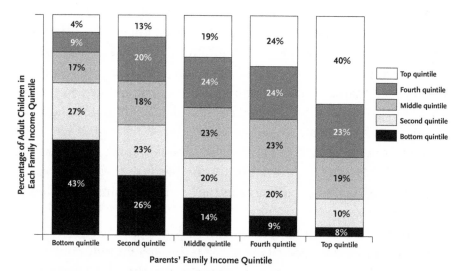

Chances of moving up or down the family income ladder by parents' income. Note: Data has been adjusted for family size. (Urahn et al., *Pursuing the American Dream*)

First, the American dream does not account for the fact that many people who get a "home run" in life started out on third base. There are data that show that economic upward mobility is actually not as common as many people would believe. That is to say, intergenerational mobility is not as prevalent as we'd like to think it is. For example, this graph shows that the Horatio Alger myth[6] applies only to about 4 percent of people (the proportion of people who move from the lowest to the highest quintile of income), while 43 percent of people who are raised by parents in the lowest quintile are likely to remain there as adults. Meanwhile, about the same proportion (40 percent) of those who were raised by those at the top are likely to stay there.

Another caveat is that you can earn good grades in US schools, sacrifice your life in the US military, pay taxes, and raise your children to love this country and still not be cloaked in the security of the American dream because you have been constructed as "illegal" and thus undeserving. We've always heard that one should pull oneself up by one's bootstraps, but it helps if at least one of your parents is a cobbler.

antiracism

foundational concept, tool of liberation

1. The practice of dismantling a system marked by **white supremacy** and anti-Black **racism** through deliberate action

2. A theory that explains and exposes multiple forms of racism: overt and covert, interpersonal and institutional, historical and present day, persistent and nascent

---

Racism is not the only source of oppression in US society. Sexism, homophobia, Islamophobia, and classism "are all important parts of the webbed package of oppressions internal to U.S. society"; thus, it is unnecessary and unwise to reduce all oppressions to one kind.[7] However, following Omi and Winant, we argue that **race** is a "master category" or fundamental concept that has a hand in structuring many other kinds of oppression.[8]

By recognizing and exposing the way that **white supremacy** influences every realm of US society—the economy, politics and political institutions, education, health, the media, the family, religion—as well as other forms of oppression, we become more equipped to strategize ways to dismantle systemic, institutional, and structural racism.

Though many people argue that dreaming of utopias is a waste of time, we beg to differ.[9] It is only by orienting ourselves and working toward what we believe society should look like (regardless of the known constraints) that we can envision the fulfillment of the transformations that are required to overthrow a **racialized social system**.

Black girl magic

tool of liberation, wisdom of popular culture

1. The recognition of the beauty, ability, resourcefulness, and perseverance of Black women in a society marked by anti-Black sexism

2. An effort to highlight the role of Black women in all aspects of US life

   synonyms: #BlackGirlMagic, #ProfessionalBlackGirl
   antonym: misogynoir
   see also: intersectionality

Started as a hashtag, #BlackGirlsAreMagic, the phrase has evolved and grown through the power of social media and CaShawn Thompson, the woman who developed and popularized the phrase. She explained, "I say 'magic' because it's something that people don't always understand. . . . Sometimes our [Black women's] accomplishments might seem to come out of thin air, because a lot of times, the only people supporting us are other black women."[10] The necessity for campaigns like Black Girl Magic and #SayHerName highlights the fact that Black women are often devalued and **dehumanized**, and generally speaking, their lives do not matter as much as the lives of other Americans do. Thompson's explanation of why she employs the word "magic" is premised on the notion that Black women are often deemed invisible in US society, despite their pivotal role in it. Theories and paradigms like **intersectionality** and **misogynoir** have been key to understanding persistent inequality because they illuminate the ways in which various forms of oppression layer on top of one another to constrain the life chances, opportunity structure, and positive imagery of Black women.

Black self-love has always been seen as radical. Despite the challenges posed to Black women, social media messages like

#BlackGirlMagic and #ProfessionalBlackGirl serve to unapologetically celebrate Black womanhood.

---

capitalism

foundational concept, common sense revisited

1. An economic, political, and ideological system that centers private ownership of the means of production in order to gain profit

2. The idea that the "free" market ought to determine the way that goods are produced and how income and profit is distributed

see also: American dream

There are different kinds of capitalist systems, but it's probably more useful here to point out the ways in which capitalism, generally speaking, has served to develop and perpetuate racial inequality.

Let's take a walk down memory lane: "Where would the original accumulation of capital used in industry (in the West) have come from if not the extraction of wealth from colonies, piracy, and the slave trade?"[11] Manning Marable plainly explains, "The U.S. state apparatus was created to facilitate the expansion and entrenchment of institutional **racism** in both slave and nonslaveholding states."[12] If you read the US Constitution closely, you'll see that not only is it a political document that outlines the distribution of power among the three branches of government and between the federal and state governments, but it is also laced with matters of economics and property rights.[13] For instance, there is no mention of slavery in the Bill of Rights, but there are several references to using enslaved people for political and economic benefit: counting enslaved people as three-fifths a person for the purposes of taxation and representation (Article 1, Section 2); prevention of interference in the slave trade for two decades (Article 1, Section 9); and the demand to return people who sought to self-emancipate to those who enslaved them (Article 4, Section 2).[14]

Anti-Black **racism** and **capitalism** have worked together over time to shift Blacks from chattel slavery to sharecropping and peonage, from low-wage industrial jobs to attaining lower rates on return on education, from excluding Blacks from a legitimate housing market to exposing a disproportionate number of Blacks to the sub-prime-mortgage crisis; from convict-leased chain gangs to "factories with fences."[15] Companies can make larger and larger profits by paying people less and less—or nothing if they can.

But wait! There's more! **Intersectionality** helps us to understand the ways in which Black women, and poor Black women in particular, make up an especially vulnerable group. The tripartite combination of anti-Black racism, sexism, and classism serves to place Black women at the crosshairs of three systems of oppression. With that in consideration, the ultimate emancipation of Black people cannot be complete without a critique of **white supremacy**, patriarchy, *and* capitalism.

---

citizenship

foundational concept, common sense revisited

1. Formal or legal membership in society that entitles you to rights and privileges outlined by the laws of the land

2. A mutual recognition of full membership in society or treatment as a person of equal dignity and humanity

---

We emphasize two aspects of citizenship—one formal, the other substantive—and three kinds of citizenship rights: civil, political, and social. Formal citizenship—that is, legal membership in society—

affords you an array of rights. In the United States, one is granted citizenship by birthright (outlined in the Fourteenth Amendment) or through the process of naturalization. The sociologist Thomas Marshall explains that civil rights are "composed of the rights necessary for individual freedom—liberty of the person, freedom of speech, thought and faith, the right to own property and to conclude valid contracts, and the right to justice"; political rights concern the "right to participate in the exercise of power, as a member of a body invested with political authority or as an elector of the membership of such a body." Finally, the social element of citizenship rights deals with "the whole range from the right to a modicum of economic welfare and security to the right to share in the full social heritage and to live the life of a civilized being according to the standards prevailing in society." This slate of rights implies that citizenship is not just about relishing in the privilege of membership but also that there are "reciprocal obligations toward the community."[16] These rights are largely understood to be imbued in formal US citizenship, but they are not sufficient for people to experience what Marshall and fellow sociologist Evelyn Nakano Glenn call "substantive citizenship." Substantive citizenship moves beyond having rights in theory and emphasizes whether people can exercise those rights in practice.[17]

Though all citizens are ostensibly guaranteed the full rights and privileges of all other citizens, the fact of the matter is that this has not and does not describe the reality of US citizenship. The rally cry #BlackLivesMatter serves to illuminate the fact that though most Black people in the United States are citizens by law, they are not treated as such and thus do not enjoy substantive citizenship. One can easily think of the ways in which Black people are disenfranchised, but there is also the interpersonal aspect of persistent social exclusion from "mainstream" society; this exclusion is well marked by the daily aggregation of **microaggressions**, the state of being in constant mourning,[18] and recognizing that one's life is, in fact, more vulnerable than one's average white peers.

The history of rights in the United States is neither linear nor necessarily progressive. Many of the rights that people of color and other marginalized communities gained over the years were granted only after the arduous process of demanding them. And still, some rights may be taken away or a full sweep of rights may not be fully granted even after long, arduous fights. For example, the US Supreme Court's majority decision in *Obergefell v. Hodges* (2015) requires marriage equality. However, while Americans can marry across or within genders, there are twenty-eight states that still allow for employers to fire lesbian, gay, or transgender people because they are lesbian, gay, or transgender![19] Today, we have to keep a close watch on rights concerning abortion and access to reproductive health, voting, and even the right to protest because, while guaranteed, these are constantly being attacked and, at times, circumvented or even curtailed.

---

co-optation

tool of oppression, tool of liberation

1. Taking an idea, disassembling it, reassembling it with original pieces as well as retrofitted ones; giving the modified thing a different name than the original and then claiming originality

2. Appropriation; falsely claiming rights to or innovation of something as one's own

---

Co-optation can be used for good or for evil. For instance, it is well known that Martin Luther King Jr. famously stated (among many, many, many things), "I have a dream that my four little children will one day live in a nation where they will not be judged by the color of their skin but by the content of their character." Conservatives have suggested that Dr. King, whose legacy we all (partially) know and love, desired a **colorblind** United States. Agreed. We would take Dr. King's aspiration of colorblindness to mean that one's life chances are not influenced by one's racial group membership. But for racial conservatives, being colorblind means that you should pay attention to neither **race** nor **racism**. By co-opting Dr. King's dream, conservatives are able to suggest that people who talk about race are, themselves, racist. Though foolish, this logic often successfully serves to shut down claims of and constructive conversations around race and racism. Indeed, the dominant racial ideology in contemporary US society is **colorblind racism**.

Generally speaking, co-optation usually ends with dominant groups taking, commandeering, or appropriating an idea, concept, aspect of culture, or resistance and then using it against marginalized groups (for the nearly exclusive benefit of the dominant group). But it could also be the case that marginalized people take something from the dominant group and call it their own. In 1857, Chief Justice Roger Taney, on behalf of the Supreme Court of the United States, wrote that Black people had "no rights which the white man was bound to respect." In the majority decision of *Scott v. Sanford*, Taney meticulously explained that "We the People" did not mean "all y'all." But for centuries, Black freedom fighters have co-opted this language of "we," of "**citizenship**," of "equality," and of "democracy" to broaden the imaginations of their contemporaries and that of future Americans, connecting calls for inclusion to the fulfillment of justice. And in real time, we see today how young, undocumented people who have lived their entire lives in the United States are similarly co-opting the language of the **American dream** and forcing the nation to dream bigger, more imaginative visions of what it could be.

---

colorblind racism

foundational concept, tool of oppression

1. The worldview that suggests that since race *should not* matter, it *does not* matter

2. An ideology that insists that "everyone be treated without regard to race, accompanied by a denial of the causes and consequences of racism"[20]

The consensus among scholars who study **racism** is that today's dominant racial ideology is best understood as colorblind.[21] Put simply, "colorblind racial ideology creates a façade of racial inclusion by suggesting that in a post–civil rights era, everyone has an equal opportunity to succeed, and if differences in outcomes across racial groups continue to exist, these differences are best explained through culture, natural occurrences, or 'a little bit' of residual racism that may still exist due to a few prejudiced individuals."[22]

Colorblind racism fuels a **racialized social system** because it allows, or even requires, people to ignore structural racism and instead focus on individual behavior, while also assuming that society can be likened to a level playing field. The historian Ibram Kendi explains, "If the purpose of racist ideas had always been to silence the **antiracist** resisters to racial discrimination, then the postracial line of attack may have been the most sophisticated silencer to date."[23] Injustice thrives when the illusion of justice is perfected.[24]

Have you ever said, thought, or heard a friend say the following?

* The way to stop discriminating on the basis of **race** is to stop discriminating on the basis of race.[25]

* Sure, most people in my neighborhood are of my race, but that's because birds of a feather flock together. People are just naturally more comfortable with people who look like them.

* **Racism** exists, but it's mostly just grandmas in Mississippi and Klansmen.

* It's a coincidence that all of my friends are white.

* I believe in equal opportunity. That's why it's unfair to consider race in admissions or hiring.

* All of the Mexican kids sit together. That's self-segregation.

* If Black people worked harder, they would be much better off. Pulling up your bootstraps is key to success in this country.

* It's not that I have **white privilege**; it's just that my parents, through their hard work, ingenuity, and a little financial help from my grandparents who benefited from the GI Bill, were able to put me in the best schools and extracurricular activities.

* There are major disparities between Blacks and whites, but this is best understood as a matter of class rather than race.

These are classic examples of colorblind racial ideology frames.[26] They are tied together by an insistence that the playing field is level and the assertion that racism is not a key mechanism in the way the United States works. These very common utterances suggest that racial phenomena like residential segregation, racially homogeneous social networks, and the resegregation of public schools are best explained by nonracial explanations such as culture and class. We will be very clear on this matter: there is no high-quality, empirical data that support these ideas!

---

colorism

tool of oppression

A practice whereby privileges and disadvantages are systematically doled out on the basis of skin color, with a disproportionate amount of advantages provided to lighter-skinned people

synonym: light-skin privilege

While white Americans have a range of privileges afforded to them due to their **race**, it is also the case that even within various racial groups, people who are of a lighter hue are provided more benefits than their darker-skinned counterparts are, on average. Research shows that among African Americans, Asian Americans, and Latinxs, lighter-skinned individuals earn more money, are more likely to live in racially integrated neighborhoods and own their home, gain more education, have lower poverty rates, and marry people with higher socioeconomic status than do those who are darker skinned.[27] Darker-skinned people are less likely to get married, receive longer prison sentences, and have higher rates of unemployment than their lighter-skinned counterparts do.[28] We tend to see lighter-skinned individuals in advertisements, movies, and modeling agencies because light skin is viewed as more aesthetically and culturally normative (and superior). Taken together, we see that the United States is not just a **racialized social system**, whereby racial groups are hierarchically ordered, but also a pigmentocracy, or a society that privileges lighter skin.[29]

We cannot separate colorism, or the "process that privileges light-skinned people over dark in areas such as income, education, housing, and the marriage market,"[30] from a wider system of **white supremacy** because it is by no means a coincidence that people who more closely mimic whiteness are rewarded for doing so. In recog-

Photo by Mariah Warner

nizing the rewards that come with European physical features, such as light skin and straight hair, people across the world—reflecting the global nature of **white supremacy**—go through dire straits to attain those features. Skin-bleaching creams are common in countries that range from Saudi Arabia to India to Nigeria. It is common to get "double eyelid" surgery among Asian and Asian American women, and similarly, it is a normal graduation gift to get a nose job in parts of Mexico.

Scholars like Yaba Blay turn the notion of pigmentocracy on its head, pointing out the ways in which light-skinned individuals are, at times, disadvantaged, particularly when they are faced with **micro-aggressions** about their group identity, challenges to racial authenticity, or even exclusion by members of their own racial group.[31] **Intersectionality** helps us think through the idea that what may be an advantage in one space may lead to oppression in another. Though psychological discomfort that light-skinned individuals may face cannot and should not be compared to the material disadvantages faced by dark-skinned people, we should remain cognizant that Black people and other people of color are marginalized due to their **race**, and the effects of **racism** can be "mitigated" or intensified by colorism.

---

cross-cutting issue

extra credit

1. An issue that is salient and relevant to members of seemingly opposed groups in a similar way

2. An issue that could potentially lead to coalition across groups

---

There are a number of issues that are in the interest of some members of different groups. Poverty is an excellent example. There are poor and working-class people of various racial and ethnic groups and of various partisan identities. One might intuit that low-income Blacks, whites, Latinxs, Asian Americans, and indigenous people ought to work together around issues related to raising the minimum wage, universal health care, or at least a strong social safety net for low- and no-income individuals and families. To be sure, history is peppered with instances of interracial coalition building around cross-cutting issues, but race has often been used by white political elites as a wedge to prevent these alliances from forging and taking hold (take the 1898 Wilmington Coup d'État as just one overlooked example).[32]

Toward the end of Dr. King's life, a lesser-known, economic-minded King worked toward developing a Poor People's Campaign that would loosen that wedge of racial division and seek economic justice for people across racial groups. Today, folks like the Reverend William Barber endeavor to revive that multiracial campaign by organizing around the cross-cutting issues of universal health care, quality jobs and employment, affordable housing, mass incarceration, and the fortification of voting rights.[33] These issues are cross-cutting because they affect all sorts of people across political, ideological, and racial groups.

When we reflect on why there aren't more coalitions built around cross-cutting issues, we realize that too many people believe themselves to be playing a zero-sum game, one premised on the notion that if someone gains, someone else must automatically be losing. If I immigrate to the United States, a native-born American automatically loses a job. If your child is getting ESL lessons in school, my child is losing already-tight resources in public education. This way of thinking has also extended to other realms of US society, such that "if the country is asked to mourn and show sympathy for a slain black woman or man, it must necessarily mean that [white people] will, at least, lose favor in their own society, or worse, be the categorical target of retribution and disdain."[34] The philosopher Christopher Lebron asserts, "No one who looks at the world in this way can be prepared to sacrifice. And here, by sacrifice, I do not mean to lose. Rather, I mean, to make oneself vulnerable to new political possibilities and personal relations."[35]

culture of poverty

tool of oppression

1. The notion that poor and working-class people are poor because they do not know how to work, do not have the motivation to work, or are too dependent on public assistance

2. An idea that poverty is intergenerational because poverty is (psychologically) pathological and cyclical

I think that if we are going to have a change in this whole cycle of failure, we've got to get at the heart of it, that's at the elementary school level. I suggest that we simply take young people out of the environment where they have no motivation because their parents don't understand it, they never had any motivation when they were youngsters, they had their children when they were 16 and they never have gotten into this success cycle that many of us think of.

—Mayor of Los Angeles Tom Bradley, 1985[36]

The ideological stance called "culture of poverty" is rooted in the idea that poor people are poor because they do not know how to work toward the **American dream**. Though this idea has been used to explain poverty generally speaking, it is most often used to explain persistent racial disparities. One of the best-known historical references to such an idea comes from the now very (in)famous Moynihan Report, which essentially argued that while **white supremacy** was a barrier for Black people, Black culture—marked by female-headed households—was the greatest barrier preventing Black folks from living up to their full potential. Since then, others have mimicked this notion, combining structural factors with "cultural" ones to explain why Blacks fall behind whites on important socioeconomic indicators.

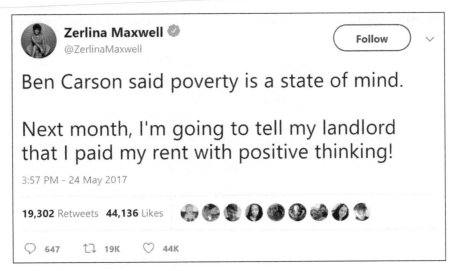

Zerlina Maxwell ✔
@ZerlinaMaxwell

Follow ⌄

Ben Carson said poverty is a state of mind.

Next month, I'm going to tell my landlord that I paid my rent with positive thinking!

3:57 PM - 24 May 2017

19,302 Retweets **44,136** Likes

💬 647   ↻ 19K   ♡ 44K

Commentary from the Twittersphere.

Racial differences in "employment and earnings, educational attainment, and family structure" cannot be explained by "culture" or values. Research shows that Blacks are systematically discriminated against in employment, get lower returns on their investment in education, value education more than whites do, and are actually more "family oriented" than whites are in conventional terms. What we ought to be cognizant of is that being poor and Black looks much different than being poor and white, in large part, due to the racial wealth gap. The prominent economist William Darity explains, "When wealth is taken into account virtually every group-based disparity in behavior customarily attributed to racial differences in cultural orientation disappears."[37] Culture matters, just not as an explanation for racial disparities.

---

dehumanization

foundational concept, tool of oppression

1. The notion that some people are less than human

2. The routine association of Blacks with demons and animals, such as apes

---

because white men can't
police their imagination
black men are dying

—Claudia Rankine, *Citizen*[38]

Anti-Black **racism** is undergirded by dehumanization, or the idea that Blacks are less than human. Indeed, the advent of **race** is fundamentally rooted in dehumanization. We know now that whites were able to rationalize the enslavement of Black people using the logic of dehumanization. On the same plantation, enslaved Black women were used as tools of labor, for sexual gratification, as breeding factories to produce more people who could be enslaved, and as live subjects of scientific and medical experimentation. Enslaved people, like houses, were taxed and insured as property.[39]

Research shows that many whites still routinely dehumanize Blacks, implicitly associating them with apes. When provided with an image depicting the "Ascent of Man," some whites rated their racial group as being more evolved than Blacks.[40]

There are other ways this dynamic plays out. For example, in Officer Darren Wilson's testimony about how and why he fatally shot eighteen-year-old Michael Brown, he said that Brown reached into the police SUV and punched him. Then he explained, "When I grabbed him, the only way I can describe it is I felt like a five-year-old holding onto Hulk Hogan." Michael Brown was six foot four and 292

0	20	40	60	80	100

"Ascent of Man"

pounds at the time of his death. Wilson, six foot four and 210 pounds, went on to testify, "And then after he did that [attempted to grab his gun], he looked up at me and had the most intense aggressive face. The only way I can describe it, it looks like a demon, that's how angry he looked." He went on to say that Brown began to flee but then turned around. At that point, Wilson explained, "it looked like he was almost bulking up to run through the shots, like it was making him mad that I'm shooting at him. And the face he had was looking straight through me, like I wasn't even there, I wasn't even anything in his way."[41] Michael Brown was dehumanized and believed to be superhuman all at the same time!

The poet and essayist Claudia Rankine asserts, "Blackness in the white imagination has nothing to do with Black people."[42] **Antiracism** requires us to keep in mind that there is absolutely nothing wrong with Black people. Racial inequality and injustice are not produced by **race**, but instead they are "products of socio-historical processes of racialization and **white supremacy**."[43]

diversity

common sense revisited

1. The presence of an array of different things or attributes

2. Diverse (adjective)

    a. Multicultural, multiethnic, or multiracial

    b. Sometimes used with grammatical abandonment to describe the presence of a single person of color, as in "Candis is diverse."

3. Happy talk[44] about multiculturalism

Everybody loves diversity. Indeed, most people view racially homogeneous spaces, such as classrooms or boardrooms, as morally suspect. In turn, we are seeing an increasing number of people of color in institutions of higher education, in the government, and in the corporate world; there are even some signs of increasing integration in US neighborhoods. Yet, if we look more deeply, we find that neither the value of diversity nor the increased presence of underrepresented racial groups has led to a major reshaping of the US racial hierarchy. How could this be?

Diversity initiatives largely evolved from **affirmative action** policies, but an increasing number of critical diversity scholars, like the sociologist Sarah Mayorga-Gallo,[45] suggest that diversity, as it is understood and constructed in contemporary US society, is mostly hamstrung from producing a more equitable society. First, researchers like Mayorga-Gallo show that diversity is understood to mean anything from having a multiracial group to a group of people with different personalities or tastes. By equating structurally contingent identities (e.g., **race**, ethnicity, gender) with idiosyncratic ones (e.g., preference for flip-flops or horror movies), it becomes easy to see how one can walk into a board of trustees meeting with all white men and believe that space to be diverse. Second, diversity is very much commodified. Diversity is viewed as a marketable commodity, and people of color are viewed and used as things to help whites accomplish their goals rather than as people who have value separate from their experiences shaped by their racial identity.[46] That is to say, today's construction of diversity is **neoliberal**, placing profits over people.

Third, research shows that while people value diversity and intend for their spaces to be more representative of the population, they do not necessarily follow up on the full incorporation and inclusion of people of color; only intentions matter, not necessarily results. Finally, there is an increased awareness that though whites value diversity in the abstract, when it comes down to it, many are able to undermine diversity initiatives by suggesting that diversity is mutually exclusive from quality, **merit**, and comfort, while some suggest that it may require additional policing of bodies of color.

"Diversity" has been **co-opted** by racial conservatives. In this iteration, "people can simultaneously recognize diversity, but not oppression; deny difference and appreciate diversity; be conscious of racial differences, but nonconscious of continuing race injustice."[47] This rendition of the concept hinders diversity from being used to realize its full potential to eradicate disparities faced by historically marginalized groups. We should note, however, that there are people who call for increased diversity for the purposes of social justice, including us. We file this under "common sense revisited" because we believe it is important for students of **antiracism** to recognize that just because people are using the same words, it is not safe to assume that we are using those words to mean the same thing.

dog whistle politics

tool of oppression

Coded racial appeals

see also: racial euphemisms

The Nixon campaign in 1968, and the Nixon White House after that, had two enemies: the antiwar left and black people. You understand what I'm saying? We knew we couldn't make it illegal to be either against the war or black, but by getting the public to associate the hippies with marijuana and blacks with heroin, and then criminalizing both heavily, we could disrupt those communities. We could arrest their leaders, raid their homes, break up their meetings, and vilify them night after night on the evening news. Did we know we were lying about the drugs? Of course we did.

—John Ehrlichman, counsel and assistant to the president for domestic affairs under President Richard Nixon[48]

A dog whistle is an instrument used to call a dog; the sound that the whistle makes is at a pitch that dogs can hear but humans cannot. Metaphorically, dog whistle politics is a means to clandestinely solicit and rally certain people using particular phrases that resonate with the targeted audience. Ian Haney López penned a beautifully written book about this as a tool of oppression, called *Dog Whistle Politics*.[49] He explains that this tool works in three basic moves: "A punch that jabs **race** into the conversation through thinly veiled references to threatening nonwhites, for instance to welfare cheats or illegal aliens; a parry that slaps away charges of racial pandering, often by emphasizing the lack of any direct reference to a racial group or any use of an epithet; and finally a kick that savages the critic for opportunistically alleging racial victimization."[50] López and others show that during and just after the civil rights era, there was real

potential to undermine a racial hierarchy marked by **white supremacy**, but dog whistle politics were employed to rally (poor) whites
around their racial group identity rather than against the political
representatives who failed to develop more equitable policies for all,
including poor whites and white women.[51] The political right used
dog whistle politics to steer US governance policy toward **neoliberalism**, starting in the 1970s and 1980s. How else could you have
convinced low-income whites to support the dismantling of New
Deal and post–World War II economic policies than by suggesting
that these policies served undeserving Black people at the expense of
hard-working whites? Dog whistle politics are aimed to undermine
efforts toward racial equality but ultimately serve to exacerbate the
enormous gap between the top 20 percent and the rest of the US
citizens and denizens.[52]

FREQUENTLY ASKED QUESTION

Donald Trump's campaign used dog whistle politics as well as outright **racist** stereotypes to garner the support of a large swath of the
American public. Are people who voted for Trump racist?

We would encourage you to ask a different question: Is it racist
to vote for a candidate whose campaign and policy platform seek to
maintain or exacerbate existing racial disparities, while developing
new ones?

The answer to that question is, "Hell yeah."

AN EXERCISE IN ACTIVISM

Can dog whistle politics be used to rally racial egalitarians? If so,
which phrases would be used? Who would "hear" them?

epistemology of ignorance

tool of oppression

1. A militant, aggressive willingness to not know[53]

2. A process of knowing designed to produce not knowing about white privilege and white supremacy[54]

It is common to hear that **racists** are ignorant. Another common refrain is that if white people knew more about structural racism and **white privilege**, they would behave differently, be more benevolent and sympathetic, and practice **antiracism.** The philosopher Charles Mills insightfully notes, "ignorance is usually thought of as the passive obverse to knowledge, the darkness retreating before the spread of Enlightenment," but he argues that *white ignorance*—ignorance about **white supremacy** and white privilege—is often militant and aggressive.[55] Many white people do know about white privilege and persistent racial inequality but actively bypass this knowledge and tacitly maintain white supremacy. **Colorblind racism** is rooted in this epistemology of ignorance.

The sociologist Jennifer Mueller points out that there are four ways that people actively bypass their knowledge about embedded systems of racial inequality. One way is to simply evade learning about racial matters. Another way is to introduce "alternate factors to facilitate misanalysing, ignoring and/or rejecting the racial dynamics" of racial inequality.[56] For example, a person might assert something like, "Yes, my grandparents benefited from a policy that was implemented in a racist way, but they worked hard. **Meritocracy** is a better explanation for their accumulation of assets." A third mechanism that produces not knowing is to suggest that people only participate in perpetuating racial inequality because they do not know they are doing so; this mechanism assumes that whites are inherently virtuous, failing only because they do not know, and assumes that whites' knowledge will automatically lead to better results. Finally, people mystify practical solutions or suggest that the problem of **racism** is too big to tackle, thus rendering change impossible.

People learn about what they want to know and actively avoid knowing what they do not want to know. Our goal is to make ignorance difficult to maintain.

---

false equivalence

tool of oppression

1. A logical fallacy, whereby two opposing sides of an argument are deemed equivalent when they actually are not

2. A reliance on feeble similarities in an attempt to make moot the more important observation and effect of the glaring differences

---

Most people value fairness, but sometimes we equate fairness with balance, with providing equal time for all sides of a story, or with trying to see the world through all possible sets of perspectives. It may sound counterintuitive to some people for us to argue that not all sides should get a say, but we assert such a claim because not all sides have the moral authority to take part in civil discussions that have the potential to produce more equitable outcomes for society's most vulnerable groups. To suggest otherwise provides an opening for a false equivalence.

For instance, some people would claim that calling someone a racist is just as bad as being a racist. That is a false equivalence. Or the suggestion that referring to a white woman who calls the police on people for being Black while grilling as a "Barbeque Becky" is as vicious as likening a Black woman to an "ape" is a false equivalence. Or claims of **reverse discrimination** are by definition rooted in

Trump on the "reverse racism" of the show *Blackish*.

false equivalence. Or the proclamation that there is "blame on both sides" when a neo-Nazi protestor injures a dozen people and kills a counterprotester can best be described as a false equivalence. Or the argument that Black Lives Matter movement is just as divisive as the Ku Klux Klan also requires suspension of logic because that claim is also a false equivalence. By equating the power and effect of **racism** with something that has little to no influence on one's opportunity structure or life chances is to minimize the power and effect of racism, and to equate an analysis of racism with racism itself is to ignore the power dynamics embedded in a **racialized social system**.

gaslighting

wisdom of popular culture

1. To psychologically manipulate a person or group of people into believing that they cannot trust their own memories, perceptions, or interpretation of events[57]

2. *Racial gaslighting*: a systematic effort to discredit claims of racism, typically by means of contradiction, outright denial, misdirection, and lying

Considering the fact that **racism** today has a "now you see it, now you don't" quality,[58] minorities often feel that when they are having a racialized experience, such as **microaggressions** or finding themselves on the short end of the structural racism stick, white Americans around them seem not to notice; if they do notice, the experience often gets downplayed as an isolated event or is invalidated entirely as nonracial. This persistent denial of racism is now known as "racial gaslighting," a form of psychic violence.

An excellent example of racial gaslighting is the use of the words "incident" and "bad apple," as in "Police shootings of unarmed Black people are not indicative of a larger system of racism but instead are isolated incidents caused by a few bad apples." The Department of Justice (DOJ) under Loretta Lynch's leadership tells us otherwise (as mentioned in chapter 1). After investigating the police departments of Chicago, Baltimore, and Ferguson, the DOJ found systematic abuses of power and widespread patterns of constitutional violations that were skewed in racially biased ways. Police brutality is not a figment of the imagination, but some people would like to frame it that way. Another means to manipulate people of color is to misdirect attention of the true cause of the problem, especially when that problem is racism.

Bearing the brunt of a constant bait-and-switch and enduring the barrages of **whitesplaining** that interpret one's own reality in nonsensical terms can wear a person down. As an act of resistance and well-being, the contemporary Movement for Black Lives encourages Black people to love and care for themselves and other Black people because dealing with interpersonal and structural **racism** is mentally and emotionally taxing. Black people and other marginalized human beings must be free to speak their truths, confess their intuitions, and heal themselves in community. We should take note of the sage advice attributed to Zora Neale Hurston: "If you are silent about your pain, they'll kill you and say you enjoyed it."

implicit attitudes

extra credit

Unconscious associations between value-laden characteristics and/or stereotypes and various groups of people or things

Almost nobody we know wants to be racist, but most people, without even thinking about it, associate positive characteristics with some groups (e.g., white, able-bodied, Christian, cisgendered, wealthy) and negative stereotypes with other groups (e.g., Black, immigrant, differently abled, Muslim, transgender, low- or no-income). Because Americans are socialized within the same social and political milieu, we all tend to be exposed to the same set of associations, especially by the media. What this means is that people across racial groups are likely to have racial biases that run in the same direction (though some may be stronger than others). While unconsciously making connections between one group and a set of positive or negative characteristics doesn't automatically cause a person to behave in a racist manner, it should be noted that implicit attitudes "shape one's deliberative thoughts without

Trump in the Rose Garden. (Photo by Amanda Holland)

the person knowing how this influence actually occurs or that it has even taken place."[59]

The political scientist Efrén Pérez explains that when political topics such as immigration (or **affirmative action, diversity**, welfare, crime, gun control, etc.) come up, "relevant implicit attitudes are spontaneously activated and made mentally accessible to people. . . . These implicit attitudes can affect not only the political opinions citizens express but also the very interpretation of the information they use to arrive at those opinions."[60] As such, unconscious thinking plays an incredibly important part in the way we think and behave.

There are mounds of research on the effects of implicit bias. Pérez's data show that implicit attitudes about Latinxs influence immigration policy preferences. In lab experiments, people across racial groups are more likely to shoot unarmed Black people than whites in video games, and people are more likely to believe that the items that Blacks are holding are guns.[61] Recent research shows that in places where whites have a higher-than-average bias against Blacks, Blacks are more likely to be victims of police shootings.[62] In the photo above, the video producer Amanda Holland Photoshopped Rep. Mark Meadows's face on *all* of the men who took a picture with Donald Trump in the Rose Garden after the House passed a bill to "repeal and replace" Obamacare. Did you notice? The fact that most people don't notice is because the mental road that connects "political power," "elite," and "white men" is very smooth and incredibly fast. Taken together, we see that our implicit attitudes reflect the United States' racial order, and the actions and policy preferences that are, in part, shaped by unconscious thinking perpetuate that order.

It's important to know that a recognition of implicit attitudes is a necessary but not sufficient step toward **antiracism**. Some people are very fatalistic about this possibility, suggesting, "We're hardwired to stereotype in order to deal with a very complex world, so yeah . . . let's move on." This type of thinking not only undermines the power of human agency but also forsakes a degree of morality. It's time to hold our brains accountable to our principles. This not only means becoming more cognizant of our biases, implicit or otherwise, but also entails changing the systems and institutions that train us to connect certain characteristics with certain groups.

---

intersectionality

foundational concept, tool of liberation

1. A theory that highlights the heterogeneity of privileges and layers of oppression that individuals within a group may experience

2. A paradigm, rooted in the analysis of Black women's experiences, that reveals that Black women are "doubly bound," due to overlapping layers of oppressions, including racism and sexism; this paradigm asserts that race constructs the way women experience gender, and gender influences how women experience race[63]

see also: Black girl magic, misogynoir

Coined by the critical **race** theorist Kimberlé Crenshaw, "intersectionality" helps to expose the fact that people are situated in multiple, structurally contingent identity groups and that the advantages and disadvantages that are related to each identity are "mutually constructing phenomena."[64] Loosely worded, the burdens and benefits that come with your different identities influence each other and thus influence your opportunity structure. Consequently, people who share membership in one group may experience that identity differently because of the good stuff or bad stuff that comes with some other identity they may have.

Here's what intersectionality is not: It's not about all the different identities you have. It's not what makes you special! That is a superficial first step in understanding the contribution of the theory. As an analytical strategy, "intersectionality is based on the idea that more than one category should be analyzed, that categories matter equally and that the relationship between categories is an open empirical question, that members within a category are diverse, that analysis of the individual or a set of individuals is integrated with institutional analysis, and that empirical and theoretical claims are both possible and necessary."[65]

Another thing: intersectionality helps us to realize that there are almost no groups that have all the power in all situations, and there are almost none that have never had any power. Even within a racial group, for instance, there are various ranges of life chances due to gender, class, skin color, sexuality, and the like. Upper- and middle-class Black people face racial discrimination, but it may look very different from a low-income Black person's experiences. Or, as another example, the #SayHerName hashtag was developed in order to highlight the fact that Black women are also susceptible to racial terror committed by the state and fellow citizens, though those experiences tend to be made invisible in the popular media, as well as in Black people's conversations.

It's important not to go down the Oppression Olympics rabbit hole. The point of intersectionality is to make us cognizant of the fact that the lives of Black people are vulnerable to anti-Black **racism**, but that vulnerability manifests itself in very different ways for members across the racial group.

---

meritocracy

American mythology, common sense revisited

1. A system based on merit

2. An incentive system that rewards the actions that society values[66]

3. An American myth based on the idea that opportunities are presented in direct proportion to individuals' hard work, skills, and talents

antonym: nepotism

They say they want you successful
But then they make it stressful
You start keepin' pace,
They start changin' up the tempo

—Mos Def, "Mr. Nigga" (1999)

Meritocracy is not a myth, in and of itself, but the way meritocracy is constructed in the United States is better understood by the concept of "social closure." Social closure is a "process of subordination whereby one group monopolizes advantages by closing off opportunities to another group of outsiders beneath it which it determines as inferior and ineligible."[67]

So, in the case of most US colleges and universities, high standardized-test scores on the SAT, GRE, and even annual tests for elementary and high school children are highly valued. So one's merit is derived from attaining a high score on these tests. But the ability to score high on these tests is often dictated by other factors outside the range of one's intelligence or ability to learn, such as access to high-quality teachers, expensive preparation courses, or other resources that are unequally distributed across **race** and socioeconomic status. As such, it is more accurate to characterize the United States as a system of social closure because the things that we value that allow people access to more opportunities are disproportionately provided to some groups rather than others in a systemically **racist**, classist, and sexist way.

Relatedly, we have to think about how and why our values are shaped the way they are in the first place. Our sense of deservingness, for example, is profoundly tied to what we deem as meritorious. In many cases, this means that people who lack the most basic necessities such as food and shelter are required to *prove* that they are worthy of being valued. Sit on that for a minute. But let's also consider the fact that working-class people, agricultural workers, and stay-at-home moms often do very hard work, but not the kind of work that is "valued"; consequently, people in these occupations are often not viewed as "deserving" of help when hard times arise. For instance, the current system of meritocracy is why Wall Street got bailed out but Main Street and Martin Luther King Boulevard did not.

In order to work toward an **antiracist** society, Americans must, at a minimum, reassess their shared values and develop standards of merit that are not highly correlated with **race** due to sociohistorical processes rooted in racism.[68] Such a reassessment would actually serve to broaden opportunity structures across class, gender, and racial groups. Better still, we should question why in a nation of so much wealth we are thinking about merit at all when it comes to hunger, preventative health care, and a safe place to rest for the night.

microaggression

tool of oppression

1. Small, subtle, pernicious acts of racism

2. Brief remarks, vague insults, casual dismissals, and nonverbal exchanges that serve to slight a person due to the person's race[69]

see also: gaslighting

A lot of (white) people don't buy the idea of "microaggressions" for a few reasons. One is that in isolation, microaggressions often look like the good intentions of a (white) person gone awry. Two, people of color are often depicted as overly sensitive about racial issues and prone to political correctness; thus, they are just "making something out of nothing." Three, if it doesn't involve a noose or a "whites only" sign over a water fountain, it can't, they believe, be *that* bad.

Here's what you should know about microaggressions: from the perspective of a person of color, experiences with microaggressions are not isolated incidents. When aggregated over the course of one's lifetime, these brief exchanges ultimately send a larger, disparaging message: You do not belong (in this society) because of your **race** or ethnicity.[70]

Most people are not even aware that they are communicating via microaggression because it isn't their intention to do so. However, just like many unintentional acts, these words can still wound. For many people of color, microaggressions serve as daily reminders that they are not viewed as full members of society. Microaggressions recycle the harmful stereotypes that people have about various groups of people; they are insulting; they highlight patterns of **implicit attitudes**; they reveal that what is viewed as "normal" in society does not include people of color; they pathologize marginalized people; and they are rooted in an **epistemology of ignorance**.

TRANSLATING MICROAGGRESSIONS

Research shows that when it comes to matters of **race**, white people generally tend to privilege the intentions of the speaker rather than the feelings of the message receiver, thus leading white people to ask people of color to feel differently about a "racial gaffe," rather than to require whites to think before they speak.[71] Here, we translate common microaggressions:

Message sent	Message received
You speak English very well.	You don't look or sound like an American, and therefore you are not a full member of society.
To a Black woman: Can I touch your hair?	You're so exotic and different from anyone/anything I've ever seen before.
To an Asian American person: You're smart. You'll definitely get into your top choice.	Racism isn't real, especially not for Asians.
What are you?	You're some kind of nonwhite person/thing, and I need to know which one you are.
Where are you *from* from?	You cannot be an American because you are not white (or Black).
To a Latinx person: No prob-blem-o!	I'm using mock Spanish to suggest that I value diversity even if that comes at the cost of devaluing the language of your heritage.
You're being paranoid. / It's not that deep. / You're being overly sensitive.	Racism isn't real. Your experiences are invalid.
It would be easier to get into / be hired by [college/corporation] if I were [fill in any underrepresented racial group].	Racism isn't real, but reverse racism is.

Message sent	Message received
I never think of you as a Black/Latinx/ Native American/Asian guy/gal.	I am minimizing what might be an important identity for you so that I can show that I am "**colorblind**" and progressive.
Oh, I'm sorry. I didn't see you standing right in front of me.	You're invisible. And I don't pay close attention to invisible people.
You're pretty for a Black girl.	White women hold the standard of beauty.
No, you're white.	I am minimizing what might be an important identity for you, but I am identifying you as white because you fit my personal criteria.
Your name's too hard to say. I'm gonna call you ——.	Let me help you conform to my version of whiteness.
As a white woman, I totally understand what you're going through as a racial minority.	All oppression is the same. Also, I am disqualified from the possibility of perpetuating racial inequities.
I have a Black neighbor/friend.	I believe association with people of color automatically disqualifies me from the possibility of perpetuating racial inequities.

misogynoir

wisdom of popular culture

1. Misogyny directed toward Black women

2. The ways in which Black women are disrespected and disregarded in US society due to the combined forces of racism and sexism

   antonym: Black girl magic
   see also: intersectionality

Grounded in the theory of **intersectionality**, "misogynoir" is a word that Moya Bailey, a queer Black woman, writer, and scholar, "made up to describe the particular brand of hatred directed at black women in American visual & popular culture."[72] Misogynoir pinpoints the way in which Black women's gendered experiences are influenced by anti-Black **racism** and how Black women's experiences with racism are simultaneously shaped by sexism. Bailey's explanation of what motivated her to come up with the term illuminates the various ways

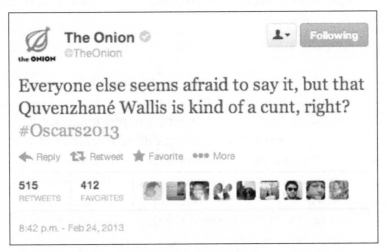

A deleted tweet from @TheOnion when Wallis was nine years old.

that anti-Black **racism** and sexism are directed at Black women, specifically: "I was looking for precise language to describe why Renisha McBride would be shot in the face, or why *The Onion* would think it's okay to talk about Quvenzhané the way they did, or the hypervisibility of Black women on reality TV, the arrest of Shanesha Taylor, the incarceration of CeCe, Laverne and Lupita being left off the *TIME* list, the continued legal actions against Marissa Alexander, the twitter dragging of black women with hateful hashtags and supposedly funny Instagram images as well as how Black women are talked about in music."[73]

---

nationalism

foundational concept, tool of liberation, tool of oppression

1. As it relates to nation-states, a type of attachment to one's country that is marked by chauvinism and a sense of superiority over others[74]

2. As it relates to broader notions of "nation"—including the conception of a racial or ethnic group as a type of nation—an ideology that emphasizes in-group solidarity and prioritization and, in some cases, political autonomy

---

Despite the important distinctions between these definitions, it should be noted that nationalism is foundationally about one's sense of affection, admiration, and/or loyalty to one's imagined group, be it one's country or **race**. Importantly, different strands of nationalism advocate the idea that one's country should be composed of and controlled by people of one's own racial group. Relatedly, some racial nationalists believe that a new country or some other kind of political jurisdiction should be created for the sake of giving their racial group exclusive sovereignty.

One might argue that the founding of the United States of America was a white nationalist project. Yes, it is important to know that the legality of slavery and the status of nonwhite people was and has been fiercely debated and contested from the founding through the Civil War and still today, but we must acknowledge that the laws and institutions of this nation—and nearly all of its states—intentionally and explicitly privileged white people over people of color for most of their history. Only with the culmination of the modern civil rights movement do we start to see the formal extension of belonging and acknowledgment of **citizenship** to people of color. White Americans are still disproportionately in control of various seats of power in civil society, which makes the United States a **white supremacist** nation even though the vast majority of white Americans today do not advocate a white nationalist agenda as they did with, say, the doctrine of Manifest Destiny, the Johnson-Reed Act of 1924, or the "Segregation Now, Segregation Forever" campaign.

While different types of white nationalists may debate about a strategy of racial separatism from people of color, their agendas tend to coalesce around the goals of maintaining their status as the racial majority, exercising political control over the jurisdictions in which they live, celebrating white racial identity, preserving various aspects of their white heritage and culture, and purporting a biological and/or cultural notion of racial superiority.

Black nationalism is not the black version of white nationalism. On the surface, the two hold in common the pursuits of sovereignty, control, self-determination, loyalty, and positive affect for the in-group, but black nationalism is at its roots primarily a resistance to white supremacy; it is not a movement for black supremacy. Brands of Black separatist nationalism can be identified in the "Back to Africa" movement of Marcus Garvey and Louis Farrakhan's advocacy for a separate country and/or civil institutions for Blacks within the United States. Scholars of Black politics find that a pragmatic type of black nationalism is more concerned with black solidarity as a strategy for racial uplift and defense for Blacks living in a pluralistic society.[75]

The era of Black Lives Matter, the election of Donald Trump, and the increasing polarization of the American people is ushering a new relevancy for racial nationalism of all stripes—be they supremacist or anti-**white supremacist**. It will be crucial for you as a player on this stage to know the difference.

---

neoliberalism

extra credit

A governing ideology "grounded in the belief that markets, in and of themselves, are better able than governments to produce, in particular, economic outcomes that are fair, sensible, and good for all"[76]

see also: capitalism

In this present crisis, government is not the solution to our problem, government is the problem.
—President Ronald Reagan, Inaugural Address, 1981

Neoliberalism is today's hegemonic economic ideology that shapes not only a great deal of US public policy but also what is understood to be common sense in the way Americans deal with and think about each other. There is a lot we can say about neoliberalism, but we will just focus on neoliberalism's role in perpetuating racial inequality. Neoliberalism gained traction in the 1980s and represents a major break from the policies that were developed after the Great Depression and World War II, which actually helped to grow a (white) middle class in the United States. In contrast to policy packages like the New Deal and Great Society, neoliberalism eschews "economic redistribution, state-guaranteed economic security, publicly provided services, domestic ownership, control of key economic sectors, and government protection and provision of better compensated and more stable jobs."[77] Poor people and people of color are the most likely to be hurt by curbing the role of the government and shifting resources and power from the government to private companies, especially resources that have historically been thought of as public goods (e.g., schools, water, roads, hospitals). The way neoliberalism has played out in the United States has served to exacerbate inequality in the country, well evinced by the fact that the white-Black racial wealth gap went from huge to gargantuan after the Great Recession.

Neoliberalism normalizes a market mentality and gives rise to a "cult of individualism."[78] One of the dangers of neoliberalism is how its logic bleeds together with **colorblind racism** to dismiss the interconnected ways that people's lives are shaped by matters beyond their immediate control as individuals. At its worst, neoliberalism works in concert with identity-based oppressions like **racism** and sexism to blame disadvantaged people for their own marginalization.

---

race

foundational concept, common sense revisited

1. A social construction, whereby people are (semihaphazardly) grouped by some combination of their physical characteristics and (geographic) ancestry and ranked hierarchically to confer systematic advantages and disadvantages

2. A social identity

3. An organizing principle[79]

Race is the child of racism, not the father.

—Ta-Nehisi Coates[80]

Everybody thinks they know what race is, and yet when asked for a definition, it becomes quite difficult to put words to common sense.

A SMALL SAMPLE OF ANTIMISCEGENATION LAWS, 1963

State	Marriage prohibited between . . .	Penalty for intermarriage	Marriage automatically void?	Penalty for functionary performing interracial marriage
Georgia	Whites and any person with Negro, West Indian, or Asiatic Indian ancestry	1 to 2 years' imprisonment	Yes	If the marriage ceremony is performed with knowledge of the illegality of the marriage, the functionary is guilty of a misdemeanor but no punishment specified
Indiana	Whites and Negroes or descendants of Negroes through the fourth generation	$100–$1,000 fine and 1 to 10 years' imprisonment	Yes	If done "knowingly," $100–$1.000 fine
Kentucky	White and Negroes or mulattoes	$500–$5,000 fine and 3 to 12 months' imprisonment if cohabitation continues after conviction	Yes	If done "knowingly," up to $1,000 fine or 1 to 12 months' imprisonment or both
Louisiana	Whites and Negroes; Indians and Negroes	For marriage between whites and Negroes, up to 5 years' imprisonment; for marriage between Indians and Negroes, none	For marriage between whites and Negroes, no; for marriage between Indians and Negroes, yes	If done "knowingly," fine or imprisonment or both
Maryland	Whites and Negroes or descendants of Negroes through the third generation; whites and Malaysians; Malaysians and Negroes or descendants of Negroes through the third generation	1½ to 10 years' imprisonment	Yes	$100 fine whether or not functionary was aware of the illegality of the marriage

Source: Barnett, "Anti-Miscegenation Laws."

One particularly knowledgeable gut reaction is to say, "There is no genetic basis for race because race is a social construction." Yes! Correct! But let's take a step back. We think of race in three different but intertwined ways.

First: a social construction. A social construction is a shared understanding of what something means or signifies. As such, you can move to another space (e.g., town, state, country) or another era in time, and the construct may mean something totally different. For instance, prior to the *Loving v. Virginia* (1967) Supreme Court decision, interracial marriage was illegal in many states. In order to enforce such a law, one would first have to determine who was of what race. The table of antimiscegenation laws describes states' legal definitions of who was Black or American Indian as well as the penalty for interracial marriage. What we see here is that by going from one state to another, one's race would legally change!

Institutions such as the US judicial system, the Census Bureau,[81] and state legislatures have had a great deal of influence on instructing members of US society how to categorize themselves into racial categories. If you look at the census from 1790 to 2010, you'll notice that almost no two census lists of racial categories are identical, with most subsequent lists being longer than the previous ones. It is not necessarily that ancestrally and phenotypically distinct groups come into being in any given year because of immigration or cross-group baby-making; instead, political institutions create new criteria for grouping in racial categories.

This is going to get circular, but ultimately, political institutions' constructions of race are influenced by members of society, and vice versa. The US Census Bureau explains that its racial categories "generally reflect a social definition of race recognized in this country. They do not conform to any biological, anthropological, or genetic criteria." This is another way of saying that race is a social identity. One's race is partially shaped by whatever the "shared criteria" for racial group membership is. Today, the criteria in the United States largely rely on phenotype and (perceived) ancestry in the United States. (Some people do not feel connected with or identify with the racial group that most people want to put them in. One's self-identification matters in this calculus as well, but it should be noted that some people have greater latitude to "choose" which race or racial groups they want to identify with.)

In addition to self-identification and institution-based identification, there is another process called *racialization* that categorizes people and shapes their lives. Racialization is the attachment of value-laden characteristics to otherwise-value-neutral physical attributes and ancestral lines. By associating shiftlessness to Blacks, notions of illegality to Latinxs, myths of the model minority to Asian Americans, terrorism with people believed to be Muslims or from the Middle East, and power, wealth, beauty, objectivity, and morality to whites, race becomes an organizing principle in our society. Or in other words, race becomes a key category that structures inequality across political, economic, and social realms of our society.[82] It structures identity; it structures individual and collective agency; it structures life chances and opportunity; it structures a **racialized social system**.

Thinkers and scholars like Ta-Nehisi Coates, Ibram Kendi, and Audrey Smedley all reveal that racial groups were constructed and racialized only in efforts to rationalize an apparent contradiction: the American creed is rooted in ideals of freedom, equality, justice, and humanity, but genocide, slavery, disenfranchisement, and purloined land were constitutive to the founding of the country. The founders of what is now known as the United States of America created racial groups and deemed some inferior and others superior in order to maintain **capitalist** endeavors that profited from the labor of enslaved people who became Black on land stolen from people who are now known as American Indians. Walter Rodney explains, "Oppression follows logically from exploitation, so as to guarantee the latter. Oppression on purely racial grounds accompanied, strengthened, and became indistinguishable from oppression for economic reasons."[83] However, over time, **racism** has become so enmeshed in the United States' social fabric that the maintenance of the existing racial hierarchy often supersedes profit maximization as a motive for oppressing people.

racial euphemisms

extra credit

1. Words and phrases that we use to avoid directly talking about race and racism

2. Misnomers and other means of racial circumlocution

see also: microaggression

People in US society use all sorts of words to circumvent matters of **race** and **racism**. Part of this stems from the terribly misguided notion that talking about race makes you a racist. This just isn't the case. Talking about rape doesn't make you a rapist, does it?[84] Talking about **antiracism** doesn't make you antiracist either. You get the point.

It is common for people to conflate terms or make a **false equivalence** between concepts in order to make racism sound as if it is neither ubiquitous nor *that* bad. There are probably three major reasons why people use these words. First, there may be a deliberate distortion of words for nefarious reasons. Second, we notice that people use euphemisms because being called a racist these days amounts to character assassination. Third, the use of racial euphemisms has become the dominant way of talking about racism. Ultimately, this all serves to whitewash (no pun intended) the inhumanity of racism.

In the following table, we outline a list of common euphemisms. Ultimately, we hope that students of antiracism become sensitive to the omnipresent nature of racism and notice the ways in which our everyday language can be used to uphold a **racialized social system** marked by **white supremacy**.

Euphemism	Another way to think about it
alt-right	The Alternative Right is a **white supremacist, racist** ideology.
Caucasian	The term is perceived as a softer, more politically correct way to say "white." "Caucasian" is a holdover from nineteenth-century scientific racism; its corollaries are "Negroid" and "Mongoloid." Do you hear those words being used today? If so, where?
diverse	As in "Tehama is diverse." What they mean to say is either "Tehama is some kind of ambiguously nonwhite person" or "Tehama is biracial." The term is also used to mean that a space has at least (and perhaps only) one person who is different on a structurally contingent axis of identity.
diversity hire	The term is generally used to describe the hiring of a racial minority (but it is also used to suggest that an organization hired someone that is not like the other people who already work there). Sometimes it implies that the person of color who is hired is not as qualified to work there, but any place that needs a "diversity hire" probably has its own history of institutionalized exclusion of "diverse" people. Just saying.
ethnicity	People often use this term in place of saying "**race.**" If you don't have a distinguishing criterion between "race" and "ethnicity," you're probably trying to describe "race." Just say "race"!
exotic	The term is usually gendered, as in a reference to a woman of color who is beautiful (despite the fact that she is not white). It is also used to describe something that is not white or derived from "Western civilization," thus reinforcing white normativity.
fascist	Though this term has a very specific definition, after the election of Donald Trump to the US presidency, it seems to be used to describe not only an authoritarian **nationalism** but also "white supremacist," "racist," and "Islamophobic." Why conflate terms when you could use them all?
gaffe	As in "I know I said something that you could have interpreted to be racist, but it was just a gaffe." This term is a means to shirk responsibility for saying something racist. Looks like that **"implicit" attitude** found a voice.

Euphemism	Another way to think about it
identity politics	This term is usually employed to suggest that Black people, other people of color, and other marginalized people use their identity in "divisive" ways, rather than to home in on the fact that their life chances are influenced by their identity and membership in groups that have historically gotten the short end of the stick.
personal responsibility	As in the "Personal Responsibility and Work Opportunity Reconciliation Act of 1996." The term is a **neoliberal** ideological frame used to imply that increasing racial and socioeconomic inequality can primarily be chalked up to the way people behave rather than the structure and the outcome of neoliberal policies.[85]
politically correct	It used to be the case that people tried not to be mean in public, but we are in an age of social meanness. When people call for an end to political correctness, they are essentially taking the liberty to give their honest, plainly spoken opinions, regardless of whether it hurts or offends anybody else. As such, resistance against political correctness is another way to say, "Fuck you. If you're offended by my words and misrepresentation of reality, then that's on you."
populist	At the most basic level, populism is a call for average people to work together to resist the elite, but in practice, it is typically used to refer to those times when politicians dip into the reservoir of **racism** among working-class white people and convince them that Black and Latinx people are getting free stuff and taking jobs from whites, in order to create policies that only help political and economic elites.
race	As in "Black parents have to give their sons a talk about **race** that white parents do not." It should be noted that Black parents give their children multiple talks about racism. That's what they are doing.
race card	See "identity politics."
race relations	When people use this term, they often do so with the assumption that there are no power asymmetries between racial groups. But power asymmetries do exist. The next time you hear someone use this term, ask them what they mean. What are they talking about exactly? We think you'll have a clearer conversation.

Euphemism	Another way to think about it
racial incident	"Incident" connotes that an event happens once or that the event is an exception to the rule, but typically this term is used to explain the presence of nooses on campuses, Klan marches, or hate crimes. As such, this term is a euphemism for racial terrorism, which is a regular feature of US society.
racial undertones	As in "The ugly racial undertones that panicked our response to Ebola."[86] This is another way to say "**racist.**"
racially biased	Discrimination.
racially charged	As in "So-and-So celebrity is in hot water for a racially charged joke about [fill in underrepresented minority here]." This is another word for "racist."
racially divided	As in "Americans' attitudes are so racially divided these days." This means that people across racial groups have different attitudes, but as we pointed out in chapter 1, people across racial groups have very different experiences in a **racialized social system**, on average. Also, as in "Neighborhoods are very racially divided." This is just a less controversial way of saying "segregated."
racially insensitive	See "gaffe."
racially motivated	This term usually refers to an action done out of racist and hateful motivation.
standard, proper	As in "Please speak standard English." This term is usually a reference to whiteness.
thug	Debatably, the twenty-first-century version of the N-word.
tough on crime	This term is **dog whistle politics** language, whereby political representatives implicitly promise to develop and enforce laws aimed to disproportionately control and incarcerate Black and Brown people.
unpatriotic	As in "Colin Kaepernick's protest is unpatriotic." This term is used in many ways, but when it comes to matters of race, it is usually a reference to Black and Latinx people who critique the current state of racial inequality.

racialized social system

foundational concept

A society where social, economic, political, and psychological benefits
and disadvantages are doled out along racial lines

synonym: white supremacy
antonym: postracial society

The United States is a racialized social system,[87] marked by **white
supremacy**. That is to say, the United States is a society where people who are believed to be white are allocated a disproportionate
amount of political, social, economic, aesthetic, and psychological
benefits and advantages, while racial others receive a disproportionate amount of disadvantages in nearly all realms of life in the United
States. Contemporary society's racial structure can be conceived of
as "the totality of the social relations and practices that reinforce
white privilege," whereby the dominant (racial) ideologies of the
day serve as important mechanisms that reproduce racial privilege.[88]

Think about all the ways in which you see whites, on average, in a
better situation than Blacks and other people of color in social, political, and economic spheres of life in the United States. For instance,
standards of beauty are largely based on whiteness (we might think
of this as a feature of the social sphere), Black Americans get a lower
return on their investment in education than whites do (the economic sphere), and felon disenfranchisement laws have a disproportionate effect on Black and Latinx communities (the political sphere).
Can you think of other examples? Some of the racial disparities you
see in day-to-day life occur because consciously **racist** people want
them to and **antiracists** have not yet stopped them. But many of
them occur unintentionally or because they were set in motion
long before any of us were born and we have not yet implemented

practices to correct them. Bottom line: as long as there is a litany of racial disparities that we can point to, we have evidence that we live in a racialized social system.

A THOUGHT EXPERIMENT

Tomorrow, everybody residing in the United States will wake up without an ounce of racial bias or bigotry in their being. They will not know any racial stereotypes. They will not have any **implicit attitudes** toward any racial group. What will change in the realm of racial inequalities?

Answer: Not a thing. Changing people's attitudes will not immediately influence the fact that most people who wake up in mansions are white and those who wake up in the ghetto are Black and Brown. It will not change the makeup of the prison population, residential segregation, or wealth distribution. These inequalities are structural. Nobody needs to do anything intentional to keep them going. Things will just move on, business as usual, until **antiracists** implement change.

racism

foundational concept, common sense revisited,

tool of oppression

1. A feature of a society, whereby patterns of public policy, institutions, dominant ideologies, and popular representations serve to perpetuate social, political, and economic inequities between racial groups

2. The array of anti-Black practices, policies, and ever-perpetuated inequalities that maintain white privilege and power

3. The connection among the racial disparities that we outlined in chapter 1

   antonym: antiracism
   see also: racialized social system, respectability politics, white supremacy

When most people think of racism, they tend to think about it as negative attitudes about or actions against people or groups due to their **race**. Sometimes people conflate this term with bigotry, chauvinism, prejudice, xenophobia, and interpersonal discrimination. While *partially* accurate, these definitions of racism are incredibly narrow and, therefore, lead to a faulty assumption about how to rid ourselves of this defect in our society: if we change attitudes, we fix the problem.

We encourage people to think about structural racism. Structural racism in US society is like the sand embedded in concrete. You can't really see it, and yet it's foundational. In previous eras of US society, racism was overtly codified in law (de jure). Segregation, antimiscegenation laws, and general racial terror were completely legal, or at least widely condoned or ignored. However, in today's iteration of structural racism, there are few unambiguous symbols and signs of intentional perpetuation of persistent racial inequalities. Evidence of structural racism is best seen when *differential impact* occurs, or "when individuals are treated equally according to a given set of rules and procedures but when the latter are constructed in ways that favor members of one group over another." This includes "decisions and processes that may not themselves have an explicit racial content but that have the consequence of producing or reinforcing racial disadvantage."[89]

Structural racism is neither fully apart from intentional, overt racial animus nor absolutely necessary for a policy, person, or institution to intentionally work toward perpetuating the existing racial hierarchy. To be clear, there is human agency involved—indeed, some clearly identifiable racially disparate policies are codified in law by today's lawmakers (e.g., voter identification, "show me your papers," "stop and frisk," "stand your ground")—but structural racism can be likened to a well-oiled machine that reproduces racial inequalities and enhances **white privilege** without the need for very much maintenance.

---

respectability politics

foundational concept, tool of oppression

An ideology based on the notion that by presenting oneself in the way that is pleasing to members of the dominant group, one will be able to assuage their fears about one (and one's group), and as a consequence, racial animus will dissipate among white Americans

see also: meritocracy, neoliberalism

Evelyn Brooks Higginbotham coined the term "politics of respectability" to describe an ideology and strategy of nineteenth-century middle-class Black women who sought to improve their racial group's

standing in US society. They suggested that through a specific standard of personal comportment and practicing particular behaviors,
such as proper dress, thrift, cleanliness of property, temperance,
polite manners and language, and sexual purity, Blacks could mitigate the ongoing threats of racial terrorism.

Today, proponents of respectability politics believe that focusing
on Blacks' behavior is a clever survival strategy, arguing that Blacks
"should not obscure an essential fact: any marginalized group should
be attentive to how it is perceived."[90] This sentiment is predicated on
the assumption that Blacks can convince whites that they deserve
the rights guaranteed to them by the US Constitution. This logic is
useful only in that it reveals the recognition on the part of Blacks that
they have to work harder than others to prove that their lives matter.

It should be noted that while the thread of respectability politics
has been needled through Black politics for nearly a century and a
half, resistance to this ideology has a similarly long lineage. Black
intellectuals and activists like Anna Julia Cooper (1858–1964) disputed notions of respectability politics and instead called for "undisputed dignity." The Black feminist scholar Brittany Cooper explains
the difference: "Demands for dignity are demands for a fundamental
recognition of one's inherent humanity. Demands for respectability
assume that unassailable social priority will prove one's dignity. Dignity, unlike respectability, is not socially contingent. It is intrinsic
and, therefore, not up for debate."[91] Ultimately, the logic of respectability politics implores "an oppressed community [to] implicitly
endorse deeply flawed values, including many that form the foundation of their own oppression," such as "hegemonic articulations
of gender, class, and sexuality."[92] The contemporary Movement for
Black Lives is over all of this with receipts in hand: this strategy is
not working, and it's morally reprehensible to suggest that Blacks
are responsible for reshaping whites' imagination of them. The Black
Lives Matter movement instead demands the recognition of the full
humanity of all Black people no matter how respectable others think
they are.

---

reverse discrimination

tool of oppression

There. Is. No. Such. Thing.

see also: affirmative action, diversity, white supremacy

Claims of "reverse discrimination" are generally made to suggest that efforts to (a) ameliorate racial inequality, (b) reduce historically produced racial disparities, and (c) actually "level the playing field" are unfair to white people.

There are a multitude of renditions of how claims of so-called reverse discrimination play out. Some people suggest that by taking **race** into consideration, whites are automatically disadvantaged. Historically, however, we see that when race is considered, whites are usually made better off.[93] Some folks suggest that efforts made to create a more egalitarian society end up sacrificing **meritocracy**, as if the two are mutually exclusive. Still others argue that it is unfair for today's white people to have to pay for the sins of their ancestors, as if they are not reaping the benefits of historical de jure policies and de facto **racist** norms. In all, claims of reverse discrimination help to prop up a system of **white supremacy** by implying that racism is an equal-opportunity mechanism of oppression, which it is not. White people have never been on the bottom of the racial hierarchy.

But you may still be wondering, "But can't Black people be racist too?" Great question! Here's the thing, when most people ask that question, they are asking if a Black person can treat a white person differently or badly simply because the person is white. In that case, the answer is yes. But we would call that "bigotry" or "prejudice." Some people might even call it "discrimination." We reserve "racism," however, for those aggregated actions, behaviors, stereotypes, policies, institutions, and so on that maintain or exacerbate the existing racial hierarchy, which is currently one characterized by **white supremacy**. To be sure, there are Black people who work to maintain the existing racial hierarchy, and that, we would argue, is racist.

___

transracial

extra credit

1. In the context of adoption, a transracial adoptee is a person who is raised in a family of a different race than his or her own.

2. In the context of self-identification, a transracial person adopts (or attempts to adopt) a new racial identity through self-identification.

___

In both definitions, "transracial" is linked by the idea of adoption, or taking on. The first, conventional use of "transracial" refers to when a person of one racial identity is adopted by parents or a family of a different racial identity/identities. The parties of a transracial adoption make a choice to become members of each other's family (in the case of babies, we might say that this reciprocity is manifested, if at all, later in life). A more recent use of "transracial" refers to the choice made by a person to adopt a racial identity other than the one given to him or her at birth. The most well-known contemporary case is that of Rachel Dolezal, a woman born white who is attempting to take on a Black racial identity.

There are grievances from members of the transracial adoptee community about this recent **co-optation** of the word "transracial," as they believe it conflates and confuses their experience—in which individuals of different **races** become part of each other's family while maintaining their original racial identities—with that of someone like Dolezal, who is actually trying to become a person of a different race. At stake is a matter of privilege. If a person with a non-white identity joins a white family, the person may have increased access to **white privileges** via their relationship with white people, but this does not mean he or she becomes white. The person lives as a person of color with white people. Dolezal, on the other hand, has white privilege because of her original racial identity and can ostensibly, at any time, retreat to that whiteness if she no longer chooses to present herself as Black. There are also concerns from the transgender community that gender expression and racial identity are being inappropriately paralleled to each other.[94] While gender expression is in many ways a social construct, it is also one that is believed to emanate from or be misaligned with one's biological sex. Racial identity, on the other hand, is not an attribute of an individual but rather a social construct that is tied to ancestry and phenotype.

While the term "transracial" as it relates to self-identification is relatively new, the practice of *passing* has long been a phenomenon in which people of non-European descent are presumed to be white and/or intentionally present themselves as white—either permanently or temporarily—in an attempt to enhance their own life chances (and possibly the life chances of others) by positioning themselves as entitled recipients of the privileges afforded to people at the top of the racial hierarchy.[95]

Like passing, the act of transracialism seems to be predicated on the idea that someone is trying to move from one monoracial category to another (i.e., from white to Black, or Asian to white). This effort is different than being a biracial person who wishes to be perceived as monoracial but has difficulty convincing others. In this case, biracial individuals may "cover" or downplay one aspect of their biracial identity or "accent" or draw attention to an aspect of their identity or ancestry as a way to mitigate a stigmatized aspect of one of their racial attributes or to increase the likelihood of accessing a resource or beneficial status.[96]

SPACE FOR DEBATE

The very notions of transracialism, passing, covering, and accenting raise questions and debates that entreat us to think critically about **race**:

1 When people of color pass as white, are they in effect reinforcing the **white supremacist** racial hierarchy, are they undermining the rigidity of the hierarchy, or are they simultaneously doing both?[97]

2 Does one's self-identification have to align with one's ascribed racial identity in order to be considered an authentic member of either the self-identified or ascribed racial community? Are there other measures besides identification that validate someone as a "real" member of a racial group?[98]

3 If Jessica can convince Austin that she belongs to Racial Group A rather than Racial Group B, should Jessica actually be allegiant to Racial Group A? If so, what does that allegiance look like? Does the requirement of allegiance rest on whether Jessica's original racial identity is white or not?[99]

4 Under what conditions, if any, can a transracial individual speak for and represent his or her adopted racial community? Does using one definition of "transracial" over the other change your answer to the question?

5 Does one's ability to pass necessarily mean that the person can empathize with members of the racial group that he or she is presumed to belong to? How long must someone live as a transracial person (using the second definition), and what experiences must that person have in order to "know what it's like" to be an original member of the group—or is this even possible?[100]

white fragility

tool of oppression

"White Fragility is a state in which even a minimum amount of racial stress becomes intolerable, triggering a range of defensive moves. These moves include the outward display of emotions such as anger, fear, and guilt, and behaviors such as argumentation, silence, and leaving the stress-inducing situation. These behaviors, in turn, function to reinstate white racial equilibrium."[101]

The multicultural-education scholar Robin DiAngelo coined the term "white fragility" to pinpoint whites' perception of vulnerability when confronted by racial matters. DiAngelo explains that because many whites are not socialized to think critically about **race, racism**, and **white privilege**, they lack the stamina to engage in conversation about these topics. The issue of stamina is not problematic in and of itself—that can be built up over time and experience. It is the act of disengaging from racial discourse that raises our concern. Racial inequality must first be identified before it can be dismantled. By disengaging from discourse, whites largely end up withdrawing from **antiracism** altogether. This retreat often occurs when dominant ideologies and taken-for-granted "common sense" (e.g., **meritocracy**, individualism, whiteness, **colorblindness**) are challenged, rendering the challenged person feeling unauthoritative and epistemologically insecure.

It should be noted that Black people, in particular, are well aware of white fragility. Black folks and other people of color often treat white folks with kid gloves, particularly around matters of race. Indeed, they are socialized to do so. The "talk" that Black parents give their Black children on driving, living, walking, and breathing while Black includes a lesson on white fragility. This is why we try to smile and talk to white people in a way that assuages fears and makes them feel good. We recognize that white people are easily threatened and may respond accordingly (or recklessly).

We bring all of this up because it's important for (white) allies to recognize that you have to develop stamina if you're going to be **antiracist**. It's really hard. There will be times when you may *feel* fragile, vulnerable, or even like a total asshole. But that's okay! No antiracist is infallible. Think things through. Learn from your misunderstandings. Keep your eye on the prize.

---

white privilege

tool of oppression

1. An advantage, good, or resource that people with ascribed white racial identities receive and/or have greater access to and that people with ascribed nonwhite racial identities are denied and/or have less access to, primarily as a consequence of their ascribed racial identity and not because of what they do or do not do as individuals

2. A condition of whiteness, whereby one is not, nor needs to be, cognizant of the racial dynamics that systematically benefit white people and disadvantage people of color

see also: epistemology of ignorance, racism, white supremacy

There are a few important things to bear in mind when using this term. First, the word "privilege" connotes that the benefits of being white have been accrued over hundreds of years and are essentially unearned. To believe otherwise is to unequivocally accept the myth of **meritocracy** and, by extension, also to believe that the reason that white people have better life chances is because they somehow deserve them and nonwhite people do not.

A second thing to bear in mind is that privilege is relative. In other words, every white person is not better off than every person of color. The term "white privilege" can be used to note the aggregate experience, where the likelihood of not being pulled over by the police for "a broken taillight," for example, is much greater for whites *on average* than it is for Blacks.

Third, some white people have more privilege than other white people. A white person who makes $100,000 a year is in a much better position to acquire and enjoy the **American dream** than, say, a white person who makes $20,000. Where the "white" part of the privilege becomes particularly evident is when you compare the life chances of that wealthier or poorer white person to her or his $100,000- or $20,000-earning counterpart in the Latinx, Black, or Arab community.

Peggy McIntosh theorizes that there are two types of privilege: "unearned entitlements" and "conferred dominance." The first type consists of those things that all people should have. The latter refers to the power that people with privilege have over others.[102] Meanwhile, Allan Johnson describes three paradoxes of privilege: First, you do not have to belong to the privileged class (i.e., the white racial group) to receive the benefits of whiteness; you just need to be perceived as white by others. Second, one can be privileged without feeling privilege. Third, being privileged doesn't guarantee happiness. Johnson asserts, "To have privilege is to participate in a system than confers advantage and dominance at the expense of other people, and this situation can cause distress to those who benefit from it. White privilege, for example, comes at a huge cost to people of color, and on some level white people must struggle with this knowledge."[103]

whitesplaining

wisdom of popular culture

A portmanteau that combines "white" and "explaining" to describe those times when whites try to explain matters that are well understood by people of color to people of color in a way that is condescending, ultimately revealing the overconfidence and cluelessness of the "splainer"

see also: gaslighting, microaggression

Let's get something off the table right now—not all white people who verbally make sense of **race** and **racism** are guilty of whitesplaining. Maisha Johnson explains that whitesplaining is a problem because "it's not just harmlessly discussing racism, but implicitly acting on racist ideas that say that people of color are ignorant and wrong, even about their own experiences."[104] Whitesplaining has a certain condescending, paternalistic, **gaslighting** quality. Whitesplainers tend to

* imply that secondhand learning about negative experiences with racism are just as qualifying as the firsthand experiences of a Black narrator;

* erroneously alert individuals that talking about race is racist;

* make suggestions of paranoia and oversensitivity about racism;

* argue that the person of color who has faced racism is being cynical about the intentions of the offender;

* base one's ideas about what Black people really think on the only other Black person they may have been exposed to, such as Stacey Dash or Ben Carson; and

* get offended and then lash out from a place of **white fragility** when claims and observations about racism are made about the "splainer."

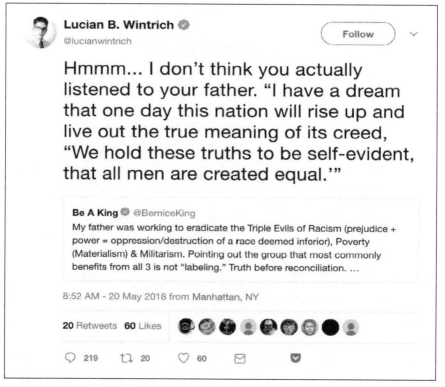

Whitesplaining to Bernice King.

Here's the rub: **white supremacy** "depends on whites socializing each other not to empathize fully with people of color. This emotional disconnect helps legitimize, and prevent a critique of, the racial status quo."[105] The sociologist Joe Feagin calls this "social alexithymia," or the inability to understand or relate to the painful experiences of those who are targeted by oppression.[106] Whitesplaining is rooted both in social alexithymia and the idea that white people are objective observers of the world.

white supremacy

foundational concept, common sense revisited, tool of oppression

1. The systematic provision of political, social, economic, and psychological benefits and advantages to whites, alongside the systematic provisions of burdens and disadvantages to people who are not white

2. A set of norms and expectations predicated on white habitus, or the preferences, tastes, emotions, and perceptions of white Americans[107]

3. The belief that white people are inherently superior to people of color and should dominate over people of color

   synonyms: racialized social system, whiteness
   antonym: antiracism
   see also: racism, white privilege

Many people may balk at our definition of "white supremacy," but we think it is helpful nonetheless. First, let's note that in our definition, the term primarily refers to a *system* that produces racial inequality whereby white people are made better off, on average. Second, there are multiple cultural standards that buttress and justify this systemic arrangement. While white supremacists (à la our third definition) are among the most obvious opponents of racial egalitarianism, we contend that you don't have to actively engage in overt **racist** behaviors and espouse old-fashioned, biological racist attitudes in order to uphold a system marked by white supremacy; you don't even have to be white.

The philosopher Charles Mills helps us to understand the historical and theoretical foundation of a society shaped by white supremacy in his book *The Racial Contract*. In it, he asserts that racism is not an unintended aberration or mistake but instead is woven into the fabric of US society. For instance, when Thomas Jefferson wrote that "all men are created equal," it was not his intention to suggest that "all humans are created equal," best evinced by the fact that he enslaved and raped people of African descent. Relatedly, history shows that **white privilege** was forged through the law as a means to prevent poor people of European descent from rallying around their shared class status with people of color (Blacks and indigenous people) for purposes of seeking collective gains in their life chances. Those privileges inscribed in the law included the franchise, property ownership, exclusive legal access to white women, the right to bear arms, the right of self-defense, and the ability to profit from one's own labor or the labor of (enslaved) others.[108]

Though the US has come a long way from where it once was, we must also keep in mind that US society is still a **racialized social system**. A racialized social system marked by white supremacy confers privileges that are neither earned by whites nor easily recognizable to most whites because they are deeply embedded in white supremacist culture (à la our second definition), including such features as the implicit assumption that whites are more moral, humanistic, rational, and objective; the presumption of white innocence; the easy application of labels such as "vulnerability" and "victimhood" to describe the state of white people; the disproportionate positive images of whites juxtaposed against the disproportionate negative images of people of color in the media; the duality that whites are both unique individuals and emblematic of the universal human experience; the mainstream standard of white beauty; the disproportionate political power of white people; the economic prestige afforded to white income earners / wealth generators; whites' enhanced access to exclusive opportunities due to "legacy" and restricted social networks; credit to white people for appropriated innovations; and so on. Taken together, white lives matter more in a society marred by white supremacy. **Antiracism** is the antidote.

Questions and Debate

1 Which words and concepts did we miss but ought to be taken into consideration? Are any of the words and concepts highlighted in this chapter becoming obsolete or falling out of use?

2 Which concepts do you view in a completely different light from what has been presented here? Which words and concepts are viewed differently or are highly contested across generational groups?

3 Some people use their knowledge of certain concepts as credentials for self-declared "wokeness." To what extent is "wokeness" predicated on being fluent in the words and concepts we presented here? Are there other ways of knowing that produce racial awareness and actions toward **antiracism**?

4 Have you ever used hushed tones when talking about racial matters, such as in describing someone's racial identity or skin color? If yes, what were you trying to achieve in doing so? If not, why not?

5 Think of a time when you had a hotly contested conversation about **race**. What position, issue, concept, or word was at the heart of the debate? Would you use any of the highlighted terms from this chapter to describe the scenario?

Additional Materials to Consider

BOOKS

Collins, Patricia Hill. *Black Feminist Thought: Knowledge, Consciousness, and the Politics of Empowerment.* New York: Routledge, 2002.

Delgado, Richard, and Jean Stefancic. *Critical Race Theory: An Introduction.* New York: NYU Press, 2017.

Feagin, Joe. *Systemic Racism: A Theory of Oppression*. New York: Routledge, 2013.

Guinier, Lani. *The Tyranny of the Meritocracy: Democratizing Higher Education in America*. Boston: Beacon, 2015.

Katznelson, Ira. *When Affirmative Action was White: An Untold History of Racial Inequality in Twentieth-Century America*. New York: Norton, 2005.

López, Ian Haney. *Dog Whistle Politics: How Coded Racial Appeals Have Reinvented Racism and Wrecked the Middle Class*. New York: Oxford University Press, 2015.

Mills, Charles W. *The Racial Contract*. Ithaca, NY: Cornell University Press, 2014.

PODCASTS

Code Switch. National Public Radio. www.npr.org.

Our National Conversation about Conversations about Race. Hosted by Anna Holmes, Baratunde Thurston, Raquel Cepeda, and Tanner Colby. www.showaboutrace.com.

Still Processing. Hosted by Wesley Morris and Jenna Wortham. *New York Times*. www.nytimes.com.

3

The Politics of Racial Progress

Folks on the political right and left have berated Black Lives Matter activists for protesting in "all of the wrong ways"—for being "too aggressive," for being "disrespectful" of their elders, for taking over highways, and for forcing political candidates to account for their policy agendas that may have only alluded to addressing racial injustice. Athlete activists who take a knee or raise a fist during the national anthem to call attention to anti-Black **racism** elicit a particular ire among those who find their protest an affront to American patriotism.[1] They are called "un-American," they are called "sons of bitches," and they are sometimes even called "terrorists." This all sounds familiar. Americans don't learn very much about this aspect of the civil rights movement, but people said the same things about the young freedom fighters of the 1940s, '50s, and '60s. In fact, by 1966 only 28 percent of Americans had a favorable opinion of Martin Luther King Jr., and many freedom fighters were deemed criminals.[2]

Two years after breaking ground on the memorial to honor the now almost universally beloved Dr. King, the United States celebrated the 2008 election of Barack Obama as historic, as an absolution to US racism, and as evidence that the nation is moving forward

Clockwise from top left: Winonah Myers, Doris Castle, Travis Britt, and Clarence Melvin were four of the more than four hundred Freedom Riders of the 1960s. By traveling across state lines in interracial groups and violating the local segregationist laws and customs that restricted the use of facilities associated with interstate travel (such as bus terminal restrooms, shoeshine stands, and restaurants), Freedom Riders tested the enforcement of the *Morgan v. Virginia* (1946) and *Boynton v. Virginia* (1960) decisions, which declared the racial segregation of interstate buses and bus terminals unconstitutional. These activists were arrested for a variety of alleged offenses, including breach of the peace, trespassing, and unlawful assembly, and many were targets of mob violence. Today, they are considered heroes. (Mississippi Department of Archives and History)

on its inevitable path of racial progress. But nearly a century and a half prior, the country forced itself to do things that were seemingly impossible just decades before. Hundreds of years of chattel slavery were summarily ended and quickly followed by the near-full incorporation of Black men into the political sphere. So, yes, the election of the son of a Kenyan man and a white woman from Kansas was historic, but an achievement of that magnitude was not unmatched. Soon after the Civil War, men who were *previously enslaved* were *elected into the US Congress.* The progress of that short era—Radical

Reconstruction—was dissolved by white backlash and rage so quickly and with such little reckoning that it is now unknown to most Americans today.[3] "The misuse of history often provides distorted instruction on the process of change,"[4] but by getting our facts straight, remembering that today's heroic agents of change were yesterday's villainous subversives, and knowing that wondrous gains in racial progress can be lost, and also regained, we cultivate a clearer sense of the political struggle we're joining when we declare that Black lives matter.

The United States of America has already done the impossible. But can we do it again? Sure. So what's the hold up? First, too many Americans believe that progress toward racial equality is inevitable, so they don't feel it's necessary to drive forth a future they believe is already fated. Relatedly, numerous Americans believe that what they do or do not do in their own lifetime matters little to none when it comes to societal advancement. There are other Americans who simultaneously believe that the civil rights movement was a clear success, but they also recognize that daily life for many people of color in the twenty-first century is precarious. That is, they are in a state of cognitive dissonance in which they believe two contradictory things to be true. One of the ways people relieve the discomfort of their cognitive dissonance is to reduce the importance of one of their conflicting attitudes. Rather than advocating for policies and practices that dignify the humanity of people of color, scores of Americans have tacitly decided that today's racial inequities are something they can ignore. And still, there are other people in this country who have given up on the project of racial progress altogether because, quite frankly, they believe we have already made enough progress (for some, perhaps, too much).

If we are more intimately familiar with our history, perhaps more of us will set our sights toward a grander and, dare we say, more radical vision of an **antiracist** society. In this chapter, we get you thinking about why staying woke has as much to do with the past as it does with the present and the future. We demonstrate that progress toward racial equality is neither inevitable nor inherently linear and therefore requires the unabating will and labor of its champions. We illustrate how political institutions and dominant society can make concessions to Black movements while also **co-opting** the movements' messages. By considering vestiges of the past and today's new challenges, it will become clearer why the progress we've made is not enough to quiet the calls for equality—there is still unfinished business. Finally, we examine what it means to be radical when lives are at stake, and we assert that this brand of political imagination and activism are both American and necessary for racial progress.

DÉJÀ VU: ARTISTS REFLECT ON HISTORY TO MEASURE OUR RACIAL PROGRESS

One year after Los Angeles Police Department officers who beat the Black motorist Rodney King* were found "not guilty," the hip hop artist KRS One released "Sound of Da Police" (1993). Questioning the notion of progress, he begs listeners to draw a parallel between antebellum and modern forms of policing:

Yeah, officer from overseer
You need a little clarity?
Check the similarity!
The overseer rode around the plantation
The officer is off patrolling all the nation
The overseer could stop you what you're what doing
The officer will pull you over just when he's pursuing
The overseer had the right to get ill
And if you fought back, the overseer had the right to kill
The officer has the right to arrest
And if you fight back, they put a hole in your chest!

* On March 3,1991, after removing King from his vehicle, numerous Los Angeles Police Department officers encircled King and repeatedly beat and kicked him on the ground. The violence was filmed, unbeknown to the officers, by an amateur photographer using his home video camera.

This cartoon was published in 1992 when the four officers who beat Rodney King were pronounced not guilty of a variety of charges including assault with a deadly weapon and excessive use of force as a police officer. The artist calls into question the fulfillment of Dr. King's dream by ironically using his phrasing here. (Cartoon by Pat Oliphant. Oliphant © 1992 Andrews McMeel Syndication. Reprinted with permission. All rights reserved.)

A Lesson in Nonlinearity

At the conclusion of the US Civil War, a political battle heated up in Washington, DC, over how to reunite the nation. The plan of the Unionist and Southern Democrat President Andrew Johnson to "restore" the South to the Union was to require only that Southern states ratify the Thirteenth Amendment, which abolishes slavery and involuntary servitude except as a punishment for crime, repudiate the secession of the Southern states from the Union, and cancel the debts of the Confederacy to its loaners. Johnson, a former slaveholder, included no consideration for the incorporation and well-being of newly freed people. Instead, it seemed that Johnson was intent both to forgive rebel Southerners and to comfort Southern and Northern whites alike who feared that an end to slavery also meant the end of

white supremacy. He steered clear of civil rights talk and was keen to withdraw the Union army from its Southern posts.

The majority-Republican Congress had a different idea of how to proceed. With nearly 620,000 lives lost in battle, many members of the legislature were leery to so openly and easily embrace their seceding brethren who drew them into war. Still grieving the assassination of their party leader, Abraham Lincoln, Republicans were arguably more mindful about what policies should accompany emancipation. Congress passed the Civil Rights Act of 1866, overriding Johnson's veto, and granted Black people basic civil rights by federal law. The ensuing struggle between the president and the Congress galvanized a referendum vote against Johnson in the fall election of 1866, resulting in a Republican gain of seats in Congress. Newly energized, Republicans seized the opportunity to reinvent the social and political order.

A ten-year era of Radical Reconstruction began with the passage of the Reconstruction Acts of 1867, which divided the vanquished South into five military districts and installed a presiding military governor in each district until new state constitutions could be drafted and ratified by Congress. Men of any **race**—with the exception of former Confederate leaders—were allowed to participate in the constitutional conventions that crafted the new state governments. The Reconstruction Acts required that the new state constitutions both recognize universal male suffrage and ratify the Fourteenth Amendment, which extends **citizenship** to "all persons born or naturalized in the United States," including all freed persons, and grants "equal protection of the laws" to all. In 1869, Congress ratified the Fifteenth Amendment to the Constitution, prohibiting *all* states from denying the right to vote because of race, color, or previous condition of servitude.[5] The Enforcement Acts of 1870 and 1871 were adopted to curb intimidation and violence against newly enfranchised Blacks, and the Civil Rights Act of 1875 made racial discrimination in public accommodations illegal. Radical Reconstruction was nothing short of a revolution.

During the era of Radical Reconstruction (1867–1877), sixteen Black men (nine of them born into slavery) were elected to Congress

Hiram R. Revels of Mississippi became the first Black senator in 1870. Five years later, Blanche K. Bruce, who was born into slavery, was elected into the Senate, a Republican from Mississippi. The next Black senator was not elected until ninety-one years later, when Edward Brooke was elected by popular vote in 1966. To date, there have only been ten Black senators. The first time that two Black senators served simultaneously was in 2013. (Brady-Handy Photograph Collection, Prints and Photographs Division, Library of Congress, LC-DIG-cwpbh-00554)

(two serving in the Senate).[6] One Black man became governor of Louisiana, and six hundred others became members of their state legislatures. Additionally, at least fifteen hundred Black men held other public offices, such as mayors, sheriffs, tax assessors, treasurers, and justices of the peace.[7] Black men were voting and being elected to serve the public, often forming coalitions with poor whites and white Republicans in an interracial democracy.

Black women, though still barred from voting on account of their sex, participated in political organizations. The sociologist Evelyn Glenn explains that though Black women were not allowed to vote, "outside convention hours, [Blacks] gathered at mass meetings to discuss and vote on the positions that black male delegates should take. Community votes were taken by voice or by rising, and all in attendance—men, women, and children—voted"; thus, for Black women, "participating and voting in internal political meetings was rooted in an alternative conception of democratic representation,"[8] or what the anthropologist James Holston calls "insurgent **citizenship**."[9]

In order to usher newly emancipated Blacks from slavery to freedom and to aid destitute whites in the South in the aftermath of the war, the federal government set up the Freedmen's Bureau (short for the Bureau of Refugees, Freedmen, and Abandoned Lands). The bureau was charged with protecting the new political freedoms of and securing economic stability for Black people, and the expanse of its services was broad—providing food and clothing, helping people locate their family members lost to one another in slavery, monitoring elections, and regulating labor relations between planters and former slaves. It built orphanages and hospitals and invested in infrastructure to redevelop the Southern economy. To prepare Blacks and whites alike to more fully participate in US society, the Freedmen's Bureau introduced public school education to the Southern states, one of the few remaining vestiges of the postwar era. In only a few years, the same people who labored tirelessly in bondage, whose bodies and familial bonds were broken by the whips and whims of their masters, were now undergoing a radical political and civic metamorphosis.

Radical Reconstruction was a deliverance for formerly enslaved Black people and an abomination to **white supremacists**. Angry white Southerners who detested the elevation of Blacks to equal civic status as whites and resented the dominance of the Republican Party in the formerly seceded Southern states formed the Ku Klux Klan and other white **racist** paramilitary groups like the White League and the Red Shirts. They did so in order to terrorize Black people and intimidate them from exercising their new political freedoms. One in ten Black people who participated in state constitutional conventions were either killed or physically harmed by vigilante violence.[10] By using brutal violence to keep Blacks away from the polls and by threatening the lives of Black and white Republicans who ran for political office, these Southerners worked to return power to Southern Democrats who were keen to preserve white racial domination.

Not only did violent mobs kill or threaten voters, activists, and candidates who envisioned an interracial democracy; in some cases, they literally forced Black and white Republicans out of office through violent means. Both attempted and actual race-based coup d'états—or sudden, often violent, and illegal takeovers of government—occurred and went unpunished in Southern states after the Civil War. In the spring of 1871, a white mob in Meridian, Mississippi, killed more than thirty Black men and forced out the white Republican mayor, William Sturges, sending him out of town on a north-bound train.[11] In June 1874, a white mob in Coushatta, Louisiana, killed five freedmen and six white Republican officeholders, two who had already surrendered and were on their way out of town.[12]

In September 1874, thousands of rioters led by the White League flooded Canal Street in New Orleans, Louisiana, and seized the statehouse for days before federal troops and gunboats restored Republican order.[13] On Election Day, November 3, 1874, in Barbour County, Alabama, near the town of Eufala, armed white rioters drove away at least one thousand (mostly Black) Republicans from the polls, killing at least seven and wounding seventy. They then stole the ballots, refused to count the Republican votes, declared Democrats the victors, forced out the Republican officeholders, and installed Democrats throughout every office in the county. If any Republican attempted to testify to election fraud, the judges of the Democratic Party would convict them of bogus charges and publicly lease their labor.[14] Perhaps the most well-known coup occurred after Radical Reconstruction, on November 10, 1898, in Wilmington, North Carolina. White mobs killed an untold number of Black people, drove hundreds into the surrounding wintry woods, and forced the remaining Black and white Republican officeholders on a train out of town.[15]

The casualties of coups and other acts of racial violence amounted to more than the murder, maiming, injuring, and disabling of Black men, women, and children. Many fled their besieged towns, never to return. In search of refuge, they left behind their homes, their few precious heirlooms, their land (had they any), and whatever new, budding wealth they amassed. They would have to start over again, but where? They would have to begin anew, but how? Some bore the physical wounds of racial violence; others suffered material dispossession. But the legacy of racial terrorism haunted millions of Black Americans for subsequent generations, not just in the South but throughout the United States.

Radical Reconstruction came under attack in the South at the hands of violent **white supremacists**, while in the nation's capital, elected officials' political will dwindled, and they subsequently withdrew the monetary investment to sustain its development. When the financial crisis of 1873 drove the country into an economic depression, fewer and fewer Northern Republicans believed it was imperative to continue funding the Reconstruction of the South. The private Freedman's Savings Bank, chartered by the federal government, which served as the premier banking institution for Black veterans and former slaves, went bankrupt in 1874 due to corrupt management and fraud. Contrary to what depositors had been told, their funds were not backed by the government, and thousands of Black individuals, families, and organizations lost their entire savings.[16]

Once the "custodians of freedom,"[17] Congress soon became lackadaisical in protecting the freedoms of Black Southerners. The disputed election of 1876 sealed the coffin of Radical Reconstruction. In exchange for the presidency of Rutherford B. Hayes, Republicans agreed that Hayes would withdrawal federal troops from the South. By giving home rule to the South, Hayes effectively conceded to Northern and Southern white supremacists. With racial mob violence run amok and almost entirely unaccounted for, Southern states under Democrat majorities quickly enacted a web of racially suppressive laws that disenfranchised Blacks and codified at virtually every level of social and civic life a separation of racial groups that came to be known as Jim Crow segregation. It was not until another hundred years had passed that the tide began to turn again during the modern civil rights movement—sometimes called the Second Reconstruction—and that people of color, fighting for their political rights, began to radically change the nation once more.

Numerous race-based acts of mass violence were carried out by white militia and laypeople against Blacks, indigenous peoples, Chinese, Mexicans, other people of color, and their white allies. Here is a short list of such events:

New York City Draft Riots (NY), July 13–18, 1863
Sand Creek Massacre (CO), November 29, 1864
Memphis Massacre (TN), May 1–3, 1866
New Orleans Riot (LA), July 30, 1866
Pulaski Riot (TN), summer 1867
Opelousas Massacre (LA), September 1868
Eutaw Riot (AL), October 25, 1870
Colfax Massacre (LA), April 13, 1873
Hamburg Massacre (SC), July 8, 1876
Seattle Riot (WA), February 6–9, 1886
Thibodaux Massacre (LA), November 23, 1887
Wounded Knee Massacre (SD), December 29, 1890
Slocum Massacre (TX), July 29, 1910
East Saint Louis Massacre (IL), July 2–3, 1917
Ocoee Massacre (FL), November 2, 1920
Tulsa Race Riot (OK), May 31–June 1, 1921
Rosewood Massacre (FL), January 1923
Zoot Suit Riots (CA), June 1943
Greensboro Massacre (NC), November 3, 1979
Charleston Church Massacre (SC), June 17, 2015
Unite the Right Rally (VA), August 11 and 12, 2017

——

A Lesson in Concessions
and Co-optation

At the end of the Reconstruction era, Southern states were allowed to reimplement a **racialized social system** that would keep Black people in a subordinate status relative to whites. States and local governments adopted Black Codes and Jim Crow laws that explicitly barred Black people from certain domains of society and restricted upward mobility or any semblance of equality with whites. Share-cropping replaced chattel slavery, tying agricultural laborers to the land and often plunging sharecroppers into debt to the landowners, forming a new kind of bondage. Vagrancy laws made it permissible for police to arrest people who *appeared* to be out of work or without a home and gave wide discretion to white law enforcement officers to put Black men, women, and children into state control. There they were frequently put into forced labor to serve private interests through the convict-leasing system or "chain gangs." (Remember that loophole in the Thirteenth Amendment?) Policies of racial segregation were upheld by the United States Supreme Court in *Plessy v. Ferguson* (1896), in which the court allowed public accommodations to be separate, so long as they were equal. The enforcement of this ruling (as with the enforcement of any law) was the responsibility of the executive and legislative branches, especially at the state level, and it was here for decades that the separate-but-equal doctrine was either actively or passively denied.

Racial terrorism was rampant across the country. White mobs lynched and mutilated Black people in weekly, sometimes daily acts of vigilantism. Contrary to minding "law and order," racial terrorists deliberately broke the law with expressed intent to restore the **white supremacist** social order. For decades, the journalist and activist Ida B. Wells raised awareness and outrage about this endemic practice, drawing the ire of numerous white men and women in the process.

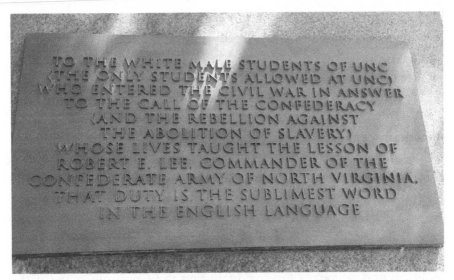

TO THE WHITE MALE STUDENTS OF UNC
(THE ONLY STUDENTS ALLOWED AT UNC)
WHO ENTERED THE CIVIL WAR IN ANSWER
TO THE CALL OF THE CONFEDERACY
(AND THE REBELLION AGAINST
THE ABOLITION OF SLAVERY)
WHOSE LIVES TAUGHT THE LESSON OF
ROBERT E. LEE, COMMANDER OF THE
CONFEDERATE ARMY OF NORTH VIRGINIA,
THAT DUTY IS THE SUBLIMEST WORD
IN THE ENGLISH LANGUAGE

Many Confederate statues were erected well after the Civil War. These statues have raised many debates: Should they be torn down, or should their plaques be replaced to provide greater context? The students at the University of North Carolina, Chapel Hill, constructed their own "new" plaque, pictured here, for a statue dedicated to the university's alumni who fought in the Confederate army. Student-activists later tore down the entire statue on August 20, 2018. (Photo by Oliver Mitchel-Boyask)

Even in these oppressive times, however, the federal government made concessions to the women and men who resisted **racism**, sexism, and **capitalism**.[18] For instance, on August 18, 1920, after over a century of activism by women suffragists and women's rights advocates, the Nineteenth Amendment was ratified, giving women the right to vote. This law largely applied to white women, as women of color, especially Black women, were disenfranchised through other loopholes in the law, such as white primaries, grandfather clauses, poll taxes, and literacy tests (which many Harvard students still have difficulty in completing)[19] as well as the threat of extralegal violence.

Or as another example, during World War II, Black Americans in the defense industry enjoyed some federal protection when President Franklin D. Roosevelt created the Fair Employment Practices Committee after A. Philip Randolph, president of the Brotherhood of Sleeping Car Porters, threatened to call a March on Washington.

Later, in July 1948, President Harry Truman used an executive order to end racial discrimination in the military, and under the Eisenhower administration (1953–61), the military was fully desegregated on the basis of **race**.[20]

It would be futile to try to single out one reason why the modern civil rights movement (1954–68) occurred when it did, but we know that many of the people who organized, strategized, and participated in the movement cut their teeth in a variety of other struggles for freedom and social justice. Some led the antilynching campaigns and the prounion labor movement; others shaped the New Negro Movement / Harlem Renaissance. Still others fought in the all-volunteer, interracial Abraham Lincoln Brigade during the Spanish Civil War or in World War II. Meanwhile, others were active in an array of political and advocacy groups, including the Communist Party, the Socialist Party, the Congress of Racial Equality, the Community Service Organization, the Fellowship of Reconciliation, and the National Association for the Advancement of Colored People, whose partner,

Johnnie Carr's early activism included raising legal funds for the Scottsboro Boys, nine Black teenagers falsely accused of raping two white women. (Photo by Jim Peppler; Alabama Department of Archives and History)

Bayard Rustin was a pacifist and member of both the Fellowship of Reconciliation and the War Resisters League. (Photo by Warren K. Leffler; U.S. News & World Report Magazine Photograph Collection, Prints & Photographs Division, Library of Congress, LC-DIG-ppmsc-01272)

the Legal Defense and Education Fund, is widely considered the legal wing of the movement.

With an ethos of collective responsibility and through coordinated but occasionally spontaneous collective action, Black Americans initiated and led a movement of largely nonviolent civil disobedience in opposition to laws and social rules that subordinated Blacks and other people of color relative to whites. With the Cold War well under way and the United States government intent on showing

Hosea Williams fought in World War II in Patton's army and earned a Purple Heart. (Photo by Jim Peppler; Alabama Department of Archives and History)

the world that its **capitalist** democracy was morally superior to the Soviet Union, activists used all the leverage they could in a growing technology called television that would demonstrate as never before the images and sounds of terrible inequities taking place in the United States.[21] Under pressure from peaceful demonstrators and their more militant agitators, President Lyndon B. Johnson and a coalition of Northern Democrats and Northern Republicans passed the Civil Rights Act of 1964 (prohibiting racial segregation in schools and outlawing discrimination on the basis of **race**, color, sex, or national origin in employment, public accommodations, and voter registration requirements), the Voting Rights Act of 1965 (providing, among other things, federal oversight to prevent voter suppression), and the Fair Housing Act of 1968 (creating equal housing opportunities irrespective of race, religion, and national origin).

These three legislative concessions brought the United States into a new world of racial norms. Racial equality, while not a new idea nor even fully actualized, gained authority and set the stage and rules for how Americans were supposed to act with each other from that moment on. Blacks had the vote now firmly in hand, but the implementation of desegregation and the expansion of opportunities for upward mobility were inconsistent across states and localities and met notable resistance. On the ground, resentful whites reacted in various ways, some using violent tactics to intimidate Blacks from integrating with whites, while others who did not care to stay and put up a fight moved further away from desegregating areas in a wave of white flight.

Segregationist politicians and pundits, now out of step with the new wave of legal doctrine and growing norms of racial equality, were busy strategizing ways to preserve white, middle-class privileges. With explicit segregationist and **white supremacist** language becoming publicly reprehensible, Republicans devised a new strategy to draw segregationist Southern and Northern Democrats to their party and remain relevant in national politics. At the time, civil rights lawyers employed the language of colorblindness to argue that de jure segregation was unconstitutional because it treated people differently on the basis of **race** (i.e., it treated people of color as inferior to whites). In stark contrast, over time Republicans **co-opted** this language to articulate an anti-interventionist politics that ignored the unevenness of the playing field and emphasized individualism in order to argue that race, and thus existing racial inequality, should not be considered in any manner, to enforce neither segregation nor integration.

This dialect of colorblindness proved to be ideologically versatile for white racial conservatives in the decades to come. Whether the issue was desegregating schools by busing, **affirmative action**, welfare reform, health care, or congressional redistricting, they could be found invoking a reappropriated memory of the civil rights movement while arguing against state-led remediation for racial inequality and, in some cases, even advocating for policies that were known to exacerbate racial disparities.[22] In the most twisted form of this line of argument, some conservatives have gone so far to say that the consideration of race is itself a betrayal of the civil rights movement. Ha!

Republicans are not alone in their use of **colorblind racism**. Moderate and conservative Democrats have in many ways capitulated to the now-hegemonic use of colorblind language either by agreeing with its ideological logic or by being unwilling or unable to mount a repudiation of it. Yet again, we see the two-steps-forward-one-step-back dance of racial progress. Or, as the historian Ibram Kendi explains, just as we see racial progress, we also see **racist** progress.[23]

The Allure of the Almost There

The call for racial equality cannot be quelled because the concessions made in the post-civil-rights era have not adequately addressed the compounding inequities of the past, nor have they inoculated our society from contemporary mechanisms that produce new inequities. There are *vestiges* of older **racialized social systems** that continue to keep people of color and poor whites at a profound disadvantage. The logic of vagrancy laws, alongside the erosion of the Fourth Amendment (protection against unreasonable search and seizure), informs policing practices today; one can still be arrested and jailed for being out in public while not actively working or lacking the intent or ability to spend money. Depending on how someone appears, police may investigate the immigration status of a person already stopped, detained, or arrested if they suspect (for any reason) that individual is an undocumented immigrant (see *Arizona v. United States* [2012]) or a gang member in the company of other gang members (through the use of gang injunctions). In both instances, the practices are deemed constitutional if the police use **race** as one but not the sole reason for suspicion (see *United States v. Brignoni-Ponce* [1975]). As in the days of Reconstruction, those who are under the custody of the state as prisoners can still be forced to labor for private interests. (Remember the season of *Orange Is the New Black* in which Piper and several other prisoners made expensive panties for very little pay? That is a real thing.)

The Supreme Court has served as an obstacle to the elimination of racial disparity and injustice in other ways. The court's decision in *Washington v. Davis* (1976) established that, in order to succeed, plaintiffs bringing constitutional challenges to facially neutral government actions with disparate racial effects must prove that the challenged action is purposefully discriminatory. This requirement operates as a substantial burden on minority plaintiffs.

Though we often romanticize the Supreme Court, it is hardly a progressive institution. For instance, in *San Antonio Independent School District v. Rodriguez* (1973; 5–4 decision), the court held that the financing of public schools using local property taxes does not violate the Fourteenth Amendment's Equal Protection Clause, in essence ruling that it is permissible to discriminate in education on the basis of wealth and poverty, even if the disparities between poor schools and wealthy schools more deeply entrench racial segregation. *Milliken v. Bradley* (1974; also a 5–4 decision) drew a constitutional line between intentional, explicit discrimination (de jure segregation) and the machinations of growing suburbs, school boundary making, city planning, and tax structures that facilitate white flight and the resegregation of schools (de facto segregation), embedding racial inequality even further by treating white-flight-enabling politics as somehow racially agnostic.[24]

We see the *overturning* of signature civil-rights-era legislation, thus providing new opportunities for inequity to flourish. In *Shelby County v. Holder* (2013), the Supreme Court struck down section 4 of the Voting Rights Act, which prohibited certain districts with a history of racialized voter suppression (including many Southern states as well as counties in several states across the country) from changing their election laws without authorization from the attorney general or a three-judge panel in the US District Court for Washington, DC, verifying that they did not have the intent or outcome of negatively impacting the right to vote on the basis of **race**. The immediate implication of this decision is that voter-suppression tactics, such as voter ID laws and reducing early voting periods, proliferated across many of the previously covered states.

Structural **racism** is a central focus of this book, but we would be remiss to ignore that in addition to the crisis of excessive force employed by police on Black people and the accompanying trend that those who kill Black people are infrequently brought to justice,

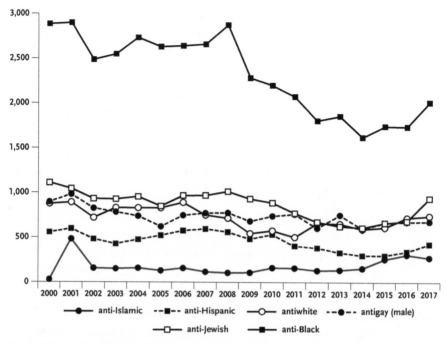

Single-bias hate crime incidents per group, 2000–2017. (Data compiled from FBI statistics)

Black people are far and away the most targeted group of single-bias hate crimes in the country. Though the trend of hate crimes against Black people has largely declined over the past two decades (save the period's sharpest spike over a one-year time span that occurred during Donald Trump's first year as president), the lives of Black folks are incredibly vulnerable to both state-initiated and citizen-induced violence.

In addition to grappling with remains of the past and working to hold onto the progress that activists have made through arduous struggle, there are *new balls of wax,* issues that did not emerge in the past because social and historical context did not produce the social-political question of constitutionality and social justice. For example, although people have had same-sex sex throughout human history, a social identity as gay, lesbian, or transgender did not emerge until rather recently. In the wake of the modern civil rights movement, the civil rights of gays, lesbians, and eventually transgender

Americans gained their own but related platform. During the Obama administration, we witnessed important advancements in the civil rights of these groups, but many significant forms of legal discrimination still exist. People of color who also identify as lesbian, gay, bisexual, queer, or transgender thus face multiple axes of oppression. As a point of evidence, the average murder rate for all Americans between ages fifteen and thirty-four is about one in twelve thousand, but for Black transgender women, it is one in twenty-six hundred.[25]

There is also a political fight being made at the time of this writing over the fate of Deferred Action for Childhood Arrivals (DACA), of Dreamers (people who were born in other countries and brought to the United States as children by their undocumented parents), and of children who have been separated at the border from their parents by US Customs and Border Protection. To be sure, if we look at the intersection of anti-Black animus and current immigration policy, we find that Black undocumented immigrants make up a disproportionate number of those who are deported from the United States.[26]

How far, then, are we from attaining what previous generations of Black freedom fighters aimed to accomplish? Just over a decade ago, in 2007, Barack Obama asserted that the civil rights generation "took us 90 percent of the way there," as if the remaining 10 percent is "not a fundamental, woven-into-our-institutions **racism** requiring policy and institutional transformation but a remnant racism."[27] This kind of narrative is where the historian Jeanne Theoharis locates the *allure of the almost-there.*[28]

A Note on Being Labeled "Radical" and "Un-American"

Many people in the past who agitated mainstream society and challenged political institutions with the primary objective of fulfilling the rights of the US Constitution and achieving the necessary conditions for all people to have what they need to stay alive and make a living were called "radicals." By calling them radicals, defenders

Whites protest the admission of the "Little Rock Nine" into Central High School at the Arkansas state capitol, August 20, 1959. (Photo by John T. Bledsoe; U.S. News & World Report Magazine Photograph Collection, Prints & Photographs Division, Library of Congress, LC-DIG-ppmsca-19754)

of the status quo framed egalitarians as "out of place" and "out of line." During the early to mid-twentieth century, for example, many whites claimed that the idea of racial equality was fundamentally un-American. By framing the redistribution of resources to the poor and marginalized as anticapitalist and conflating **capitalism** with patriotism, **white supremacists** argued that the integration of white and nonwhite bodies in public space and the integration of white and nonwhite tax dollars for public goods was a usurpation of the American way. This nefarious narrative ignored and disregarded two indisputable facets of our American heritage: a long tradition of **anti-racist** resistance in our country and a rich, "homegrown" socialist and communist politics.[29] (If you have ever enjoyed a two-day weekend or a forty-hour work week, you have socialist and communist activists to thank.) With this legacy in mind, egalitarians *were* radical, but only if we think of radicalism as "the imagination and will to think and act outside of the bounds of what is normally acceptable."[30]

THE STRUGGLE FOR FREEDOM AND EQUALITY REMAINS UNDER SURVEILLANCE

The FBI placed the following individuals and organizations under surveillance because it deemed them to be radical and subversive. What these surveilled Americans wanted was an egalitarian society.

James Baldwin

Black Panther Party

Stokely Carmichael
(aka Kwame Ture)

César Chávez

Congress of Racial Equality

Deacons for Defense and Justice

W. E. B. DuBois

Medgar Evers

James Farmer

Fannie Lou Hamer

Fred Hampton

Highlander Folk School

Coretta Scott King

Martin Luther King Jr.

Paul Robeson

Jackie Robinson

Bayard Rustin

Betty Shabazz

Southern Christian Leadership
Conference (SCLC)

Student Nonviolent Coordinating
Committee (SNCC)

United Farm Workers

Roy Wilkins

Richard Wright

Malcolm X

In August 2017, the FBI reported that "Black Identity Extremist (BIE) perceptions of police brutality against African Americans spurred an increase in premeditated, retaliatory lethal violence against law enforcement and will very likely serve as justification for such violence."[31] According to a *Foreign Policy* investigation, "former government officials and legal experts said no such movement exists, and some expressed concern that the term is part of a politically motivated effort to find an equivalent threat to white supremacists."[32] *Will this new categorization of extremism be used as a tool of obstruction for the Movement for Black Lives?*

Kwame Ture (formerly Stokely Carmichael) once attributed the following quote to George Bernard Shaw: "all criticism is an autobiography."[33] That is, how one judges others says a lot about how one thinks about oneself. Like critique, the history we construct reflects a great deal about what we value or disapprove of in our past, and it reveals what it is that we are willing and unwilling to reckon with in the present day. Today, we commemorate the key leaders, strategists, and foot soldiers from the Underground Railroad to the civil rights movement—people who were once stigmatized as dangerous and even criminal. We consecrate (and at times **co-opt**, yet again) nonviolent, civilly disobedient Black people in children's books, public school curricula, Hollywood motion pictures, political speeches from both major parties, postage stamps, and a federal holiday. But we must keep in mind that what is *omitted* from (state-authorized) history books is a function of power.

The superficial way that Americans tend to celebrate Black freedom fighters from Harriet Tubman to Rosa Parks does a disservice to us all because it distorts and dilutes the grander vision that these people had in mind—a society where Black people have the authority to protect their lives and where Black lives, and thereby all lives, matter. The congratulatory stories we tell ourselves treat the existence of the Underground Railroad and the civil rights movement as an emblem of the American people's freedom-fighting spirit rather than as an emblem of the deeply ingrained **racism** that these folks sought freedom from. The stories we tell ourselves are ones that highlight the reluctant concessions of US lawmakers, rather than the remaining structural barriers against which radical activists fought. The stories we tell ourselves make us feel that we are making progress.[34] In other words, we focus on measuring how far the arc of the moral universe has bent but not how long the arc is or how tight the grip of historical inequity. This is a history of vanity. For a better today and even better tomorrow, we must be vigilant of over-congratulations. Don't let your love of country lull you into complacency. Staying woke—calling out injustice, advocating for the vulnerable, and working against the forces of anti-Black racism—is patriotic.

Questions and Debate

1 How do you measure racial progress? How far have we come, and how far do we have to go to attain a postracial society? Is it even possible? Is it even desirable? How do we know when we've gotten there?

2 Several Southern states are reckoning with their history. The administration of Duke University removed a statue of Robert E. Lee from the Duke Chapel, which was designed by Julian Abele, an African American architect. Who could or should be placed in this spot?

The empty space where the Robert E. Lee statue once stood at Duke Chapel. (Photo by Candis Watts Smith)

3 This chapter focuses primarily on the historical struggles of Black Americans. How are the struggles of Black Americans tied, if at all, to those of other racial and ethnic groups? Consider the role of genocide, colonialism, imperialism, eugenics, exclusion, and recruitment and exploitation of low-wage labor.

4 At what age should we introduce children to historical aspects of US racism?

5 Americans laud the violence relied on in the American Revolution, Civil War, both world wars, and to some extent, the ongoing conflict in Afghanistan. But Americans also praise the nonviolent strategies of the civil rights movement and even require it of activists at the center of the contemporary Movement for Black Lives. Should violence occur in the wake of a Black protest, it is often referred to as racial rioting or mob rule. Do we have a double standard for the use of violence?

Additional Materials to Consider

BOOKS

Adams, David Wallace. *Education for Extinction: American Indians and the Boarding School Experience, 1875–1928*. Lawrence: University Press of Kansas 1995.

Brown, Dee. *Bury My Heart at Wounded Knee: An Indian History of the American West*. New York: Holt, Rinehart and Winston, 1970.

Cecelski, David S., and Timothy B. Tyson. *Democracy Betrayed: The Wilmington Race Riot of 1898 and Its Legacy*. Chapel Hill: University of North Carolina Press, 2000.

Foner, Eric. *Reconstruction: America's Unfinished Revolution, 1863–1877*. New York: Harper and Row, 1988.

Francis, Megan Ming. *Civil Rights and the Making of the Modern American State*. Cambridge: Cambridge University Press, 2014.

Franklin, John Hope. *From Slavery to Freedom: A History of African Americans*. New York: Knopf, 1947.

Gómez, Laura E. *Manifest Destinies: The Making of the Mexican American Race*. New York: NYU Press, 2007.

Kelley, Robin D. G. *Hammer and Hoe: Alabama Communists during the Great Depression*. Chapel Hill: University of North Carolina Press, 1990.

Kendi, Ibram X. *Stamped from the Beginning: The Definitive History of Racist Ideas in America*. New York: Nation Books, 2016.

Ngai, Mae M. *Impossible Subjects: Illegal Aliens and the Making of Modern America*. Princeton, NJ: Princeton University Press, 2004.

Rigueur, Leah Wright. 2015. *The Loneliness of the Black Republican: Pragmatic Politics and the Pursuit of Power*. Princeton, NJ: Princeton University Press.

Theoharis, Jeanne. *A More Beautiful and Terrible History: The Uses and Misuses of Civil Rights History*. Boston: Beacon, 2018.

Zinn, Howard, adapted by Rebecca Stefoff. *A Young People's History of the United States: Columbus to the War on Terror*. New York: Seven Stories, 2009.

FILMS

Black Power Mixtape 1967–1975, The. Directed by Göran Hugo Olsson. 2011.

Eyes on the Prize: America's Civil Rights Years, 1954–1965. Blackside, 1987.

Eyes on the Prize II: America at the Racial Crossroads, 1965–1985. Blackside, 1990.

I Am Not Your Negro. Directed by Raoul Peck. 2016.

Slavery by Another Name. Directed by Samuel D. Pollard. 2012.

3½ Minutes, Ten Bullets. Directed by Marc Silver. 2015.

When the Levees Broke: A Requiem in Four Acts. Directed by Spike Lee. 2006.

WEBSITES

Facing History and Ourselves. www.facinghistory.org.

PODCASTS

Stuff You Missed in History Class. www.missedinhistory.com.

4

Are You Upholding White Supremacy?

Are you a **racist**? No? Great! Are you sure? Few people are willing to raise their hand to provide an affirmative response to this question, but this presents a paradox: why is there such a preponderance of evidence that racism exists, and yet we have so few racists? If you are reading this book, chances are you're not a card-carrying member of the Ku Klux Klan, the National Alliance, or any other neofascist, anti-Black, anti-Semitic, **white supremacist** organization. With that said, is it possible, even despite your best intentions, that you may still be contributing to or enabling ongoing racial disparities?

It would be a hard pill to swallow if you had to respond "Yes" to this question. Indeed, there are some who would reject the question out of hand. Some people argue that racism doesn't mean anything anymore because people use the word "too often." It's true that describing something as racist has become a common, inaccurately deployed quip, a verbal equivocation, or a default insult. But arguably the word is used frequently because there's plenty that can be accurately described as such. Maybe we should, in fact, be using the word more often and for a wider array of social, political, and economic processes, phenomena, and outcomes. But maybe we should also be more pointed and more specific about what we mean when we say that someone or something is **racist**. Let's ask the question another way, and we'll give you some nuanced ways to answer:

Do you live your day-to-day life in a way that may—intentionally or otherwise—uphold white supremacy?

a. Yes, because I'm an overt racist.
b. Yes, because I'm a structural racist.
c. Yes, because I'm a complicit racist.
d. No, I'm an antiracist.

Let's think through these options one by one and perhaps use the process of elimination. Most people have gotten pretty good at pointing out the *overt racists* in the world. He's the guy who drove a car into a group of counterprotestors at the Unite the Right rally in Charlottesville, Virginia. She's the family member at Thanksgiving dinner who makes derogatory remarks about . . . (fill in name of an underrepresented racial group here). Their behavior evinces racial animus, bigotry, and prejudice. Their violence and epithets are interpersonal and, more importantly, individualistic.

The *structural racists* are the Supreme Court justices who have written or concurred with decisions to dismantle the Voting Rights Act or allow police to pull people over who "look illegal."[1] They are the teachers, principals, and resource officers who discipline children of color more harshly and more frequently than they do white children.[2] They are the doctors who are less likely to prescribe certain medicines to or do necessary surgery on Black patients.[3] And they are voters who support candidates who disparage whole groups of vulnerable populations on a regular basis in order to garner and maintain the support of people who are racially resentful.[4] Their behavior affects others in a structural way, shaping institutions and contributing to patterns of racial disparity. (Let's also be clear that some people are both overtly and structurally racist.)

The *complicit racists* are people who do absolutely nothing in their day-to-day lives to prevent either overt or structural racists from further enmeshing racial inequality into our society. This group of people may not intentionally work to perpetuate negative stereotypes, support candidates whose policies exacerbate racial inequities, inundate people with **microaggressions**, or **whitesplain**, but they are not **antiracists** either. By latching onto hegemonic ideologies like **colorblindness** and **respectability politics**, however, many people *across all racial groups* enable the perpetuation of **white supremacy**. They fail to recognize that the lives of white people are more greatly valued by a variety of institutions and that interpersonal racial hostility and prejudice alone cannot fully explain persistent racial disparities.

Being a complicit racist is easy because it only calls for you to stay out of the way. Being a complicit racist is easy because it's business as usual, it's normal, and almost everyone is doing it. Being a complicit racist is easy because we all have a script in our hands, ready to be recited when something looks suspicious but doesn't completely raise up our red, that's-so-racist flags.

Staying woke, on the other hand, is a process of developing habits of antiracism, such as vigilance, speaking out, stepping up, using one's privilege to undermine **racism**, and broadening your understanding of how racism works. Staying woke means honing your skills to notice when the racial rules of the game are changing, becoming cognizant of the underlying assumptions of dominant racial ideologies, and listening to the ways in which racial grammar evolves so that you can combat new forms of oppression.

The purpose of this chapter is to highlight some of the scripts that many of us have learned in order to be good, friendly complicit racists. These scripts are coded as ostensibly progressive, but their purpose is to avert or diminish accusations of racism and to allow people to maintain a humanist image of themselves and of US society. The everyday repetition of these scripts sounds normal and innocuous, but they inadvertently uphold white supremacy. In deconstructing common narratives that are rooted in **colorblindness** and **respectability politics**, we hope to get you thinking about how you can intervene in the socially acceptable reproduction of racial inequality.

———

"It Doesn't Matter If You're Black or White or Green or Blue!"

Colorblindness has become the dominant racial ideology in the US (though not the only one), putting us in what the anthropologist Lee Baker calls the "color-blind bind."[5] Sociologists like Ruth Frankenberg explain that a colorblind ideology is a "mode of thinking about race organized around an effort not to 'see' or at any rate not to acknowledge race differences," because this is perceived as the "'polite' language of race."[6] A colorblind narrative suggests that we can get rid of the last, lingering vestiges of racial inequality by ignoring **race** altogether. There are two assumptions here. First, the logic erroneously presumes that there is only a "little bit" of **racism** left, and second, it suggests that ignoring the problem will solve it. Taken together, these assumptions serve to perpetuate racial inequity because they lead us to falter in addressing the issue for what it is: *racial* inequity.

Though it has become a common belief that being colorblind is best for everyone, colorblindness is actually an evolved form of previous, harmful racial ideologies and attitudes. This ability to transform and appropriate the values of contemporary (middle-class) whites and to discard the parts that would make it irrelevant or too obviously transparent is what makes some people call racism a "scavenger ideology."[7] We have to keep in mind that a racial ideology is simply a story we tell ourselves to explain what we see in this world. So during the "Jim Crow" racism era, people relied on a narrative that suggested that Black folks' subordinate social, political, and economic status resulted from their inherent inferiority. After Jim Crow was dismantled through civil-rights-era policies—such as the Civil Rights Act of 1964, the Voting Rights Act of 1965, and the Fair

Housing Act of 1968—many whites, arguing that the playing field was now leveled, became indignant over additional **race**-conscious efforts, such as **affirmative action**, which sought to close the racial disparities in opportunity. These racially resentful people asserted that if any trace of the racial inequities that were developed during the previous four hundred years still existed, it was because Black people did not live up to their newly presented opportunities to succeed. Today, **colorblindness** leads people to rely on logic that claims that since race *shouldn't* matter, it *doesn't* matter; in fact, some believe we would be better off if we just didn't "see" race altogether.

The claim to "not see race" does us all a disservice because race *does* shape the lives of every living person in the United States. Relatedly, many people on the left claim that "identity politics" is the opposite of colorblindness and thus is harmful because white **nationalists** use the same identity-based "rationale" as people of color to demand redress for their perceived loss of racial privilege. This logic and argument are lazy and careless. As is often said, when you're accustomed to privilege, equality feels like oppression. If we shift our perspective from a position of privilege to that of the most marginalized, then we can more easily understand that identity politics is not "just about who you [are], it [is] also about what you could do to confront the oppression you [are] facing." The women who founded the Combahee River Collective, a Black feminist organization in the late 1970s, used the term "identity politics" to highlight the fact that "Black women's social positions made them disproportionately susceptible to the ravages of **capitalism**, including poverty, illness, violence, sexual assault, and inadequate healthcare and housing, to name only the most obvious."[8] Though identity politics is yet another concept **co-opted** and abused to maintain **white supremacy**, its originators conceived of it as a means not only to bring attention to interlocking sets of oppression but also to respond to them politically and radically.

In order to buck the colorblind trend, you need not make essentialist assumptions about a person on the basis of the person's race. It is fine to notice people's race (along with other aspects of their identity, such as gender), if you plan to use that recognition for good—for compassion, empathy, or consideration of how a person might have to navigate a particular space or situation differently or to remedy the effects of **racism**. Besides, it's annoying, hurtful, and psychologically taxing to hear people say, "I didn't even notice you were Black." Ironically, straight-up overt racists admit to seeing **race**, but they just do so to actively pursue injustice or violence or to respond apathetically to injustice or violence. But those who stay woke know that simply saying nothing and doing nothing effectively makes you part of the problem, rather than part of the solution.

"I Voted for Obama"

The 2008 and 2012 elections of Barack Obama were objectively historic: Obama was the first self-identified Black person elected to the United States presidency. The first time around, the *New York Times'* front page declared, "Racial Barrier Falls in Heavy Turnout." Another headline suggested, "Change Has Come." A below-the-fold article in the *Washington Post* claimed, "America's History Gives Way to Its Future." People were excited. Jessie Jackson was crying. Tehama was crying—this guy was her professor for goodness sake! Everyone was crying! People were excited to divulge what had typically been taboo—publicly announcing the way one filled out one's secret ballot: "I voted for Obama." For many people, "I voted for Obama" denoted that they helped to usher in what many believed would be a postracial reality. But "I voted / campaigned / donated to / knocked on doors for Obama" has also become currency that can be cashed in when accusations of racism arise. "I voted for Obama" is the twenty-first-century version of "I marched with Dr. King" or "My friend/ neighbor/cousin-in-law is Black." Here's the thing: none of these things means that you are **antiracist**.

Voting for a political party or candidate that explicitly aims to reduce inequality is a step in the right direction, but it is not sufficient to dismantle an embedded system of racism. You know who else voted for Obama? Jason Kessler, the guy who organized the

Unite the Right protest in Charlottesville, Virginia, which not only gathered modern-day Nazis, white **nationalists**, and racist internet trolls but also led to the murder of Heather Heyer and the injuries of nineteen other people and provided the forty-fifth president the opportunity to double down on the bullshit idea that there was "blame on both sides." All said, your vote is a blunt instrument to translate your preferences into political action.

What people loved (or hated) about Obama was that he was a symbol of racial progress. Here's the thing about Obama. He was the safest Black candidate the Democratic Party could add to an otherwise-curated lineup of primary candidates. He's a Black man with a biracial heritage and an Ivy League background; he was a third-culture kid[9] who can code switch, a skill that he often used to speak in front of Black audiences with an authentically Black tone of voice but with messages of **respectability politics**. He has light-skinned privilege in a society where **colorism** is rampant. In experiments, researchers show that darker-skinned versions of Obama received much less support from white Americans.[10] Though he did not just stroll into the White House, he did have middle-class privilege and the cultural currency of his white family, which he cashed in regularly on the campaign trail. He never made any promises on the campaign trail to address structural **racism**; he didn't even mention racism until he was forced to.[11] While Obama did take steps to change policies and create initiatives aimed to help people of color and sometimes spoke eloquently on racial issues, racial wealth inequality actually increased under his presidency, and his words of racial uplift were often laced with messages of Black blame.[12]

We have to be careful how we talk about racism and also racial progress because the words, rationales, and concepts that political liberals and racial progressives use often get **co-opted** by racial conservatives. Case in point: while many white liberals proxy "I voted for Obama" to mean "I cannot be racist," racial conservatives have co-opted the election of Obama to argue that we live in a postracial society. If Obama, a Black man who was raised in a female-headed household, could become president, neoconservative logic leads us to the notion that it's quite obvious that structural racism is not what

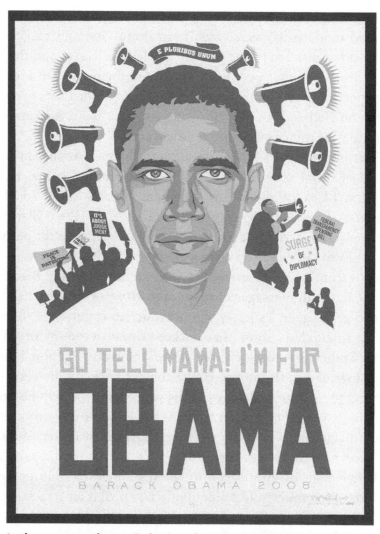

In the run-up to the 2008 election, the artist Ray Noland was commissioned by Obama for America to create posters for the presidential campaign. Noland says, "After numerous talks with Director of New Media, Scott Goodstein, I realized the campaign had an issue with the way I presented Barack Obama's image. From their comments, I felt they thought I made [Obama] look 'too black.'" After parting ways with the official campaign, Noland continued to create artwork supporting Obama's run. In creating this poster, Noland presents Obama as "unapologetically brown and at times jet black, to stress the point" of his racial identity. (Designed by Ray Noland; first-edition printing, 2006, by Steve Walters, Screwball Press, Chicago; second-edition printing, 2007, at Crosshair, Chicago; quotations from email correspondence, September 2, 2018)

While many people understood Barack Obama's election as being made possible by a legacy of struggle for freedom and equality, as depicted in this cartoon, it was by no means the culmination of their efforts. We must continue to build on their victories. (Cartoon by Matt Wuerker)

prevents Blacks and other people of color from *earning* the same life chances and enjoying the same opportunities as whites.

Antiracists have to resist not one but three sets of logic that uphold a society marked by a racial hierarchy: that of well-meaning complicit **racists**, that of structural racists, and that of overtly racist conservatives—all of whom rely on Obama's election either to suggest that individuals should be absolved from the fact that they enjoy **white privilege** or to assert that large-scale policies to eradicate racial disparities need not be developed because the United States in toto became postracial on November 9, 2008. An antiracist is aware of the misuse and abuse of political symbols and works instead to produce tangible outcomes that produce racial equity.

"I Did Not Vote for Trump"

There are plenty of people who honestly believe that their choice to support a candidate who claimed that he could shoot a person in public and not lose any votes, declared that most Mexican immigrants are rapists who bring drugs into the United States, mocked people with disabilities, asserted that if time travel were possible, he would still intern Japanese citizens, argued that Muslims should be banned from the United States, promised to appoint Supreme Court justices who would overturn marriage equality and rights to access abortion services, believes that Black people have "nothing to lose," and admitted that he likes to grab women "by the pussy" was not in and of itself a choice to support the oppression of whole groups of people. A number of these people will even say they voted for him begrudgingly; embarrassed by his crude immorality, they clung to something redemptive they saw in his brash speech, his late-in-life cozying up to the religious right, his eight-year utter revulsion of Barack Obama, or the fact that he wasn't Hillary Clinton. Then there are the hardcore Trump voters with no reservations, no qualms, no disclaimers—this was their guy, the man they've been waiting for

The Women's March, the largest single day of protest in US history, was organized by a cadre of seasoned activists. Galvanized to speak on issues of political, social, and economic inequity, millions of people across all seven continents protested on January 21, 2017, the day after Trump's inauguration. But it will require persistent activism and the regular exercise of the franchise to upend the structural problems that participants sought to highlight. (Photo by Candis Watts Smith)

their entire lives, MAGA all the way. Are these two groups of people exactly the same? No. Did they cast their one and only ballot for the same man? Absolutely.

Meanwhile, there are also plenty of liberals who in their efforts to distance themselves from the so-called Basket of Deplorables[13] pridefully note that they did not vote for Trump but in the very next breath suggest that during the next time around (e.g., 2018 midterm elections and later in 2020), Americans, generally speaking, and the candidates of the Democratic Party, more specifically, should focus more on the plight of poor and working-class white people, whose primary concerns include job loss due to globalization, a sense of vulnerability due to the increasing racial **diversity** of US demographics, and increased crime and drug addiction that comes from feelings of disenfranchisement. By endorsing a platform that privileges the plight of certain white people, rather than one that exploits

Americans' anxiety over and animus toward immigrants, Muslims, and people of color, these liberals fancy themselves morally superior to their Trump-voting counterparts.

But here's the thing: the problems of poor white America are problems that arise because the social safety net set up during the New Deal and Great Society has been weakened. Public schools are not well funded, and teachers are undervalued. The national minimum wage is a not a living wage. The Affordable Care Act (though imperfect) is being dismantled one piece at a time. And only time will tell whether the opioid epidemic will be treated with the crime-and-punishment tools of the crack epidemic, given that the forty-fifth president was slow to deem a pandemic that kills almost one hundred people *per day* a national emergency and appointed an attorney general who wanted to revive some of the worst aspects of the failed War on Drugs.[14] Much of this is happening because conservative political elites have led racially resentful whites to believe that undeserving, lazy people of color will benefit from evidence-based, dignity-sustaining public policy at the expense of whites.[15] "Not only do these attacks have consequences for ordinary Black people, but they are also a 'Trojan Horse' shielding a much broader attack against all working-class people, including whites and Latino/as."[16] The effects of this combination of policies have been crushing Black and Brown folks, including those in the middle class, for decades and now are more readily eating away at the lives of ostensibly dispensable poor white Americans. Ignoring any of these facts consigns anyone, even a liberal, to the Basket of Deplorables.

Okay, so you object to the "Basket of Deplorables" terminology? And you're not too crazy about the idea that Clinton-voting liberals might be deplorable too? Let's think about this in another way. We tend to associate **racism** with particular groups of people (e.g., whites) who live in certain regions of the country (e.g., the South) or particular areas of our states (e.g., rural). We also tend to focus on interpersonal racial discrimination and overt bigotry to make determinations of membership in the Basket of Deplorables. But staying woke means recognizing that the dominant mode of racial ideology is **colorblind**, and racism, generally speaking, is best understood as deeply embedded in our society—it's structural, it's almost invisible, and it's insidious.

You can use your vote as a blunt proxy for your principles, but electoral politics is only one stop on an **antiracist**'s path to making change. In fact, your vote for candidates in either major party may actually serve to exacerbate inequality. But there is no shortage of organizations to join, to donate to, to canvass for, to use your skills to make change in your community—ranging from the ACLU to local chapters of Black Lives Matter. You might join in a collective protest, picket, or boycott. Or you may still decide to join the campaign of a candidate who is *explicit* about the ways in which she or he wants to address vast racial inequalities in our society. Or you may become that candidate yourself—for school board, city council, or state representative. Doing something is better than nothing, but solely relying on your vote for or against a candidate is just enough to uphold the status quo.

"When Old People Die, We Will Finally Be Done with Racism"

Are you relying on the next generation to help us take a turn toward a postracial reality? We sure hope not. First, the problem of **racism** is an urgent one. We cannot wait for small people to grow up and become leaders and herd us to the promised land. Second and perhaps most importantly, the next generation has not come to us as fully formed people who love **diversity** and multiculturalism and support interracial marriage and have an insatiable desire to stomp out systemic injustice. Children are raised by adults who teach them stuff or, in academic parlance, socialize them. And herein lies the problem: grownups are not necessarily providing children with the proper tools to dismantle racism.[17]

Colorblindness characterizes the environment in which young whites have been socialized. Research shows that white parents, in particular, are teaching their children that they should love everyone

It's never too early to begin to cultivate an appreciation for justice. (Women's March in Washington, DC, January 21, 2017; photo by Candis Watts Smith)

regardless of their color, which is great. But it's what adults are *not* teaching children that is messing them up. Folks are teaching their children this love-everyone business through the logic of **color-blindness**. For instance, you know that game where you have a bunch of faces, and the person on the other side has to guess which of the characters is your favorite: Guess Who? Kids are failing to do well at this game because they don't want to ask, "Is your person Black?"! The social psychologist Evan Apfelbaum and his colleagues show that whites adopt what they call "strategic colorblindness," or an effort to completely avoid mentioning **race** even in a task for which pointing out someone's skin color is actually helpful.[18] This group of scholars found that by the age of ten, white kids have been fully socialized to avoid mentioning people's race altogether even if describing someone's race can help them successfully complete a task.

Children have an astute ability to connect dots. For example, on a flight to Canada, our resident mini person, André, explained, "When we go up in the air, everything will get very small," and then he consoled, "But don't worry. When we come back down, things will get back to their normal size." Correct. (Mostly.) Sometimes, children make logical connections between concepts and ideas but come to inaccurate conclusions. One of the conclusions that they may make is that if Obama, Beyoncé, and Chance the Rapper can become president or some other well-to-do public figure, then the sky is the limit for Black people who are willing to work toward their dreams. In arriving at this conclusion, they will likely arrive at others: **meritocracy** functions perfectly because the playing field has been leveled for everyone; people on welfare are failures because they don't try hard enough to make a living for themselves; and you cannot act out an implicit bias if you value **diversity**.

By avoiding conversations about race, **racism**, and inequality, we are doing a disservice to ourselves and our children. We already know that overt racists are most likely to teach their children to think and act as they do, but it's the passive act of not teaching our children about racism in all its forms—structural, implicit, overt, interpersonal, complicit—that serves to sow more seeds of inequality. We have listed a series of children's books at the end of this chapter that will help you to explore some of these tough issues with the young people in your life. It is difficult to talk about racism, but we do ourselves a disservice by keeping them in a bubble, pretending that they don't notice what's going on, and by preventing them from developing a language and ethos of **antiracism**.

"All Lives Matter"

If you walked into a room full of people and asked, "What is the purpose of saying 'Black lives matter?'" invariably somebody will say something along the lines of "Well, I think it's important to say 'All lives matter.'" Okay. First of all, that is not an answer to the question, but the response does illuminate the notion that contemporary **racism** is rooted in the **epistemology of ignorance** and apathy. Contrary to what some people believe, "Black lives matter" *is* a universal claim to value the lives of all people. The philosopher Clevis Headley explains this well:

> Most people prematurely denounced the Black Lives Matter Movement because they uncritically interpreted this movement as a particularism that is opposed to the universalist view that all lives matter. . . . We live in a society that gives lip service to this universalist recognition but behaves as though Black lives are irrelevant and are, therefore, excluded from the universalist position. Thus, the only way to include Black lives into the universal position is to explicitly assert that Black lives matter. . . . Accordingly, it expresses this recognition by calling attention to the fact that the universal declaration of the value of all lives is atrociously empty if the lives of Black people are not equally valued.[19]

The person who deflects the original question shifts attention from considering the state of Black life to, instead, focusing on a **colorblind** claim that decontextualizes the problems that Black people face in the United States. White people have been **gaslighting** Black folks since the end of the first Reconstruction, and "All lives matter" is one of the ways that self-proclaimed colorblind Americans take part in this game.

To say that it is terrible that several unarmed Black people have been killed by the police and then add that if Black people just behaved differently, they would be better off is to willfully dismiss the entire history of policing in Black communities.[20] To call Black

In this 1967 cartoon, a white military officer claims that Black opposition to the Vietnam War is costing African Americans support from white people in their quest for civil rights. The officer's rationale, critiqued here by the artist, is a good example of what we consider racial gaslighting. (Cartoon by Jules Feiffer)

people crazy for thinking that the government has a cure for AIDS or cancer or whatever but is holding back is to aggressively reject the entire history of unnecessary medical experimentation on and state-supported eugenics policies toward Black individuals and communities.[21] To claim that Black people just prefer to live in neighborhoods that have fewer amenities, low-performing schools, and slumlords because people, just like wolves and birds, naturally flock together with "their own kind" is to refuse the entire history of state-sponsored housing and zoning policies that segregated and still segregate US cities and towns. Actively refusing to engage with the many layers of history that are relevant to the discussion at hand is to uphold **white supremacy**, regardless of your intentions. Shifting the conversation to "All lives matter" is an apathetic response to the state violence that Black people face and the persistent racial inequity that people of color endure on a daily basis.

———

"If Only He Weren't Wearing a Hoodie"

Why was Trayvon Martin murdered? Everyone had something to say to try to explain why a Black teenager, walking in his neighborhood with candy and iced tea, would be stalked, shot, and killed with impunity by a neighbor under the guise of the neighborhood watch. Geraldo Rivera said, "I think the hoodie is as much responsible for Trayvon Martin's death as George Zimmerman was."[22] He was relying on the **politics of respectability**. In response to the outrage that many people felt in the wake of Zimmerman's acquittal, many people on the right wanted to know why there wasn't more dialogue about "Black-on-Black" crime. They were relying on the politics of respectability. The conservative commentator Bill O'Reilly elaborated, "The reason there is so much violence and chaos in the black precincts is the disintegration of the African-American family. . . . Raised without much structure, young black men often reject education and gravitate towards the street culture, drugs, hustling, gangs. Nobody forces them to do that, again, it is a personal decision."[23] He was relying on the politics of respectability. By saying that "Bill O'Reilly doesn't go far enough" and then providing "five things that you [Black people] should think about doing"—don't sag, do not use the N-word, don't litter in your neighborhood, finish school in order to break the cycle of poverty, and do not have unplanned, out-of-wedlock pregnancies—the Black CNN anchor Don Lemon was practicing the harmful politics of respectability.[24]

The basic assumption underlying the politics of respectability is that if Black folks could show that they were just as clean, thrifty, polite, sober, morally upright, and sexually prudish as white people, whites' negative stereotypes about Blacks would dissolve and so would **racism** in the United States.[25] It's perfectly unclear how not wearing hoodies or doing any of the five things that Don Lemon suggests will dismantle voter disenfranchisement, raise the minimum wage, integrate schools, bring jobs to predominantly Black neighborhoods, close the wealth gap, end the War on Drugs and mandatory-minimum sentencing policies, expand Pell Grants, reduce the price of SAT prep courses, build sidewalks and parks in low-income neighborhoods, or create policies that will lead to fewer police and citizen vigilantes murdering unarmed (or legally armed) Black people. Totally unclear.

The **politics of respectability** implicitly requires Black folks to prove themselves worthy to *earn* the rights that are already promised to them as citizens. It requires Black people to convince everyone else that **racism** is wrong. The most damning implication of respectability politics is that it implies that not all lives matter, or it at least suggests that some lives matter more than others. Those who do not follow traditional, white, middle-class, heterosexual patriarchal norms are (perhaps unintentionally) deemed as deviants and, thus, as not "grieveable."[26] But people have a breaking point. When Black people see that no matter what they do, they can be the next Sandra Bland, Eric Garner, Tenisha Anderson, Philando Castile, Rekia Boyd, Oscar Grant, Charleena Lyles, Amadou Diallo, Michael Brown, Freddie Gray, or Tamir Rice, it's an insult to suggest that they pull up their pants in order to avoid a similar fate. This ever-growing list of slain Black people "[drives] holes in the logic that Black people simply doing the 'right things,' whatever those things might be, could overcome the perennial crises with Black America."[27]

Again, we are in a one-against-three situation where **antiracists** are pitted against, perhaps, a relatively small group of vehemently overt racists as well as the great majority of Americans, which includes whites, Blacks, Latinxs, and Asian Americans who are well meaning, complicit racists propping up our **racialized social system**, and structural racists who are adding fuel to the fire (to mix metaphors). Overt racists couldn't care less if Black people contort themselves to a white standard. Meanwhile, proponents of respectability politics believe that it is important to keep in mind what other people think of Black people as a survival strategy. To be sure, some folks do mean well when they make suggestions about Black people's sartorial decisions, but the logic of respectability politics upholds **white supremacy**. One of the liberating ideas that Black Lives Matter advances is that the time for respectability politics is over. Black lives matter, and Black death is grieveable no matter how people are dressed, where they live, their gender identity, their sexuality, their involvement with the justice system, or their immigration status. Rather than a focus on respectability, we may all be better off to take inspiration for Anna Julia Cooper, who demanded *undisputed dignity*.[28]

Flipping the Script

Racism is not just the mean things people do, and **antiracism** is not just the nice things we say. Common narratives of what it means to be a "real" racist include white cloaks and swastikas, but this is only one part of a larger truth. These oversimplifications are effective, however, because they fit into our collective imagination of what evil looks like. Yes, racial inequality is advocated for by members of **white supremacist** organizations, but it is buttressed by regular people trying not to rock the boat.

We can do something different. Actively resisting and loudly agitating against racism can be awkward. At first, you might use the wrong words, be unaware of the entire history underlying the problems, or slip into old habits of **respectability politics**. And people might get annoyed with you as you try to convince the most well-meaning complicit racists to get a grip, face reality, and *do* something. Some people will laugh at you or look at you with dismay; they may even disown you, verbally or even physically abuse you, troll your Twitter account, call you racist and/or sexist epithets, suggest that you are overreacting or being too sensitive, or deem you a **race** traitor because you're upsetting the status quo,[29] but know this—you'll be on the right side of history. Staying woke means being aware of the fact that although racism can be reproduced in our day-to-day lives—in our personal interactions, the way we do our jobs, the way we raise our children—we can all take small (or big) corrective steps to undermine the erroneous respectability politics and **colorblind** narratives that underwrite racial oppression.

Questions and Debate

1 Now that you've read chapter 4, have you changed your answers to the questions posed in the outset: Are you upholding **white supremacy**? Do you intentionally or unintentionally contribute to or enable ongoing racial disparities?

2 Where do you hear these scripts used most, by whom, and for what reasons?

3 Are there other scripts that normalize, explain away, or rationalize racial inequality that you hear commonly?

4 Tamir Rice was a twelve-year-old Black boy playing with a toy gun at the park. A neighbor called the police to report that a boy was playing with a toy gun at the park. Tamir Rice was shot dead within seconds of the police officers' arrival. How do you explain this to a Black child? Does your explanation change if you are talking to a white child? If so, why?

5 The scripts that we outlined are common and predictable, but confronting them when they occur is sometimes intimidating. You have to learn and practice new counternarratives. Consider the six scripts we posed and develop an **antiracist** response for each of them.

Additional Materials to Consider

BOOKS

Bonilla-Silva, Eduardo. *Racism without Racists: Color-Blind Racism and the Persistence of Racial Inequality in the United States.* 5th ed. Lanham, MD: Rowman and Littlefield, 2018.

Eddo-Lodge, Reni. *Why I'm No Longer Talking to White People about Race.* London: Bloomsbury, 2018.

Hill, Jane H. *The Everyday Language of White Racism.* New York: Wiley, 2009.

Rosa, Jonathan. *Looking like a Language, Sounding like a Race: Raciolinguistic Ideologies and the Learning of Latinidad.* New York: Oxford University Press, 2018.

Tatum, Beverly Daniel. *"Why Are All the Black Kids Sitting Together in the Cafeteria?" and Other Conversations about Race.* New York: Basic Books, 2003.

CHILDREN'S BOOKS

Buitrago, Jairo, and Rafael Yockteng. *Two White Rabbits.* Berkeley, CA: Groundwood Books, 2015.

DiPucchio, Kelly, and LeUyen Pham. *Grace for President.* New York: Hyperion Books for Children, 2012.

Gonzalez, Maya. *When a Bully Is President: Truth and Creativity for Oppressive Times.* San Francisco: Reflection, 2017.

Hoffman, Mary. *Amazing Grace.* New York: Dial Books for Young Readers, 1991.

Kates, Bobbi. *We're Different, We're the Same.* New York: Random House Children's Books, 1992.

Tyler, Michael. *The Skin You Live In.* Chicago: Chicago Children's Museum, 2005.

Tonatiuh, Duncan. *Separate Is Never Equal: Sylvia Mendez and Her Family's Fight for Desegregation.* New York: Abrams, 2014.

5

It Doesn't Have to Be This Way

Consider the idea that some people have cast the prominent figures of the contemporary Movement for Black Lives—including Alicia Garza, Patrisse Cullors, Opal Tometi, DeRay Mckesson, Brittany Packnett, Aislinn Pulley, and Johnetta Elzie—as well as members of organizations that seek to amplify and eradicate the effects of anti-Black **racism**, as terrorists.[1] Or when Colin Kaepernick and dozens of other NFL team members began to protest police brutality and racial inequality in 2016, millions of people claimed that they didn't know why the players were kneeling during the US national anthem. They did know, however, that they didn't like that these well-paid, "ungrateful" (read: the new word for "uppity") Black athletes were supposedly disrespecting the flag and US veterans. Over time, the take-a-knee protest has been referred to as the "anthem protest," but these football players and cheerleaders are not protesting "The Star-Spangled Banner." The intended message of this protest, just like that of Black Lives Matter, was resoundingly clear despite indications otherwise.

Historically, Black social movements have been misunderstood or simply mischaracterized—sometimes cast as radical, undemocratic, unpatriotic, or even un-American. The same can be said for this contemporary movement. The truth of the matter is, sometimes we don't know what other people want because we *don't want* to know. So-called alternative facts circulate despite the fact that we live in a world where the truth can, in many cases, be discerned at the tip of people's fingers, or by asking Google, Siri, or Alexa. They will tell you that the NFL protest aimed to bring attention to police brutality in Black communities; that Occupy Wall Street wanted to bring attention to and close the gap between the wealthiest 1 percent of Americans and the rest of us; that the participants of the Arab Spring demanded democracy, free elections, human rights, and regime change; that signatories of #MeToo just want to work without the threat or fear of sexual assault or harassment; and that BLM and M4BL are working to assure that the humanity and dignity of all Black people is fully realized and valued by everyone—plainly and simply.

So you want to stay woke? You want to transition from being a well-meaning person to an **antiracist** who makes a difference in your community, in your state, and in this country? There are three things that we think you must know in order to accomplish this goal:

1 The Black Lives Matter movement is "not your grandfather's civil rights movement." There are a number of reasons we make this claim, but one of the main reasons is that the movement's philosophy is rooted in Black feminist ideology. The demands of the Black Lives Matter movement serve as a North Star for antiracism and racial justice advocates in the twenty-first century.

2 The figureheads of the civil rights movement were incredibly important, influential, and effective at moving US society toward its better angels, but the requirement of a single leader implies that average citizens either do not understand their own problems or simply do not have the capacity to begin to address them. As Patrice Cullors asserts, we regular people "can catalyze a movement in our own community."[2] You can be a leader in your community.

3 Good leaders know how to orient their goals and direct their energy. In the United States, most of the inequality we see on a

day-to-day basis is not produced by Congress but instead is created, maintained, and exacerbated in state legislatures and in city halls. You must know *your* political terrain so you can effectively navigate barriers that stand in between the status quo and racial equity.

We elaborate on each of these three points in this chapter, and we do so with the intention of building a foundation for a well-informed person to move toward **antiracist** advocacy and action in one's community.

Lesson #1: Here's What They Want

One of the most important things to know about the Black Lives Matter movement and the Movement for Black Lives (M4BL), which includes the Black Lives Matter Global Network and also dozens of other organizations, is that their political philosophy centers on a concept called **intersectionality** and is rooted in Black feminism. The historian Robin D. G. Kelley explains that Black feminism has "flipped the script on the black freedom movement, arguing that freedom for black women would result in freedoms for black people as a whole" and, consequently, would provide "the most thorough, sustained interrogation of sex and gender as part of a general challenge to conceptions of black liberation."[3] All told, "Black feminism is the centripetal force around which contemporary Black social movements revolve."[4] This political philosophy is well illustrated in the platform of the unified M4BL, which declares, "We believe in elevating the experiences and leadership of the most marginalized Black people, including but not limited to those who are women, queer, trans, femmes, gender nonconforming, Muslim, formerly and currently incarcerated, cash poor and working class, disabled, undocumented, and immigrant. . . . There can be no liberation for all Black people if we do not center and fight for those who have been marginalized."[5] Or, in other words, the Black Lives Matter Global network sees itself as being "guided by the fact that all Black lives matter, regardless of actual or perceived sexual identity, gender identity, gender expression, economic status, ability, disability, religious beliefs or disbeliefs, immigration status, or location," and it asserts that it is "unapologetically Black in [its] positioning. In affirming that Black Lives Matter, [members] need not qualify [their] position. To love and desire freedom and justice for [themselves] is a prerequisite for wanting the same for others."[6] This core belief runs through the tenets of Black Lives Matter's guiding principles, which include valuing **diversity**, restorative justice, empathy, and developing an intergenerational and communal network.

Relatedly, M4BL also works toward developing an **antiracist** society and outlines reforms in six policy domains. First, M4BL wants to "end the war on Black people"; this means eliminating trends of mass incarceration, police brutality, and unnecessary fatalities at the hands of police. Second, it outlines the necessity for symbolic and material reparations, which includes greater access to high-quality K–12 public schools and public universities, the enactment of legislation for a living wage, and systematic recognition of the contributions of people of African descent. Third, M4BL calls for "investments in the education, health, and safety of Black people, instead of investments in the criminalizing, caging and harming of Black people."[7] Fourth, it seeks economic justice for all, installed through policies such as progressive tax policy, federal and state jobs programs, and a right to clean air, water, and housing.

The fifth policy domain concerns the latitude that people have to control the laws, institutions, and politics that directly serve them, especially as it relates to the hiring and firing of leadership (e.g., mayor, sheriff) and street-level bureaucrats (e.g., police) and shaping budgetary decisions that are made at various levels of governance. Finally, M4BL seeks to develop a democratic society in which average (Black) people are able to effectively exercise political power, in part by reducing the influence of the money that wealthy individuals and corporations are allowed to have on elections and campaigns. This is a tall order, but it is neither unreasonable nor impractical given the depth of the racial inequity at hand.

If you study these demands and goals, one theme becomes clear: most of the issues that need to be addressed require us to shift our focus to local and state politics and policy. The contemporary Movement for Black Lives is not perfect, but it has one thing right: a one-size-fits-all approach to dismantling **racism** across the United States and globally will not happen with a sweeping set of laws at the federal level. Instead, we have to know the terrain of our state and local policy-making landscape.

Lesson #2: You Can Be a Leader!

When we think about Black freedom movements, folks like Martin Luther King Jr., Huey P. Newton, Bayard Rustin, and James Baldwin may come immediately to mind. We tend to center a solitary Black male as a necessary ingredient for a successful Black social movement because of the popularized hagiography of Black, male leadership. This narrative suggests that regular people cannot come together collectively to solve their own problems. Additionally, often overlooked are the "contributions of women, local activists, and small organizations—the lesser-known elements that enables the grand moments we associate with the civil-rights era."[8] Unlike many, though not all, previous iterations of Black freedom struggles, there is not a single (heterosexual, male) figurehead who leads the masses and speaks for all participants in the twenty-first-century Movement for Black Lives. Jelani Cobb, in his examination of Black Lives Matter, explains, "Garza, Cullors, and Tometi advocate a horizontal ethic of organizing, which favors democratic inclusion at the grassroots level. Black Lives Matter emerged as a modern extension of Ella Baker's thinking—a preference for ten thousand candles rather than a single spotlight."[9] People are well aware of what their problems are, and as we will show shortly, the contours of a community's challenges are shaped by context—local history, demographics, and politics. The Black Lives Matter movement has helped to make clear that though there are broad patterns of racial inequity across

Artwork by Victoria Garcia. (Courtesy of Amplifier.org)

the country, inequality takes many forms, often shifting in shape as it crosses state lines. Each version of racial inequality requires locally specific demands and policy innovation. What this means is that we are in need of many leaders at the local and state levels, not just a single leader at the national level. You can be a leader in your community; there is no shortage of groups and organizations that share the values and goals of the contemporary Movement for Black Lives that you can belong to or contribute to in some way. If you cannot find a local group that pushes for greater equality, you can start one yourself!

Lesson #3: Inequity Is a (Local) Policy Choice

The last thing we want you to consider in your effort toward developing an **antiracist** ethos is *federalism*. Wait! Before your eyes glaze over, let us explain. Federalism is about the division of power among different levels of government. You may have heard people talk about "states' rights." States' rights is a reference to federalism but, historically, has been sounded through a racial **dog whistle**. For instance, prior to the Civil War, Southern states fought for greater "states' rights," primarily so that they could maintain the institution of slavery in their states. Later, states called for "states' rights" so that they could maintain racially segregated public and private institutions, like schools and restaurants. The goal in both of these cases was to use the principles of federalism to reproduce, intensify, and tailor racial inequality in the states.

The framers of the US Constitution were wary of providing too much power to one part of the government (no less any one person), so they divided the power of the government into two levels—national and state—and provided each with enough power to compete with the other, thus checking the power of all involved. In turn, the US Constitution outlines a federal system of government; it outlines exactly what Congress, the judiciary, and the executive branch of government can do. Then the Tenth Amendment explains, "The powers not delegated to the United States by the Constitution, nor prohibited by it to the States, are reserved to the States respectively, or to the people."

We point this out only to illuminate the fact that the powers of the national government are actually quite limited. Though the Supremacy Clause states that if there is a conflict between state and federal law, federal law reigns supreme, the states have the most fundamental set of powers, called coercive or police powers, which essentially allows the states to regulate the health, safety, and morals of its residents. States develop and enforce criminal codes, regulate the family via marriage and divorce laws, outline the requirements for professional licenses, regulate private property; create and enforce gun laws, have the ability to expand or contract voting rights; develop policies around education (which, to be clear, is not considered a fundamental human right by the United States government), dictate health policy, determine how social safety-net resources are allocated, and a great deal of other stuff that affects your day-to-day life. The states are often viewed as "laboratories" of policy innovation, and policies created at the state level ideally allow for more specified and tailored responses to citizens' preferences.

We can turn the **white supremacist** connotation of states' rights on its head by using the principles of federalism to create an **anti-racist** society. By having a clear map of the shape of inequality in your state and in your town, you will be better prepared to navigate your terrain, to be a leader in your community, and to work toward some of the guiding principles of the contemporary Movement for Black Lives. How does this work? We outline a few examples—three, to be exact: state spending, voting, and policing—to show how racial inequity is shaped at the local level. With this information in hand, we will be better equipped to strategize around what each of us can do to dismantle structural **racism** starting in our communities.

STATE BUDGETS = STATE VALUES

Your personal budget tells a lot about your priorities, and so does a state's. A state's budget is indicative of its values. Let's consider two policy areas where states have a great deal of autonomy: budgeting for schools and prisons. On the basis of data from 2015, we find that there is not one state that invests more in its elementary and secondary school students than it does in its prisoners. At the low end, Louisiana spent about $11,000 per pupil and $16,000 per inmate under its watch in 2015. On the opposite end is California. In the same year, the US Census noted that California spent about $10,467 per pupil and a whopping $64,642 on its average inmate; that's a difference of over $54,000. Or, in other words, the great state of California invests six times more on its adults in prison than it does on its elementary and secondary school children.

We know that the War on Drugs is a mechanism that has drastically increased the prison population (and thus spending) over the past several decades, but the size of the prison population has also increased (in a racially biased way) because there are fewer resources for mentally ill and disabled people. People who need help are being funneled into prison because untreated illness and homelessness are often criminalized.[10]

We also know that a majority of the youngest living generation of Americans, babies and schoolchildren, are people of color. Not only are there vast inequalities across states, but there are savage inequalities within each state. For example, in Oklahoma, one-third of school districts have a four-day school week in order to deal with the state budget cuts to education. In Illinois, a one-hour drive between a school in the city that serves low-income, Black and Latinx students and another in a predominantly white suburb can mean a threefold difference in spending per student: $9,794 versus $28,639.[11] All in all, what should our expectations be for racial inequality if states' priorities for two of its largest institutions are aligned in opposite directions—and neither in a direction that bodes well for the full incorporation of people of color?[12] Ongoing inequity is a policy choice.

As (mandatory) desegregation efforts have drastically declined since the late 1990s, children are increasingly likely to attend racially (and economically) homogeneous neighborhood schools.[13] Children who live in low-income areas tend to go to schools with many fewer resources. The common response is, "Well, if local taxes supplement schools, then obviously the kids in wealthier neighborhoods will get better stuff." Yes, it's true that the amount of local revenues differ vastly across any particular state, but it does not logically follow that schools have to have widely different resources, as state policy makers can choose to counterbalance inequality. (And to be sure, the children of wealthy parents did nothing to deserve better schools. Why should the children of wealthy or poor parents, by accident of birth, receive better or worse *public* resources?) The immediate

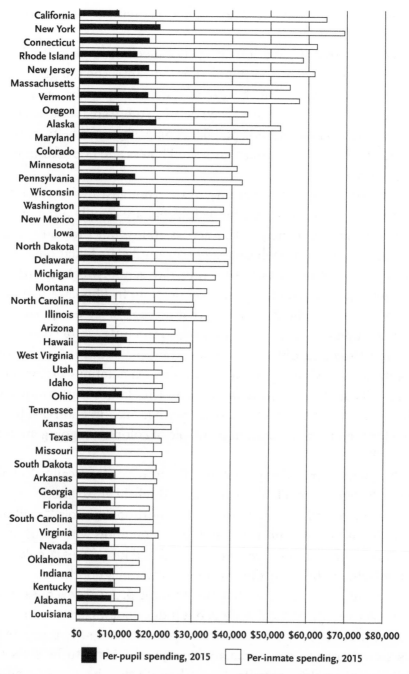

States' spending on prison inmates and pupils. (Data on prison spending retrieved from Mai and Subramanian, *Price of Prisons*; data on spending on schools retrieved from the Educational Finance Branch, "Public Education Finances: 2015")

implication of these disparities in resources is that there are increasing inequalities in outcomes for students across racial and economic groups, whereby poor, Black, and Latinx children are getting the short end of the stick.

Needless to say, we should take note of BLM and M4BL and demand that states spend more on schools and allocate public resources in a more equitable way—a way that doesn't require a person to break a law to receive drug treatment, medical care, food, or housing. *It doesn't have to be this way.* Citizens could force their states to do things differently, and the Vera Institute reveals that there are a number of states that have been able to decrease their investment in the prison-industrial complex. One way to reduce spending is by decreasing the size of the prison population. New York, for instance, has decreased spending on prisons by $302 million in five years by changing laws in police enforcement practices and thus the number of people sentenced to prison. South Carolina and Michigan have also made critical reforms in their parole and probation policies that have led to a reduction in the number of people sent to prison in those states; costs have declined, in turn. New Jersey has been able to decrease its investments in prisons "as the result of an expansion in the use of diversion programs, such as drug courts, and increased rates of parole."[14] Meanwhile, teachers are taking to the streets to squeeze funds out of state legislatures for more pay and better resources for our children; against great resistance from political elites, some have been successful.

WHOSE VOTES MATTER?

Remember when then-candidate Trump's favorite word was "rigged"? The economy was rigged, the media was rigged, and most emphatically, he warned, "November 8, we'd better be careful, because that election is going to be rigged." Trump was supposedly concerned with voter fraud, well illustrated by his oft-repeated prediction that "people are going to walk in and they're going to vote 10 times, maybe,"[15] and his claim that there were between three and five million undocumented immigrants in California who voted, and later by his creation of a Presidential Advisory Commission on Election Integrity. None of the issues that Trump raises are actual problems that reduce the integrity of Americans' votes, but elections *are* rigged in many ways—just not in the way that the forty-fifth president suggests. States and counties have a greater amount of power over local, state, and *federal* elections than the federal government itself does. We point out five facts about voting rights in an effort to motivate action to expand the franchise. What we hope to show is that some states do things that provide greater opportunity for voters to have a say in the policies that affect them. These states can serve as models of what we all can aspire and work toward in order to enhance democracy.

1. Gerrymandering dilutes the power of Black and Latinx citizens' vote. If we keep in mind that political representatives are "single-minded seekers of reelection,"[16] we recognize the incentive structure for the party in power to try to draw district lines to its political advantage. That is the very definition of gerrymandering—drawing district lines to get an outcome in your favor. Though gerrymandering is nothing new, technology provides today's political mapmakers with unprecedented precision. We've come to a point where representatives are choosing their constituents rather than the other way around. In most states, the party in power is largely responsible for redrawing the district lines, but *it doesn't have to be this way*: other states allow a nonpartisan commission to draw their lines.

2. Felon disenfranchisement policies prolong a legacy of anti-Black racism. During the nineteenth century, state legislators made it clear that felon disenfranchisement policies were aimed to reduce the chances of Blacks' having a say in elections, especially after the Fifteenth Amendment was ratified. In some states, murder was not a crime that would lead to disenfranchisement, but vagrancy—viewed as a Black crime—was. Of the 5.9 million citizens who cannot vote, 2.2 million of them are African American, resulting in the fact that, on average, one in every thirteen Blacks cannot cast a vote in the United States. This proportion increases to one in five in states like

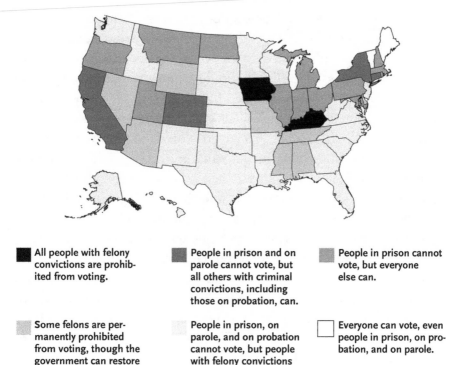

All people with felony convictions are prohibited from voting.

People in prison and on parole cannot vote, but all others with criminal convictions, including those on probation, can.

People in prison cannot vote, but everyone else can.

Some felons are permanently prohibited from voting, though the government can restore voting rights on an individual basis.

People in prison, on parole, and on probation cannot vote, but people with felony convictions can vote upon completion of sentence

Everyone can vote, even people in prison, on probation, and on parole.

Map of felony disenfranchisement laws. (Data gathered from the American Civil Liberties Union and the Brennan Center for Justice)

Kentucky, Virginia, and Tennessee.[17] This policy has become normalized, but *it doesn't have to be this way*. Two states allow people to vote while in prison![18] Laws can, have, and are changing. In 2016, California enacted a law that allows those who are serving time in county jails to vote from jail, and the year before that, Maryland changed its law to restore voting rights immediately after release from prison. In 2018, Florida's voters supported a *citizen-initiated* constitutional amendment, which vastly changed the state's policy on felon disenfranchisement; the amendment restores the rights of people with prior felony convictions, with an exception for those who were convicted of murder or a felony sexual offense. Grassroots, state-level efforts have led to reform across the United States.

3. It's difficult for underrepresented groups to vote. Voting is a two-step process. First you have to register. Young people, poor people (especially transient people), and people of color—folks who generally support more progressive policies—are less likely to be registered and thus less likely to vote because you have to reregister every time you move. Then, you can vote as long as your name has not been purged from the voter rolls because you haven't voted in a while or as long as you live in state where you can get paid time off to vote in the middle of the week. But, *it doesn't have to be this way.* Some countries automatically register citizens to vote, and there is a designated holiday to vote. Fortunately, there appears to be a groundswell of support for automatic voter-registration policies across the states. By the end of 2017, nine states and Washington, DC, had implemented policies that essentially require people to opt out of registration once they interact with government agencies like the Department of Motor Vehicles rather than opt in; thirty-two states have introduced bills to implement or expand automatic registration. In some states, citizens have successfully forced the issue through ballot initiatives.[19]

4. Voter ID policies are discriminatory. Voter ID policies aim to solve a problem that does not really exist in the United States: voter fraud. After *Shelby v. Holder* in 2013, the number of laws designed to reduce voter turnout quickly proliferated. In a Wisconsin voter identification case, US District Judge James D. Peterson asserted, "The evidence in this case casts doubt on the notion that voter ID laws foster integrity and confidence," and he went on to write, "The Wisconsin experience demonstrates that a preoccupation with mostly phantom election fraud leads to real incidents of disenfranchisement, which undermine rather than enhance confidence in elections, particularly in minority communities. To put it bluntly, Wisconsin's strict version of voter ID law is a cure worse than the disease."[20] Voter identification laws appear to reduce the turnout of Blacks, Latinxs, and Asian Americans while slightly boosting whites' rate of voter turnout.[21] And other scholars have found though some states provide "free" identification, the cost of travel, taking time off work, and paying for the documents that allow you to get the free state-issued identification

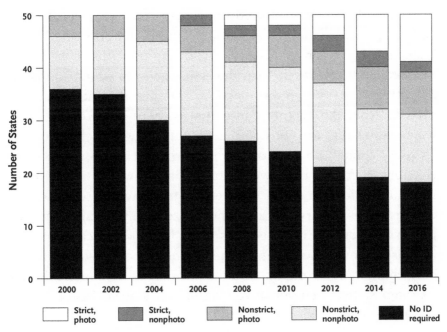

Changes in prevalence of voter identification laws. (Data retrieved from the National Conference of State Legislatures)

card can still cost upward of $172.39 in a place like Pennsylvania, $148.46 in Texas, or $166.50 (not including $1,449.75 in legal fees) in South Carolina![22] There has been a proliferation of voter identification policies, but *it doesn't have be this way*. The facts are on the side of eliminating these policies. Voter ID laws try to solve a problem that does not exist, thus doing more harm than necessary. Citizens in each state can applaud their state leaders who avoid implementing these laws, while those in states where these policies exist or are in debate can resist through direct correspondence with their representatives, voting no in state referenda, and helping others to attain identification until laws are changed.

5. Noncitizen disenfranchisement is historically uncommon. Generally speaking, noncitizens are not allowed to vote. This means that even longtime, taxpaying residents do not have a say in the laws that shape their lives. *It doesn't have to be this way.* Between 1776 and the 1930s, most states allowed noncitizens to vote in local, state, and occasionally federal elections. Or, in other words, the United States has had a longer history of allowing noncitizens to vote at the local and state levels than the status quo—in which almost no noncitizens can vote in any election.[23] Despite the anti-immigrant rhetoric from the Trump White House, there is a growing number of states that are considering extending the franchise to noncitizens. Though no state allows noncitizens to vote in statewide elections, there are now twelve states that allow noncitizen voting in local elections, and that number has the potential to grow. Several districts in Maryland allow noncitizens to participate in local policy decision-making processes, and cities like Chicago and San Francisco allow noncitizens to vote in school board elections if they have children in the district. Though most of us have never lived in a United States when noncitizen voting was a norm, history shows that things can be done differently.

CRIME AND PUNISHMENT

As a final set of illustrative examples, we focus on policing, an area where many **antiracist** advocates can step up in their local communities. There are some things we ought to be more cognizant of. First, policing is within the purview of state and local governments. However, depending on where you live, police chiefs may not be directly accountable to the people for whom they work—people like you.[24]

Second, police have a great deal of discretion, and typically scholars find that greater discretion widens the opportunity for racial discrimination. What this means is that much of what we see concerning racially biased outcomes occurs within the law. Stop-and-frisks, or Terry stops, allow police officers to briefly detain a person if they have a reasonable suspicion that the person is involved in some sort of criminal activity. Implicit-bias tests reveal that many Americans, across racial groups, are more likely to see Black people, especially men, as "suspicious." Or, as another example, we all speed on the highway, but police have the discretion to stop the speeding red sports car rather than the lead-foot dad in a minivan. Indeed, the political scientist Frank Baumgartner and his colleagues explain, "there is no requirement that speeding laws, for example, be equitably enforced; if all the drivers are speeding, it is constitutionally permissible . . . to pick out the minority drivers and enforce speeding laws selectively."[25] Once police make that stop, it is in their discretion to search the car (given that the driver does not object, but police do not have to inform drivers of that right), and Black drivers are more likely to be stopped, searched, and arrested than whites are.[26]

What happens to folks once they are embraced by the criminal justice system is also largely dictated by goings-on at the state level. Even before you are convicted of a crime, the deck may be stacked against you if you are Black or Brown. For example, if we consider the fact that registered voters are most likely to be called for jury duty, then we can see how a jury may not be composed of a group that mimics the demographic makeup of the polity. Or we might consider the fact that judges who are elected are much harsher in their sentencing than are those who are appointed. Research shows that elected judges are less likely to reverse death penalty sentences, and in the months leading up to an election, judges have been found to hand down sentences 10 percent longer than usual, perhaps under duress of political pressure to be "tough on crime."[27] Or we might consider that prosecutors are incentivized to have as many guilty verdicts as they can possibly get, given that in most states they are also elected. As it turns out, elections do not always serve to check the work and power of the prosecutors because incumbents are rarely challenged, and generally speaking, whiter, wealthier suburbanites are often more likely to turn out to vote in these local elections, even though Black people, poor people, and city dwellers are more likely to have to face the prosecutor.[28]

And then there's the issue of bail, which has been shown to be a punishment for being poor. Senator Kamala Harris explains, "More than 450,000 Americans currently sit in jail while they await trial—many of whom are there only because they don't have the money to pay to get out. Many are there for nonviolent offenses. None of them have yet been convicted of a crime."[29] Black and Latinx defendants are 25 percent more likely to be denied bail than whites are. Black defendants are assigned higher bail amounts, and they are less likely to be able to post bail than whites are; consequently, there are more people of color held in pretrial detention.

All told, this setup could be different. *It doesn't have to be this way.* For example, police officers have hundreds of reasons to stop a motorist as a pretext for racial profiling, but they tend to use excuses such as stopping someone for a broken taillight or not wearing a seat belt. The Greensboro Police Department made a two-prong policy shift: first, it stopped officers from initiating vehicle stops solely due to equipment infractions, and second, it has begun to develop programs and services to build positive relationships between the community and police.[30] There are also innovative alternatives to money bail, such as simply sending text reminders to people of their court dates rather than detaining them. These policies lead to fewer people missing their court dates (which is the goal of bail), fewer people being apprehended due to failure to show, and greater cost savings across the local criminal justice systems.[31]

BE THE CHANGE

All in all, the profile of racial inequality in many policy domains is largely dictated by state-level public policy and policy makers. Medicaid expansion is in the realm of the state. Whether children aged sixteen and seventeen are tried as adults in court is dictated by state law. The ease of undocumented parents gaining access to their citizen child's birth certificate is dictated by the state. Creating, maintaining, or dismantling laws that criminalize HIV/AIDS happens in state legislative chambers. Bail reform; assuring equal access to high-quality public schools; determining the location of hazardous waste sites, parks, sidewalks, and inclusionary zoning areas; and increasing the number or reducing the spread of polling stations all have to be addressed at the state level.

Dismantling structural **racism** seems daunting; it is so deeply embedded in our society that it can sometimes feel that nothing can be

Artwork by Hallie Jay Pope. (Courtesy of Amplifier.org)

done. But let us be clear: structural **racism** is not inevitable, and we need not mystify practical strategies that can ameliorate racialized policy practices. A great deal of work has to be done at the state and local levels because that is where a lot of the action that grows inequality is happening. Before we can take effective steps toward greater equality, we have to know our terrain. How are policies constructed? Do those constructions enhance democracy or racial disparities? Both cannot be simultaneously true. What organizations are working toward issues that you care about? How can you use your skills to inform other members of your community or members of your city council or state legislature of policies that recklessly exacerbate inequality? What small steps can you take to assure that more people have a voice in your local and state politics? What are some ways you can harness your skills, serve as a leader in your community, and chip away at racial inequity? Each of us has some capacity that can be harnessed to produce changes in our local and state communities. Here are ten things you can do to be the change you want to see in this world.

1 Half the battle of getting people to vote is to get them registered, and given the confusion of interstate differences, some formerly incarcerated individuals do not even know they can vote. Join a get-out-the-vote campaign, and help people register to vote.

2 A great majority of state legislators simply do not know enough about the issues that you care about most. Use your skills and expertise to create an at-a-glance memo that serves to bring awareness to the matter at hand. If you track legislation, you can provide information to legislators when they need it, or share your memo with an advocacy group that has the time and know-how to put pressure on your state and local representatives.

3 Attend local school board or city council meetings to speak up about an issue you care about. The issue could range from assuring that shirts with **racist** symbols are banned in the student code of conduct to advocating for the collection, analysis, and dissemination of data that focus on racial disparities in school discipline procedures. There is often a time designated for residents to voice their concerns. That time belongs to you. Use it.

4 Many local government positions go uncontested, and still many others are appointed. Run for office. There is an increasing number of organizations aimed to get women, people of color, veterans, and people across the political spectrum elected. Or if you don't want to mount a campaign, join or apply to a committee of

the city government that speaks to issues that are near and dear to you. These committees often have the ear of the mayor.

5 One thing elected officials know how to do is to count votes. Vote! Or work on a campaign for a candidate who has explicitly declared an **antiracist** platform. Keep in mind that local elections—for mayor, sheriff, school board, prosecutor, judge, county commissioner, and city council—is where the real impact is. Many local elections are won by dozens of votes or less! Your vote will matter a great deal at the local level, and the ramifications will be felt on a day-to-day basis.

6 There is no shortage of organizations that need volunteers to help push for more equitable outcomes in housing policy, immigration, mass incarceration, policing, voting rights, reproductive justice, LGBTQ+ rights, education, environment, and elections. Join the local chapter of organizations like Black Lives Matter, the ACLU, GLSEN, or Million Hoodies for Justice. If you don't have that much time, donate to antiracist organizations, such as ones listed at ResistanceManual.org.

7 Resist, protest, and campaign against policies that entrench inequality in your community, such as money bail, voter identification laws, or the development of new predominantly white or upper-class public school districts.

8 Become media literate. Write an op-ed to your local newspaper. You can use the media to communicate to a wider audience—members of your community as well as your state and local policy makers. You might highlight an issue of importance to you, explain to others how the problem is one that affects us all, and discuss the ways that other localities or states have modeled better behavior on your issue of concern.

9 Americans are really obsessed with money. Persuade local businesses and banks to donate to or sponsor an antiracist organization (they can do well money-wise by doing good social-justice-wise), or boycott a business that perpetuates racial inequity.

10 We have focused on state and local government, but do not let Congress off the hook. Members of Congress are the ones who have to strengthen the Voting Rights Act, they can create national standards for environmental protection, they can increase the national minimum wage, and they can develop a single-payer health-insurance system. We have to keep them accountable.

One last little thing about federalism: it is often the case that one city or state will see how well another city or state is doing with a new policy and will, in turn, adopt that policy. One illustrative case is the decriminalization of marijuana or the increased access to medical marijuana across several states. Every once in a while, Congress will see a locality doing well with a policy and implement it for the whole country. Political scientists call this process "policy diffusion," and it reflects the notion that good, evidenced-based policy ideas have the potential to be contagious. We can each serve to spark a change that might reverberate throughout the entire country. The many leaders of the Black Lives Matter movement have already shown us that regular working people can catalyze change at the local level, in their own communities, and so can you!

Questions and Debate

1 The Black Lives Matter movement is a leaderful social movement, and it encourages average people to make change in their community. What are the benefits of this model? What are the weaknesses of eschewing the model of a central figurehead to share the message of a large group?

2 Consider a problem in your community that you would like to address through policy. What is the role of local political leaders in dealing with this matter? What latitude do state leaders have to address this issue? What local organizations are addressing this issue already?

3 Examine the most recent local election in your community. Did any seats in the previous election go uncontested, or were any won or lost by a handful of votes? What are the implications of low competition and turnout for the policy matters you consider most important?

4 Some people argue that BLM does not value traditional politics enough. Meanwhile, others suggest that an important contribution of the movement is that it has shifted the national conversation to thinking more about racial inequality. What are the pros and cons of primarily relying on traditional modes of politics, such as voting? What are the pros and cons of primarily relying on other forms of political participation, such as protests, die-ins, and boycotts?

5 It is easy to get bogged down by depressing statistics and narratives of policies producing more and more inequality. Find an example of a successful effort that reshaped a community in a positive way. How long did it take for folks to accomplish their goal? Did they work inside or outside the political system? How are people likely to tell the story of this success ten or twenty years from now?

Additional Materials to Consider

BOOKS

Michener, Jamila. *Fragmented Democracy: Medicaid, Federalism, and Unequal Politics*. New York: Cambridge University Press, 2018.

Morel, Domingo. *Takeover: Race, Education, and American Democracy*. New York: Oxford University Press, 2018.

Sanders, Crystal. *A Chance for Change: Head Start and Mississippi's Black Freedom Struggle*. Chapel Hill: University of North Carolina Press, 2016.

Soss, Joe, Richard C. Fording, and Sanford F. Schram. *Disciplining the Poor: Neoliberal Paternalism and the Persistent Power of Race*. Chicago: University of Chicago Press, 2011.

Zepeda-Millán, Chris. *Latino Mass Mobilization: Immigration, Racialization, and Activism*. New York: Cambridge University Press, 2017.

FILMS

Revisionaries, The. Directed by Scott Thurman. Making History / Silver Lining / Magic Hour / Naked Edge, 2012.
Street Fight. Directed by Marshall Curry. Genius Entertainment, 2005.

PODCASTS

Uncertain Hour, The. Season 1. Hosted by Krissy Clark. Marketplace Wealth and Poverty Desk.

WEBSITES

Beyond I Do. https://beyondido.org.

6

Twenty-One Affirmations
for the Twenty-First Century

———

When we wrap up a semester-long course on **race**-related issues, we frequently find that our students feel a bit overwhelmed by all that they have learned. Most are so troubled by the extent to which structural **racism** pervades US society that they feel almost paralyzed. They want to be part of the solution, but they don't know where to begin. Before closing, we offer instructive encouragement and some final food for thought to help you grow the movement for racial equality.

———

1. We Are Leaderful

The contemporary Movement for Black Lives has been critiqued as leaderless and thus unorganized and unsustainable. These critics are missing the mark on more than one account. First, movements of the people are built on and sustained by collective activity. Movements are not like group projects at your school or job, where "the work can still get done" by one ardent member while others slack off. This movement will be sustainable so long as a critical mass of people come together in any variety of ways to publicly advocate for the value of Black life.

Second, we've been hearing since at least the 2003 protests against the US invasion of Iraq that movements were starting to look disorganized because seemingly disparate issues would take the stage together at a single event. That is, at an antiwar march, we might have seen environmental conservationists critique the United States' dependence on oil alongside socialists castigating Halliburton and other corporations for making money off noncompetitive wartime contracts. What some people fail to understand is that social movements are rarely, if ever, focused on one single issue or goal. What may be different in contemporary social movements is the conscious strategy to publicly articulate the connections among **racism**, patriarchy, disregard for the planet, **capitalism**, and the industrial complexes of prison and war. The willingness to incorporate these strands into a narrative for social change is in no small part due to the growing resonance of the politics of **intersectionality**. These movements are not unorganized because there is more than one message; on the contrary, the multiplicity of messages is what is being organized. The politics of intersectionality does not compel one to discipline speech or behavior so that only one issue gets addressed at a time. One is instead disciplining oneself to be mindful of the "matrix of domination"[1] and to keep that mentality when countering police brutality, gentrification, and budget cuts to subsidized school lunch programs.

Lastly, there is no one way to lead; we must dispel this myth. Not every leader is an orator or a natural in front of the camera. Leaders are people who motivate, who organize, and who do grunt work so that collective activity has momentum. Leaders make contributions and share ideas. Dependence on the presence of charismatic figures subliminally suggests that there are few leaders among us, but this is not true. The misguided belief that leadership is scarce entrenches elite representatives who either are addicted to power and looking for any justification to continue to wield power or would like to walk away from power but are afraid that their efforts and accomplishments will be squandered if no one steps up to shepherd them to

Children out front, 2006 Chicago May Day March / Day Without an Immigrant. (Photo by Tehama Lopez Bunyasi)

the next level. We can teach children how to be leaders, and we can mentor adults to become more influential and cooperative. One of the most important things we can do as leaders to ensure the progression of this social movement is to train the next generation and follow confidently behind.

2. Racism Is Tyrannical, and Democracy Is Fragile

Democracy is a radical concept because it asserts that we are all entitled and expected to participate in governance. This precious idea, that every person should have a voice in the political sphere, took millennia to cultivate. The United States of America, however, only became a robust democracy in 1965, when the federal government began to actively enforce the law of the land through the Voting Rights Act. This policy called for almost every adult citizen, regardless of **race**, to exercise the right to vote as guaranteed by the Fifteenth Amendment, which was written into the Constitution ninety-five years earlier. Up until that time, **white supremacists** at the state and local levels resisted the extension of the franchise to African Americans at every turn. Their idea of democracy was a *herrenvolk democracy*,[2] one in which the population is stratified, with only the white majority treated as "equals," and everyone else excluded from participating in a government of self-rule. Nevertheless, people of color resisted and taught the next generation to believe in and act on their natural right to be counted alongside everyone else.

Democracy is also very fragile. When we form majorities and coalitions, it is often our inclination to make decisions that are best for those who are on our team, but this cannot come at the expense of oppressing others. As we write, we are troubled by the idea that this country is slipping toward new iterations of herrenvolk democracy. Indeed, the Noble Prize–winning economist Paul Krugman declared that it is not "economic anxiety" that poses the greatest threat to US democracy today; it's "white nationalism run wild."[3] If the ascension of Donald Trump to the presidency is not evidence enough for you, consider the efforts of many state legislatures to further disenfranchise citizens of color now that an important feature of the Voting Rights Act has been eliminated. We must resist this inclination and instead find ways to make decisions that neither infringe on the rights of others nor require us to make compromises that undermine the creation of a more equitable society.

3. Progress Is Not Inevitable

Frederick Douglass famously said that "power concedes nothing without a demand."[4] These are the words spoken by someone who intimately knew the culture of **white supremacy** against which he advocated the freedom and franchise of Black people and women of all **races**. Relatedly, people often point to Martin Luther King Jr.'s assertion, "the arc of the moral universe is long but it bends toward justice."[5] When people today echo this part of his speech, it concerns us that they interpret it to mean that progress is inevitable and guided by providence but that the speed at which it progresses depends on the push of human agency. This may very well be what he wanted us all to hear. But when we listen to his speeches, we imagine something else: a man galvanizing the spirit of social justice because he believes that the *free will* and *conduct* of women and men is what makes our world a moral one and that our human souls are capable of such good things.

King, Douglass, and many other egalitarians were passionate about getting people activated for social justice because they believed *work* and *commitment over time* were necessary ingredients of social change. (Even physicists have shown that power = energy/time.) They did not trust that the momentum of any one era would carry on to the next or that the agenda of one administration would proceed naturally to some next coherent step. (Physicists also remind us of *inertia*.) Waiting around for **white supremacists** and their acquiescent partners to change their mind was not acceptable. There was no "right time"—they made their own time. This is our time to push for new ways of valuing one another, for investing in one another, and for being more humane with one another. There will never be a time riper than right now.

4. We Don't Need to Be Perfect. We Need to Be Political.

For unfortunate reasons, antihegemonic movements in the United States tend to center their campaign for rights and equality around people who they believe are virtuously above reproach. Granted, this strategy has afforded different movements some successes, but it has consistently left those who are considered "deviant" at the margins

of society. This movement is our opportunity to change this unreasonable standard. We are not perfect, and we should not have to be
perfect in order to have our basic rights recognized. People of color
and poor whites are often expected to conform to middle-class white
norms in order to be deemed acceptable or sufficient or simply to
belong. Well, here's a radical statement: We all belong here! We all
have rights, and nothing should compromise our entitlement to those
rights. If we are Black, we have rights. If we are poor, live in housing
projects or trailer parks, we have rights. If we have same-sex sex, we
have rights. If we apply for welfare benefits, we have rights. If we are
single mothers, we have rights. If we use and/or abuse substances, we
have rights. If we had an abortion, we have rights. If we wear hoodies, we have rights. If we sag our pants, we have rights. If we play our
music really loud when we drive by in our cars, we have rights. If
we are Muslims, we have rights. If we are atheists, we have rights. If
we are fat, we have rights. If we wear turbans, we have rights. If we
cannot make bail, we have rights to due process. Believe it or not, if
we are in this country without proper documentation, we still have
some rights that must be recognized. If you say you stand for justice
and cannot envision yourself defending the civil and human rights
of society's most marginalized people, then you need to rethink just
what it is that you stand for, because it isn't equality. It's all of us or
none of us. You need not be an angel to either be an agent of change
or to be regarded with dignity, respect, and humanity.

---

5. Interrogate Meritocracy

*I am, somehow, less interested in the weight and convolutions of Einstein's
brain than in the near certainty that people of equal talent have lived and
died in cotton fields and sweatshops.*

—Stephen Jay Gould[6]

It is high time that we realize that while hard work and talent are
important ingredients for opportunities and advancement, there

are many individuals with mediocre skills and personal characteristics who hold advantaged positions. Moreover, there are many folks whose hard work and talent will never be recognized, and by no fault of their own. When people explain racial inequality in terms of hard work, discipline, talent, and other virtues, they are touting a myth. The racialized myth of **meritocracy** empowers people to claim that whites work harder, are more responsible, value education more than others, and inherently possess the kind of values that make for good leaders, good home owners, good students, good police, and good Americans. This is a dangerous belief system.

We are not saying that we shouldn't value hard work or that we shouldn't want to apply ourselves in order to achieve our goals, be they ambitious or modest. Instead, we ought to realize that there are other factors that inform the life chances of Americans, and many of them have nothing to do with who people are as individuals. The circumstances of your birth, the social networks that are made available to you, the kinds of schools you go to, the financial status of your family—these all inform whether and what kind of opportunities become available to you. Be proud of your hard work and be proud of the talents that make you who you are. But bear in mind that this is not all that matters in the calculus of your success and that many people enjoy the best material and political standing in our society by little, and sometimes no, effort of their own.

6. Children Are Our Barometer

There are a lot of ways to measure how well a society is doing. When gauging the egalitarianism of our society, we'd like to encourage you to ask how the children of our country are faring. Remember, children do not get to choose the circumstances of their birth and childhood. They don't get to choose the financial status of their families or where they live. They do not get to pick their ascribed **race** or gender, even though many people will treat them on the basis of these characteristics. Children do not get to vote and do not get to make decisions about who should represent their interests. They have little say in the culture that they are born into. They are not allowed to legally work, and many of them, given their age, cannot literally speak for themselves.

Advocating for the equitable well-being of children is one of the most effective ways to make an argument for racial justice; so many of the rationalizations of and justifications for inequality are predicated on the myth of **meritocracy**, and this logic gets entirely thrown out the window once we start talking about children. How can they possibly be held accountable for the realities they have been immersed in? They have not realized their full potential, though the political choices of adults widen or narrow the path for them to do so. As adults, we should be making decisions that best support the growth and possibilities of our society's children. Indeed, it is our responsibility to do so even if we do not have children ourselves.

If we want to know how our society is doing, take a look at statistics about children. You'll learn where we are and, perhaps more importantly, where we're headed. How many kids are born into poverty, and who are they? Are babies of a certain racial group living to see their first birthday at a higher rate than those of another? How many words are in their vocabulary? Which languages do they speak, and are they authorized to use them in the classroom? Who is attending public schools, and are all public schools meeting the needs of the children? Are the kids at the private school getting a leg up? How many young citizens are denied access to developmental resources because their parents are undocumented, deported, locked up, formerly incarcerated, or dead? To what extent are adolescent behaviors legislated into adult crimes? How many children are behind bars? How many young people go hungry over the summertime and during school breaks? Do our children ever meet people of a different racial background? How many people under eighteen years old have lost a family member, friend, or classmate to gun violence? How many are allowed to preregister to vote before their eighteenth birthday? Have they all been empowered to make positive change in this world?

7. Reappropriate the Language of Morality

It is reprehensible that racial identity is an indicator of well-being in the United States. It is unacceptable that the law provides substantial room for police and citizen vigilantes to shoot and kill unarmed Black people without major legal repercussions. It is unconscionable that majority Black and Brown public schools are underfunded and overcrowded. It is shameful that politicians are more excited about being "tough on crime" than they are about being "serious about

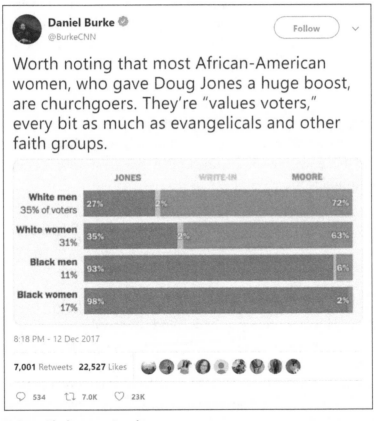

Daniel Burke ✔
@BurkeCNN

Follow ⌄

Worth noting that most African-American women, who gave Doug Jones a huge boost, are churchgoers. They're "values voters," every bit as much as evangelicals and other faith groups.

	JONES	WRITE-IN	MOORE
White men 35% of voters	27%	2%	72%
White women 31%	35%	2%	63%
Black men 11%	93%		6%
Black women 17%	98%		2%

8:18 PM - 12 Dec 2017

7,001 Retweets **22,527** Likes

💬 534   🔁 7.0K   ♡ 23K

Twitter: Black women's values.

education." It is downright deplorable that a nation such as the United States has the greatest military on earth but has neither universal pre-K nor universal health care. It is reckless to act with sloth-like reflexes, or no reflexes at all, to ensure that the water being delivered to a town and its schools is not full of lead. It is downright immoral not to care what happens to whole groups of people—children, poor people, Black people, women, LBGTQ+ people, justice-involved individuals, refugees, and so on.

The contemporary Movement for Black Lives is a moral movement because it asserts that the lives of those who have been marginalized the most should be valued as much as the most privileged members of society. By virtue of simply being alive, they should matter. Each person's life is so unique, precious in possibilities, and finite in its existence here on earth, and that is not to be trifled with.

We who advocate for policies and practices that protect the freedoms and enhance the well-being of marginalized people need to use the language of morality with full conviction. It is, after all, the native tongue for those who want to do the most good for the most people. By virtue of free speech, racial conservatives can invoke morality when they defend the reckless behavior of unprofessional police or rationalize the stinginess of public funds that could be used to help those who are in the most need, but we must not allow them to monopolize it.

---

8. Read Widely

These days it is easier than ever to immerse ourselves in an echo chamber. Hearing one's own voice and the familiar voices of others again and again is incredibly comforting, but it can also give us a false sense of consensus and power. One simple way to resist this encroaching insularity is to make time to read beyond the headlines of a news outlet that you wouldn't ordinarily look at. What topics does it believe are worth bringing to your attention? How is it

Standing in the cotton field of Mrs. Minnie B. Guice near Mount Meigs in Montgomery County, Alabama, this woman reads the *Southern Courier*, a newspaper dedicated to reporting the stories of the civil rights movement, 1966. (Photo by Jim Peppler; Alabama Department of Archives and History)

framing the major issues of the day? What arguments is it making, and do you concur?

Be intentional about reading the stories and analyses of people who have a different racial identity than you do. What can you learn from them? Does their point of view on a certain issue cause you to call your previous understandings into question? Despite the differences of your racial experiences, are there places where your ideas converge?

If we are to strive for a more inclusive society where the lives of Black people matter fully, we must be attuned to the many types of perspectives that shape discourse about Black life. Let's do more talking and engaging with and less talking at and past one another.

9. Beware of Woker-than-Thou-itis!

Striving to be educated around issues of social justice is laudable and moral, but striving to be recognized by others as a woke individual is self-serving and misguided. So, to those of you who are making a competition out of racial consciousness and progressive politicking, please get over yourself! You know who you are. Go on now and be useful to the causes you believe in by taking all your woke knowledge and making it translatable to working with others. Sometimes working with others means "meeting people where they're at" to see if you can have a meaningful conversation in which you speak your piece and attempt to understand where the other person is coming from. Who knows, you might actually learn something from them. Speaking down to someone or trying to outperform your fellow allies by being the first person to "call someone out on their privilege" or by striving to write the most searing quip on your favorite social media platform to gain "likes" is ultimately an ego-enhancing activity. Any activist or any social creature is susceptible to trying to best even those people whom they value the most. Let us all (Candis and Tehama included) orient ourselves to advocate passionately, compassionately, and in the spirit of the collective. If in our efforts to speak and act effectively we achieve some level of eloquence and are given praise, we can be grateful for those kind words and sentiments, and we should convey our praise and appreciation to others when so moved. First and foremost, however, let us ask ourselves how, when, and where we can do the most good.

10. Yield Silently to Those Who Are Seldom Heard

We can transform relationships of power by transforming how we relate to one another. One of the ways we can do this, according to the political theorist Vince Jungkunz, is through "silent yielding"—or an intentional restraint of speech coupled with active listening that "encourages participation from historically oppressed voices, and participation from historically inept listeners."[7] Possessors of privileged status commit a kind of identity suicide when they discipline themselves from speaking first, longest, loudest, and repeatedly in order for those of lesser social status to be heard and considered. By taking a position of "political and epistemological humility,"[8] the yielder creates new opportunities to differently understand and relate to the marginalized speaker. This practice is not meant to dispossess the yielder of having a role in a conversation or decision-making process; rather, the purpose is to transform the role and relationships that that yielder has with others in their shared social context. By undoing the discursive colonialism of whiteness, maleness, and other hegemonic identities, silent yielders can help create more democratic and egalitarian relationships. At times, it may not be clear who has a more privileged status; in these circumstances, people should do their best to hear from all who are present. For those underrepresented people who want to speak, please speak for yourself; everyone else, please understand that they are speaking for themselves and not as ambassadors for their **race**, their gender, or their economic class.

---

11. Second-Class Citizenship Must Be Eradicated

Over 700,000 people in the United States are denied substantive representation in the United States Congress and are required to seek congressional approval before their local government adopts budgets and laws simply because of where they live: Washington, DC. Crazy, right? What's even more absurd is that there are more people living in Washington, DC, than there are in Vermont or Wyoming! For centuries, Americans have largely accepted this disenfranchisement as a quirky state of exception. But let's think about this irony. Why should anyone be denied full rights as an American citizen as a function of calling the nation's capital one's home? We should furthermore be outraged that power is being denied to a jurisdiction whose largest population has been and continues to be Black (about 47 percent; lest gentrification completely change these figures in favor of whites). In 2016, 86 percent of DC voters cast ballots in favor of statehood. The people have spoken, but Republicans and Democrats refuse to treat the matter as a priority.

A more complicated matter that is worth being critical over is the status of Puerto Rico, the US Virgin Islands, Guam (which sometimes finds itself under threat of bombing due, in part, to the forty-fifth president's tweets), the Northern Mariana Islands, and American Samoa, among other territories. The matter of these **citizens**' vote is more difficult to advocate for given the lack of unanimity as to whether these jurisdictions should become states. These regions are vestiges of a colonial empire, and they remain in a state of disenfranchisement because of the complacency around their state of exception. If they want to become states, they should. If they want to be fully represented in Congress, they should.[9]

We must also remember that many of those who have been convicted of a felony, depending on where they live, may never get their voting rights back. There is nothing inherent in US law, history,

In this 1899 cartoon, "School Begins," the artist editorializes the expansion of the United States' territories as a necessary extension of civilization to an otherwise-uncivilized world. The pouty new pupils in lessons of self-government are the Philippines, Hawaii, Puerto Rico, and Cuba. The more assimilated and mannerly students, Alaska, Arizona, New Mexico, Texas, and California, sit nearby. A Chinese boy stands at the doorway near a Native American, who is reading a book upside down. In the far left, a Black boy washes the windows, looking on without educational materials. (Cartoon by Louis Dalrymple; published by Keppler & Schwarzmann; Prints and Photographs Division, Library of Congress LC-DIG-ppmsca-28668)

or ethos that says it must be this way. Also remember that those who are in prison or jail at the time of the census are counted in the district of the prison or jail in which they are incarcerated and not from their hometown or place of residence before incarceration. Since most prisons are located in majority-white, rural areas, this means that communities of color are being underrepresented in Congress and that white communities are being overrepresented. If this doesn't sound very different from the Three-Fifths Compromise, which enhanced the representation of white people in the antebellum South, it shouldn't. The **white privilege** of redistricting just got a makeover.

12. Reparations Can Mean Many Things

There are a great many anxieties about the idea of reparations. Outright dismissal and rejection of *considerations* of reparations to Black folks—especially American descendants of enslaved people—are often couched in worries of what reparations would cost if every Black person in the United States today were given a certain amount of money to bring about financial restitution for the intergenerational economic exploitation of slavery, Jim Crow, and racial discrimination in the post–World War II housing market. A number of scholars have argued, however, that reparations can take many forms.[10] They can be symbolic or material. Reparations could mean scholarships, tax deductions, or guaranteed access to quality food and health care. They can range from the idea of child trust accounts, or "baby bonds,"[11] to a policy akin to the reparations that the US government provided to Japanese American **citizens** who suffered in internment camps. One viable opportunity to give monetary restitution for wrongdoing by the federal government is to offer recompense (with interest) to a specific group of African Americans who descend from those who lost their savings when the Freedman's Bank went bust. The records that were kept during this financial venture are some of the nation's richest genealogical records of Black families;[12] if we follow the trail, we would be sure to find thousands of people who would have benefited from intergenerational wealth had the bank been managed more legitimately.

We can also think about reparations as relational. When Congresswoman Maxine Waters insisted on "reclaiming [her] time," we began to think about how Black people can and should reclaim what is denied them. What if we could change relationships between those who commit **microaggressions** and those whom they harm by practicing microreparations? Perhaps the ethos of silent yielding could be extended to other behavior. While we ultimately advocate for concrete and constructive ways for our society to invest in the

communities that are most harmed by inegalitarianism, some people say the act of even seriously considering reparations at all is a
valuable democratic act in itself.[13]

13. No Election Is Too Small

Many people get hyped up about presidential elections, and they
should. Choosing a president is a big decision. Voting for a US senator or member of the House of Representative is also important. But
we need to be just as concerned with our state assembly, our governor, our mayor, our school board, our district attorney, our alder-
man, our police chief, and our fricking dog catcher. These people
make decisions about our lives, and they appoint other people to
positions that cannot be held immediately accountable via elections.
We need to vet these candidates and choose the one who best represents our interests. We need to be pumped up about the midterm
elections and special referenda that appear on the ballot during the
years when we don't pick a president. There is no election too small
when it comes to picking the leaders who will either advance or
obstruct racial justice. Indeed, it is at the local and state levels where
we most directly budget for our priorities.

In most elections, there are local referenda or ballot measures that
ask voters to decide whether taxes should be spent on one public
resource or another: roads, homeless shelters, public transportation,
sidewalks, open spaces, and the like. Investing in public resources that
we can all share is an effective way to reduce inequality in our country. Everyone in this country should be able to receive a high-quality
education, live in a safe and adequate home, roam around in a clean
park, meander through a library, and be seen by a medical professional when one is ill or, better yet, before one becomes ill. We can
take steps to reduce structural **racism** by pooling our resources
together for the good of the whole. Get registered, get informed, go
vote, and proudly wear that "I Voted" sticker. Remember, one vote
can literally make a difference.[14] Local power is real power.

14. Someone Is Counting on You to Do Nothing at All

Right now, this very minute, there are political candidates (hell, political parties), corporate executives, and local officials who are calculating how much resistance they are going to get for dragging their feet when it comes to uprooting racial inequality under their helm of responsibility. Some people even put time and money into demobilizing US **citizens**, hoping they will be so disheartened and

Artwork by Lucy Holtsnider. (Courtesy of Amplifier.org)

disillusioned or feel so inefficacious that they will just stay home and accept things for how they are.

But we can't drag our feet. Casting a vote during all elections is just the beginning. We need to write letters to (and tweet and Snapchat and send Facebook messages to) our representatives, attend town hall meetings, speak up at the PTA, boycott businesses that go against our values, attend protests, and use our talents and skills to voice our opinion in any way we can. Those who show up are often the people who make decisions. We need to get involved and be counted.

---

15. Division of Labor Is a Beautiful Thing

Being a full-time activist is an exciting and demanding lifestyle, but it isn't for everyone. In fact, it isn't for most people. Instead of measuring your level of commitment against the likes of Ella Baker, César Chávez, Grace Lee Boggs, DeRay McKesson, or Alicia Garza, ask yourself instead, "How can I be a long-term advocate for racial justice given the time and resources that my current lifestyle allows for?"

Do you have more time than money? If so, there's probably a campaign out there that needs a canvasser on the weekends or a weekly tutor for a child in your neighborhood. Some people can only dedicate time to an organized effort about once or twice a year; being there and giving it your full energy can still make a difference.

Do you have more money than time? Great, there are literally thousands of high-quality, justice-oriented organizations that could use your donation. Becoming a sustaining member of a nonprofit organization can help its fiscal managers plan more effectively for the long haul.

If you are deathly afraid of crowds and can't bring yourself to attend a rally, that's fine: you can make signs for the protest. If you are barred from the ballot box, you can jump on social media to help get the word out until we win the reinstatement of the franchise for all people with felony records. Every movement needs artists, philosophers, child and elder caretakers, documentarians, phone callers, envelope stuffers, public speakers, food preparers, trash-picker-uppers, translators, door knockers, carpoolers, fundraisers, recruiters, errand runners, cheerleaders, and kind people who check in to see if anybody needs anything.

———

16. Collective Action Is and Has Been Powerful

There are a lot of things we can do as individuals. But there is nothing like working with other people to achieve a shared goal for racial justice. Participating in a march or canvassing a neighborhood with someone you just met that morning at the organization headquarters can be a moving experience. Knowing through experience that other people care about the issues you care about and that they have their own story that brought them to this shared activity can be very enlightening and quite heartening.

Logistically speaking, working with others is not always easy. People need to be organized, strategies must be developed, resources need to be mustered, and plans must be deployed and carried through. This work is energizing but also very draining; all of these sensations are valuable. When we realize how much effort goes into changing a policy or the discourse around one particular issue, it makes us aware of how much inertia and obstruction must be overcome to achieve a victory for equality. It is in the struggle for change that we can gain new appreciation for what these issues mean to us.

On a personal level, working with others to achieve social change can be emotional and challenging. Like in any relationship in which you put some piece of yourself on the line, you may find that the people you collaborate with are fallible. At some point, they may let you down, flake out on you, frustrate you, undermine your trust, or even break your heart. As you build and maintain coalitions, ask yourself whether and under what conditions you are willing to forgive and work on repairing a weakened comradeship. On the flip side, collective action can also reveal that you are fallible too. If you let someone down, undermine someone's trust, or break someone's heart, are you willing to admit fault, and would you need to be told or shown something to know that it was possible to get back to a place where you could go forward together? Being a conscientious member of a coalition requires introspection about our own humanity—could social change happen any other way?

The work you do on your own is important, but the work you do with others is crucial. Racial inequality and anti-Black oppression are collective problems, and they will require collective efforts to eradicate.

———

17. Calibrate Your Time Scales

Information has never moved faster than it does right now. Someone posts a video or commentary on a social media platform, and in the matter of an hour, hundreds of thousands, maybe even millions, of people can watch or read it. When we use our most modern technology, we can shape consciousness over the span of minutes, even seconds. The speed of this transmission, however, does not necessarily translate into political or policy change.

The disconnect between our information flow and the time it takes to build a movement, nurture a movement, and act as a movement can discourage those who do not learn to calibrate the various times scales of their lives. We can harness the speed of the internet to achieve certain goals, but other actions will take more time. The fact that some things may take more time does not mean that we can't be successful or that we will not make incremental change. Movements require a balance of urgency and steadiness. Change is often slow and arduous. Accept this fact and calibrate your time scales so that you do not mismeasure either success or failure. We need you for the long haul.

---

18. Be for Something

We should be angry and dissatisfied with the disparities we see and more so with the lack of comprehensive efforts to eliminate them. But we cannot simply be against something—we have to be for something. Complaints need resolution. We need to critique but also to create. We need to be willing to test new ideas and try many tactics. We can be almost certain that we won't "get it right" every time we put our foot forward, but that doesn't mean we give up. Working for something better is a challenging process. We create a vision, we orient ourselves toward that vision, and we struggle toward it.

---

19. Have Fun!

Let's face it, staying woke can take its toll. The inequalities and injustices of the world can evoke an array of emotions, many of them unpleasant. Working for racial justice is demanding, but it doesn't have to be depressing. It can actually be a hell of a lot of fun. Some people may even call it life-giving.

What can you do to make racial justice fun? Let's say you're a busy person who wants to build in time with friends but also wants to put pressure on your city council to change its anti-sagging-pants ordinance. Ignite your multitasking spirit, throw a potluck with all your compassionate friends, and between chip-fulls of guacamole and your second helping of chili, ask your guests to pen handwritten letters to your elected representatives. Going to a protest? Make a clever sign or create a papier mâché figurine. Are you a musician?

Protesters at the 2006 Chicago May Day March / Day Without an Immigrant use this papier mâché figurine to claim that matters of gentrification, immigration, and segregation are connected to racism, injustice, inequality, fear, and greed. (Photo by Tehama Lopez Bunyasi)

How about putting on a concert to raise money and bring attention to a social justice organization that needs your support?

You will need to renew your energy from time to time—have fun. The development of **racism** is a process, and so is building up your stamina to resist. Pace yourself and rejuvenate by celebrating the people you meet, the knowledge you acquire, and the accomplishments—big or small—that are made on this very long journey.

---

20. Do unto Others as You Would Have Them Do unto You

What would the United States be like if we all followed the Golden Rule? How different would our politics be if we all treated one another as though we would one day be in the same position as those whom we affect? What if we made this mantra our guiding political principle?

We assert that a "golden" sensibility is oriented around a view from the bottom. If we imagined what it would be like to be the most dispossessed and vulnerable people, we would want laws and practices that treat the dispossessed and the vulnerable with care and compassion—a safe place for all to lay their head; preventative and catastrophic health care for all; the presumption of innocence before proven guilty; the recognition of rights and personhood for all. Why can't the bare minimum be humane?

---

21. Dream Big!

If humane treatment is the foundation on which we build our government, what would our society look like if we dared to dream big? Everyone would wake up in an affordable home, and the kids would go to school to get a relevant, effective, and engaging education. It wouldn't really matter which neighborhood you lived in because the public schools are equally funded, the teachers are well paid, and the free after-school programs are a fun place to be. If a parent is a little late picking up a kid, the child doesn't worry that she or he will get choked, shot, or deported by law enforcement; the parent was just having one too many laughs with an interracial social network at her or his living-wage job. Tonight's dinner is another nutritious meal with vegetables from the town farm half a mile away, and that clean glass of water from the tap washes it down nicely. After eating, people promenade around the neighborhood to let their food settle and get caught up on the latest scoop. The older woman down the street has been diagnosed with breast cancer, but thankfully, they caught it early during her yearly mammogram, covered under universal health care. The nineteen-year-old who graduated from high school last year is visiting his family for the weekend; he's been working at a wind farm as part of a national program that will pay for a single year of college for each year of service. It's election week, and some folks are casting their ballots tonight, but those with other commitments are voting tomorrow or in the next few days. Two women candidates are going head-to-head again this year; one wants to build more bridges across the border with Mexico, while the other would rather expedite the conversion of our federal prison properties into job-training centers for the environmentally sustainable economy—this will be a tough choice. The night sky grows darker, but since its safe outside, people stay out a little later to watch the stars come out. The sky is clear, and the air is clean. Pop! Pop! Pop! Pop! Pop! No one ducks, but all look up—fireworks are going off over city hall. It's Harriet Tubman's birthday, and the sparkles overhead light up the faces down below. Tears well up in the eyes of the elders. They remember a time when fewer people knew her name and how she risked her life to liberate others. We carry her spirit with us a little more these days because we're attributing greater value to what we share with others and are less concerned with what we can accumulate and keep for ourselves. As we make our way home to turn in for the night, we pull our hoodies over our heads to ward off the evening chill. We feel safe in our skin, we feel safe in our country, and freedom and justice are for all.

Conclusion

WE BELIEVE THAT WE WILL WIN!

An overarching goal of this book is to shine a light on the lessons and the gifts that the contemporary Movement for Black Lives has provided to this society and the world over its six-year life span. We have aimed to show the connection between this country's violent past and its inequitable and violent present. We have also sought to bring clarity to the policy goals and political strategies of modern-day Black freedom fighters as well as to debunk some of the myths about this ongoing social movement.

We hope to have convinced you that the contemporary Movement for Black Lives can best be characterized as a movement that is "forging a praxis that centers class, gender, sexuality and empire alongside race to reflect a truly **intersectional** analysis."[1] To reiterate, this is a movement that attempts to elicit inclusion, empathy, and awareness of institutional **racism**. It relies on a Black feminist political philosophy, principled coalitions, and a collective commitment "to changing the conditions that Black communities are living and existing in" so that we can "have a real shot for living in a world that is more just, more equitable—in a world where Black lives actually do matter."[2] Not only does it aim to erase police violence and discrimination against Black people, but it also seeks to eliminate state violence that stems from structural inequalities produced in the US criminal justice system, segregated and unequal public schools, constrained residential opportunities, bad environmental policies, reduced access to the franchise, and unchecked and unregulated **neoliberal** governance.

The twenty-first-century Movement for Black Lives has successfully shifted the national narrative on racial inequality, thus helping more Americans to develop a more capacious understanding of and hold higher standards for what freedom, liberty, equity, democracy, and human dignity ought to look like in one of the world's richest and most powerful countries. Opal Tometi, one of the founders of the Black Lives Matter Global Network, explained, "What we're witnessing right now is a deepening level of commitment from people of conscience from all different walks of life. We're seeing a really vibrant, multiracial movement for Black Lives."[3] This kind of achievement is intangible, leading some people to discount it, but developing an ideological intervention that rewires more people's brains to view Black people and Blackness in a positive light will be a necessary condition for creating a world where anti-Black **racism** is not a major factor in interpersonal interactions or Americans' policy preferences. It is often the case that a paradigm shift in culture must first occur in order to build greater potential for lasting, landmark policy change. And as we will explain, there *have been* important policy successes, especially at the local level, due to the collective action of those who are committed to the improvement of Blacks' well-being. Americans are obsessed with progress. We want it fast, and we want it now; but we have to keep at least two things in perspective to really understand what capacity a young, growing social movement can have.

In 2013, when the Black Lives Matter movement began as a love letter to Black people written in response to the acquittal of the man who murdered Trayvon Martin, Barack Obama was at the helm of the US government. Although he disappointed many people on matters of racial equity, there was at least a sense that a collective movement might be able to force the next set of Democratic presidential hopefuls to commit to more progressive, **antiracist** policy stances. That hope was thwarted sometime around 2:00 a.m. on November 9, 2016, when it became clear that Donald J. Trump would be inaugurated into the US presidency.

As a consequence of Trump's campaign and election, we are now living in a time when neo-Nazis and the so-called alt-right are emboldened by the president of the United States to parade around the streets uncloaked and, in some cases, fully armed to demand greater space to perpetuate and deepen **white supremacy**. We live in a time when the US government has implemented a policy that requires migrant children, as young as toddlers, to be separated from their parents at the US border. We live in a time when a third try at a "Muslim ban" prevents many immigrants from earning an opportunity to come to the United States or even reuniting with their family members who already live in this country. The water is still bad in Flint, Michigan. The citizens of the United States who happen to live in Puerto Rico have not been fully relieved of the damage of Hurricane Maria, which occurred almost two years ago. Police shootings of unarmed Black people have not subsided. Transgender women of color still live in a state of precarity. People are fighting tooth and nail to prevent Confederate monuments from literally being toppled from their pedestals. Political representatives are working hard to dilute Black and Latinx communities' voting power. The national minimum wage is not a living wage. To say that we are not where we should be is an understatement.

The first thing to keep in mind is that any expectation that one social movement will eradicate these problems and do so quickly is an unreasonable one. But **Black girl magic** is real. It should be noted that not only have the Black Lives Matter movement and the Movement for Black Lives served to produce real policy change on a number of fronts, but together they have also started a cascading effect of social movements and protest around interrelated issues of inequality. We agree with BLM cofounder Patrisse Cullors, who argues that "we wouldn't be seeing this level of protest if we didn't have this [Movement for Black Lives] for the last five years. Black

Lives Matter really set this idea of how we fight and how we protest into action."[4] Over the past few years, the Women's March (coordinated national demonstrations that formed the largest day of protest in US history), #MeToo, #NeverAgain, and #SayHerName activists have been driven, in part, by inspiration from #BlackLivesMatter.

Additionally, various organizations that are working within and alongside the movement have largely focused on local, grassroots issues. By developing principled coalitions, average people have made significant policy change in their communities. The historian and activist Barbara Ransby notes that organizations in New York are working to overturn the city's Housing Authority policy that bars people convicted of crimes from living in public housing, and cash bail systems are being challenged across the country.[5] Organizations galvanized by this contemporary Movement for Black Lives are forming coalitions with labor groups and activists, such as the fight for a fifteen-dollar minimum wage as well as gun-regulation activists, including those who survived the mass shooting in Parkland, Florida. The successes are adding up: it is no coincidence that body cameras are increasingly common additions to the uniforms of police enforcement officers. Representatives on both sides of the aisle are starting to come to grips with the implications of unfettered spending on mass incarceration. More states are decriminalizing marijuana. California is officially ending its cash bail system.[6] The conversation is changing, and so are the policies; this movement has helped to push us in a progressive direction. Setting ambitious goals is critical to any reform movement, and many more of us will have to step up and step out to successfully combat the barriers—new and old—that are in front of us. But the contemporary Movement for Black Lives shows us that success is possible.

The second and related thing we must keep in mind is that this contemporary movement is part of a long legacy and tradition of Black freedom movements, all of which have been built on a decades-long, if not generations-long, struggle and incremental change. Sometimes these movements are stopped in their tracks but are picked back up later; sometimes they evolve; sometimes they continue but go unnoticed by the media. All of these are possibilities for this movement as well, but we ought to keep in mind that even if we don't "see" a social movement making major headway, it doesn't mean that nothing is happening.

Just think about the civil rights movement. It took *decades* of protests, sit-ins, boycotts, courtroom battles, and many acts of civil disobedience to get the Civil Rights Act of 1964 and the Voting Rights Act of 1965 written, passed by Congress, and signed into law by the president. (Today, the Voting Rights Act is being chipped away as each election passes by, which this movement is helping to reinvigorate urgency about.) To be sure, the civil rights movement did see many successes, but we also know that Black freedom fighters of the mid-twentieth century never saw all of the things they envisioned: total racial equity, full **citizenship** of people of color, rights for poor people, well-paying jobs with good benefits for people who seek them, fairness in the criminal justice system, an end to the ravages of **racism**, militarism, and **capitalism**.

Nonetheless, folks like the Reverend William Barber are taking up the mantle of the Poor People's Campaign, which demands "a right to adequate food, housing, health care, education, fair wages, and other basic necessities."[7] Here's the thing: this movement began five decades ago in 1968, the year that Dr. King was assassinated. Rev. Barber, along with women like Louise Brown and Amy Jo Hutchinson, are revitalizing the multiracial movement that never got to live out its full potential. Similarly, folks like Angela Davis and Bryan Stevenson, as well as many, many others, have been working tirelessly for decades to get greater reforms for prisoners' rights and human rights, more broadly. Davis explains, "I do think that movements require time to develop and mature. They don't happen spontaneously. They occur as a result of organizing and hard work that most often happens behind the scenes. *Over the last two decades*, I would say, there has actually been sustained organizing against police violence, **racism**, racist police violence, against prisons, the prison-industrial complex, and I think the sustained protests we are seeing now have a great deal to do with that organizing."[8] If Angela Davis needs "two decades" to do anything, what should be expected from the rest of us?! Activists and allies of the contemporary Movement for Black

Lives are "part of a movement that's been happening for hundreds of years."[9] While it seems that the historical movement for Black people to enjoy full status as US **citizens** might have ended when the Fourteenth Amendment was ratified (in 1868), we might think about the contemporary movement as an extension of that sesquicentennial legacy. Black freedom struggles persist, making new debuts when there is a critical tipping point. In this case, the tipping point came when young Black folks realized that no matter how respectable they looked or behaved, their lives did not matter in the eyes of their fellow citizens, the police who are supposed to protect them, or the political representatives who were elected to stand up for them.[10] Given the pattern of concessions and **co-optation**, two steps forward, one step back, we should not expect BLM and M4BL to do everything in their life span, but their efforts do and will scaffold onto the racial progress that their predecessors forced the United States to make. All told, the second thing to keep in mind, then, is that this contemporary movement should be best understood as a breath of new life into an ongoing Black freedom movement, which has always sought to create a world where Black lives matter.

Now what? Some people are sure that the contemporary Movement for Black Lives is dissipating, but again, if we look where the media isn't pointing their spotlight, we would see that average people and grassroots organizations are sharpening old tools as well as learning and implementing new strategies to make change at the local and state levels and even making preparations for the right time to strike at the national level. The Movement for Black Lives has never been homogeneous, especially as it concerns ideas about which tactics to deploy. As such, the only constraints to anyone taking part in this movement are in your imagination. Or, in other words, there is no shortage of ways to participate in what will very likely be a long haul, marked along the way by barriers as well as successes.

For those of us who believe in our political institutions and who think that the most practical and efficient way to make long-lasting, transformative policy change is through electoral politics, you will find to your heart's delight an enormous realm of possibilities. There is a vast array of policies that need to be addressed at the local level.

These policies range from dress codes that ban Black girls and boys from styling their natural hair in certain ways to bail reform to reallocating local budgets in a way that allows the state to provide social services to people before they are arrested for stealing food or due to behaviors that stem from mental illness. Even if you want to take a step back and assure that people who share similar values as you get elected, you have options. You can work on a campaign or simply educate yourself on the candidates and then vote. There are activists of this contemporary movement, like DeRay McKesson or members of We The Protestors, who are working inside major parties to help set new agendas.[11]

Additionally, both parties are having identity crises, which means that **antiracist** activists can have a greater say in the shape of the major political parties. Progressive political leaders like Alexandria Ocasio-Cortez, Stacey Abrams, and Andrew Gillum are upsetting so-called mainstream Democrats. When 2020 rolls around, there will be opportunities to elect a new president and at least eleven new governors, thirty-three new senators, and 435 Representatives; that's not to mention the thousands of seats in state houses, city councils, state supreme court judges, mayors, police chiefs and sheriffs, and so on. Democracy is fragile, but with vigilance, we will have new opportunities to shape our reality through the power of the ballot.

Policy reform and electoral politics are two tools in the very broad arsenal of an antiracist advocate, Black freedom fighter, or BLM activist. For those of us who have become skeptical of conventional political channels and mainstream political leadership, you are welcome to take to the streets, protest, boycott, sit-it, die-in, stand-in, and shout in the face of institutions, individuals, and businesses that are doing a whole lot of wrong or even a whole bunch of nothing. March along a highway, stand up with a labor union, feed schoolchildren when teachers are striking for better pay and more resources for students, disrupt candidates to demand that they clearly communicate their policy stances on the trifecta that Black freedom movements have been struggling against for decades: **racism**, militarism, and **capitalism**. These actions are also in the toolkit of advocates and activists.

For those of us who wish that the aforementioned group would be more like Dr. King and Ms. Parks and the activists of the civil rights movement, we say to you, be careful what you ask for. The historian Jeanne Theoharis warns that with a closer, more critical reading of history, we would find that being more like these individuals would result in "disruption, civil disobedience; an analysis that interweaves **race**, poverty, and US war making; steadfast moral witness; and a willingness to call out liberals for their inaction."[12] Just as we know that the fatally wounded Black people who make the news are neither the first nor the last people to be cut down by their government and that **racism**, poverty, and sexism continue to dog US society, it follows that there must be many more of us who will take on the ethos and actions of Martin Luther King Jr. and Rosa Parks *and* Claudette Colvin and Malcolm X and Ella Baker and James Lawson and Fannie Lou Hamer and Gloria Richardson and Elaine Brown and Paul Robeson and Shirley Chisolm. But because we face an entirely new set of circumstances that differ significantly from our predecessors'—militarized local police forces, a massive prison-industrial complex, social media, fast-moving technology, and journalists under attack by the administration in the White House—we will also need to be more like Patrisse Cullors and DeRay McKesson and Brittney Packard and Alicia Garza and Tarana Burke and Opal Tometi and Johnetta Elzie and Tef Poe and Erica Garner and Reverend Barber and Mychal Denzel Smith and Brittany Packnett and Aislinn Pulley and Aleo Pugh and Janet Mock and Tressie McMillan Cottom and . . . you.

Acknowledgments

We love our children, and we love our students. We thank them for the inspiration and motivation to write this book. We thank Lee Baker, John Biewen, Kerry Haynie, Jennifer Ho, Ashley Jardina, Kennetta Perry, Jonathan Rosa, Betina Cutaia Wilkinson, and our inspiring young-person-in-residence Megan Odum for their feedback and also for their enthusiasm for this project, bolstering our confidence to use our expertise to engage with a larger community.

Additionally, there are a number of people who provided data, helpful insights, and also encouragement along the way: Erin Acquaviva, John Aldrich, Ashley Amaya, GerShun Avilez, Frank Baumgartner, Jennifer Bennett, Kimberly Bickham, Cedrick Bright, Rose Buckelew, Yea-Wen Chen, Sam Cykert, Cassandra Davis, Ashley Day, Christopher DeSante, Heather and Philip Duhart, Lily Farel, VaNatta Ford, Megan Ming Francis, Michael Gillespie, Marissa Guerrero, Hannah Hardaway, Ayesha Hardison, Emily Hertz, Annie Howell, Amenah Ibrahim, Sarit Johnson, Vince Jungkunz, Rebecca Kreitzer, Laura Larson, Nell Lyons, Sarah Mayorga-Gallo, Anna McKinsey, Ellen McLarney, Gladys Mitchell-Walthour, Masato Nakazawa, Noa Nessim, Matt Newcomb, Chera Reid, Leah Wright Rigueur, Blayne Amir Sayed, Tim Schwantes, Colleen Scott, Joshua Sellers, Kristan Shawgo, Danielle Spurlock, Bonnie Weir, Fatimah Williams, Ethel

Wu, Ayesha Yousafzai, Chris Zepeda-Millán, and Candis's first-year seminar students and brave Racial Equity in Medicine students. We appreciate the support of the Duke Council on Race and Ethnicity, the faculty at the School of Conflict Analysis and Resolution, and Tehama's neighborhood friends.

We will never be able to thank our parents, Jane Wakeham-Lopez, Dan Lopez, Jennifer Lopez, and Sheila and Anthony Watts, enough. And our husbands, Sakwa Bunyasi and Terrell Smith, are invaluable. Thank you both, with our whole hearts.

We thank our editor, Ilene Kalish, for providing the space to write this and for her handwritten and scanned-in feedback. We also thank Caelyn Cobb and the anonymous reviewers for giving us permission to do something innovative and fun. We would be remiss if we did not acknowledge the guidance of Sonia Tsuruoka, the wonders of copy editor Andrew Katz, the skills of the folks at NYU Press, and the magic of laurie prendergast. All remaining errors are our own.

Notes

INTRODUCTION

1. Edson, "Affordable Housing."
2. Bonilla-Silva, *Racism without Racists*, 243.
3. As explained by Jelani Cobb in "The Matter of Black Lives."

1. ON THE MATTER OF BLACK LIVES

1. Thanks for the inspiration, Brandon Perez!
2. Galtung, "Violence, Peace, and Peace Research"; Galtung, "Cultural Violence."
3. Hutchings and Valentino, "Centrality of Race."
4. What is this "x" in "Latinx," and why are we using it? Many of you know that the words "Latino" or "Latina" are meant to describe somebody who is Latin American or someone who descends from those in the Americas who were once colonized by Spain. The term is both ambiguous and contested. When the label ends with an *o*, it refers to someone who is male, and when it ends with an *a*, it refers to someone who is female. After many waves of feminist, womanist/womynist, and queer politics, a number of people are now advocating the use of "Latinx" and "Latinxs" to describe someone who fits (or multiple people who fit) or something(s) that describe(s) this ethnoracial category without privileging the male as the universal. See, in the Spanish language, all nouns are gendered, and when a group of people are described, their gender is accounted for in a patriarchal fashion. For example, if we are talking about a male child, the conventional Spanish grammatical rules require that we describe the child as "niño." If a female

child is being described, we would say "niña." If we are talking about two or more male children, we say "niños," and when we are talking about two or more female children, we would say "niñas." But if we are talking about two children, one who is male and the other female, conventional Spanish grammatical rules require that we say "niños." If we were talking about one male child and one *hundred* female children, the rules of Spanish grammar would require us to use "niños." See the inequity? What's more is that there are a growing number of people who see their gender as nonbinary or even fluid, and so these old grammatical rules not only are inappropriate but can also be oppressive. In this book, we join the linguistic activism of those who aim to resist the patriarchy and colonization embedded in this grammar by using "Latinx" or "Latinxs" as our defaults unless we are trying to specify the gender of a person or group of people. If we are describing people who do not identify with a binary gender category, we will use "Latinx" or describe the person or people in greater detail. We should also note that there are people who are both Latinx and Black but are not necessarily biracial.

5. Masuoka and Junn, *Politics of Belonging.*
6. Ingraham, "Three Quarters of Whites Don't Have Non-White Friends."
7. Dr. King lamented that Sunday at 11:00 a.m. is one of the most segregated hours in "Christian America" during an interview on *Meet the Press*, April 17, 1960 (transcript at the Martin Luther King Research and Education Institute: https://kinginstitute.stanford.edu). Since then, many others, such as Cathy Lynn Grossman, have provided evidence that this observation still describes Sundays in the US.
8. Aslam, "Future of Bad Collectivity."
9. Baldwin, "Open Letter to My Sister."
10. K. Taylor, *From #BlackLivesMatter to Black Liberation*, 182.
11. M. King, "Testament of Hope," 174.
12. Garza, "Herstory of the# BlackLivesMatter Movement," 26.
13. K. Taylor, *From# BlackLivesMatter to Black Liberation.*
14. DeSante and Smith, *Racial Stasis.*
15. Wilkerson, "Where Do We Go from Here?," 61.
16. Rickford, "Black Lives Matter toward a Modern Practice," 38.
17. Instructively, Eduardo Bonilla-Silva, Amanda Lewis, and David G. Embrick say the same thing about colorblindness. Bonilla-Silva, Lewis, and Embrick, "I Did Not Get That Job," 561.
18. New York Civil Liberties Union, "Stop and Frisk Facts."
19. Ford, "Leader of the Unfree World."
20. Baumgartner and Epp, *North Carolina Traffic Stop Statistics Analysis.*
21. Baumgartner et al., "Racial Disparities in Traffic Stop Outcomes."

22. US Department of Justice, *Investigation of the Ferguson Police Department.*

23. US Department of Justice, *Investigation of the Baltimore City Police Department*, 5.

24. US Department of Justice and United States Attorney's Office, Northern District of Illinois, *Investigation of the Chicago Police Department*, 4, 25–28.

25. Sentencing Project, "Criminal Justice Facts."

26. American Civil Liberties Union, "Facts about the Over-incarceration of Women."

27. Ford, "Leader of the Unfree World."

28. Baumgartner, Grigg, and Mastro, "#BlackLivesDon'tMatter."

29. Purdie-Vaughns and Williams, "Stand-Your-Ground Is Losing Ground," 341.

30. Darity, "Revisiting the Debate"; Young, "Demythologizing the "Criminal-blackman."

31. Young, "Demythologizing the 'Criminalblackman.'"

32. Rothstein, *Color of Law*, xvi.

33. Nelson et al., "Redlining Richmond."

34. Smith and Weis, "Dividing Durham."

35. Hudnall, "In Durham, Rich Neighborhoods Have Plenty of Trees."

36. Massey et al., "Riding the Stagecoach to Hell."

37. Rugh, Albright, and Massey, "Race, Space, and Cumulative Disadvantage."

38. Massey et al., "Riding the Stagecoach to Hell," 118–19.

39. Coates, "Case for Reparations."

40. Baptiste, "Them That's Got Shall Get."

41. Hannah-Jones, "Choosing a School for My Daughter."

42. Reardon and Owens, "60 Years after *Brown*," 206.

43. Ibid., 205.

44. Barton and Coley, *Black-White Achievement Gap*, 6.

45. R. Johnson, "Long-Run Impacts of School Desegregation."

46. Williams and Houck, "Life and Death of Desegregation Policy."

47. Hannah-Jones, "Segregation Now."

48. Ibid.

49. Reardon and Owens, in "60 Years after *Brown*," provide a great summary of the scholarship on the effects of desegregation.

50. Billings, Deming, and Rockoff, "School Segregation, Educational Attainment, and Crime."

51. Darity, "How Barack Obama Failed Black Americans."

52. Pager and Shepherd, "Sociology of Discrimination."

53. Bertrand and Mullainathan, "Are Emily and Greg More Employable than Lakisha and Jamal?"

54. Pager, *Marked.*

55. Patten, "Racial, Gender Wage Gap Persist."
56. Ibid.
57. Wilson and Rodgers, *Black-White Wage Gaps*, 1.
58. Editorial Board, "College Does Not Close Racial Pay Gaps."
59. Hamilton et al., *Umbrellas Don't Make It Rain*.
60. Darity, "How Barack Obama Failed Black Americans."
61. Oliver and Shapiro, *Black Wealth / White Wealth*. On the flip side, it should be noted that debt can also passed down from generation to generation.
62. Katznelson, *When Affirmative Action Was White*.
63. Satcher et al., "What If We Were Equal?"
64. Acevedo-Garcia et al., "Toward a Policy-Relevant Analysis," 322.
65. Ibid., 324.
66. Gordon et al., "Measuring Food Deserts"; Smith and Morton, "Rural Food Deserts."
67. Whiteis, "Hospital and Community Characteristics."
68. Kreitzer and Smith, "'Contraception Deserts' Are What You Get."
69. Center on Society and Health, "Mapping Life Expectancy."
70. Florido, "Why Do Black Infants Die So Much More Often."
71. Beckles and Truman, "Education and Income," 15.
72. Boehmer et al., "Residential Proximity to Major Highways," 27.
73. Baldwin, "Open Letter to My Sister."
74. Schneider and Ingram, "Social Construction of Target Populations."
75. López, *Dog Whistle Politics*.

2. ALL THE WORDS PEOPLE THROW AROUND

1. Kelly and Dobbin, "How Affirmative Action Became Diversity Management."
2. On June 4, 1965, President Lyndon B. Johnson delivered the commencement address at Howard University. In his speech, titled "To Fulfill These Rights," Johnson articulated the rationale for affirmative action as the next step in the march toward equality. A videotape of the full speech can be found at the YouTube channel for the LBJ Presidential Library: https://www.youtube.com/watch?v=vcfAuodA2x8.
3. Omi and Winant, *Racial Formation*, 128.
4. Berrey, "Diversity Is for White People."
5. For more thoughts on this matter, see Alexander, *New Jim Crow*.
6. The Horatio Alger myth is the classic "rags to riches" story, a classic plotline of Horatio Alger Jr.'s books.
7. Feagin, *Racist America*, 6.
8. Omi and Winant, *Racial Formation*, 106.
9. Lopez Bunyasi and Smith, "Get in Formation."

10. Thomas, "Why Everyone's Saying 'Black Girls Are Magic.'"
11. Harry Magdoff, quoted in Marable, *How Capitalism Underdeveloped Black America*, 3.
12. Ibid.
13. Murray, "Historical Development of Race Laws."
14. Though there is a debate about whether the US Constitution should be considered an "economic document," there are a number of references to make sure trade and commerce flourished and to manage Indian land, debts, currency, trade, tariffs, and the like. One might also point out that the participants of the US constitutional convention were unrepresentative of the general population, being all white men of elite political and socio-economic status.
15. Numerous products and services are made or provided by incarcerated people; see Unicor as one example of this industry: www.unicor.gov (accessed August 27, 2018).
16. Glenn elucidates Marshall's ideas in "Constructing Citizenship," 3.
17. Ibid.
18. Rankine, "Condition of Black Life."
19. Bellis, "Here's Everywhere in the U.S. You Can Still Be Fired."
20. Berrey, *Enigma of Diversity*, 5.
21. Bonilla-Silva, Lewis, and Embrick, "I Did Not Get That Job"; Carr, *"Color-Blind" Racism*.
22. Smith and Mayorga-Gallo, "New Principle-Policy Gap," 891; Mayorga-Gallo, *Behind the White Picket Fence*.
23. Kendi, *Stamped from the Beginning*, 499.
24. Chiasson, "Color Codes."
25. *Parents Involved in Community Schools v. Seattle School District No. 1*, 551 U.S. 701 (2007).
26. Bonilla-Silva, *Racism without Racists*, 10.
27. For an excellent overview, see Hunter, "Persistent Problem of Colorism."
28. Hochschild and Weaver, "Skin Color Paradox."
29. Telles, *Pigmentocracies*.
30. Hunter, "Persistent Problem of Colorism," 237.
31. Blay, *(1)ne Drop*.
32. Cecelski and Tyson, *Democracy Betrayed*.
33. McClain, "Rev. William Barber."
34. Lebron, *Making of Black Lives Matter*, 158.
35. Ibid.
36. Clayton, "Bradley Has an Idea."
37. Darity, "Revisiting the Debate on Race and Culture."
38. Rankine, *Citizen: An American Lyric*, 135.

39. Owens, *Medical Bondage*.
40. The image comes from Jardina and Piston, "Dehumanization and the Role of Biological Racism."
41. Wilson, testimony to grand jury.
42. Kellaway, "Claudia Rankine."
43. Mueller, "Producing Colorblindness," 221n3.
44. Bell and Hartmann, "Diversity in Everyday Discourse."
45. Mayorga-Gallo, *Behind the White Picket Fence*; Smith and Mayorga-Gallo, "New Principle-Policy Gap"; Berrey, *Enigma of Diversity*; Warikoo, *Diversity Bargain*.
46. Leong, "Racial Capitalism."
47. Andersen, "Fiction of 'Diversity without Oppression,'" 17.
48. John Ehrlichman, quoted in Baum, "Legalize It All."
49. López, *Dog Whistle Politics*. There is also an episode of *Scandal* by the same name.
50. Ibid., 4.
51. A great example is the Wilmington Race Riots, well explained in Cecelski and Tyson, *Democracy Betrayed*.
52. Occupy Wall Street highlighted the enormous gap between the 1 percent and the 99 percent, but those in the top 20 percent are not necessarily struggling financially either, according to Reeves, "Stop Pretending You're Not Rich."
53. Mills, "White Ignorance."
54. Mueller, "Producing Colorblindness."
55. Mills, "White Ignorance," 13.
56. Mueller, "Producing Colorblindness," 227.
57. The term "gaslight" is derived from Patrick Hamilton's 1938 play *Gas Light* and subsequent movie adaptations.
58. Bonilla-Silva, Lewis and Embrick, "'I Did Not Get That Job.'"
59. Pérez, *Unspoken Politics*, 4.
60. Ibid.
61. Payne, "Weapon Bias."
62. Vedantam, "Thumbprint of the Culture."
63. Gay and Tate, "Doubly Bound."
64. Crenshaw, "Mapping the Margins"; Collins, "Definitional Dilemmas."
65. Dhamoon, "Considerations on Mainstreaming Intersectionality," 231.
66. Guinier, *Tyranny of the Meritocracy*, xi.
67. Murphy *Social Closure*, 8.
68. Lani Guinier provides a compelling case for this argument in her book *The Tyranny of the Meritocracy*.
69. Upkins, "Denying Racism."

70. Sue, *Microaggressions in Everyday Life*.
71. Hill, *Everyday Language*.
72. Bailey, "They Aren't Talking about Me."
73. Bristol, "On Moya Bailey."
74. Nationalism is different from "patriotism," which is a national attachment marked by love of country and is predicated on neither animus toward others nor feelings that one's country is better than another. See McDaniel, Nooruddin, and Shortle, "Proud to Be an American?"
75. Brown and Shaw, "Separate Nations"; Shelby, "Two Conceptions of Black Nationalism"; Dawson, *Black Visions*; J. Taylor, *Black Nationalism in the United States*.
76. Cohen, *Democracy Remixed*, 11.
77. Centeno and Cohen, "Arc of Neoliberalism," 324.
78. Centeno and Cohen, "Arc of Neoliberalism," 331. Omi and Winant, in *Racial Formation*, also do an excellent job in discussing the history of neoliberalism in US history.
79. Omi and Winant, *Racial Formation*, 263.
80. Coates, *Between the World and Me*, 7.
81. Nobles, *Shades of Citizenship*.
82. Omi and Winant, *Racial Formation*.
83. Walter Rodney, quoted in Marable, *How Capitalism Underdeveloped Black America*, xxi.
84. Tehama Lopez Bunyasi, in *Race 2012*.
85. For several examples of how this plays out, see F Schram, Soss, and Fording, *Race and the Politics of Welfare Reform*.
86. Culp-Ressler, "Ugly Racial Undertones."
87. For a full explication of the theory of racialized social systems, see Bonilla-Silva, "Rethinking Racism."
88. Bonilla-Silva, *Racism without Racists*, 9.
89. Pager and Shepherd, "Sociology of Discrimination," 182.
90. Kennedy, "Lifting as We Climb."
91. Cooper, *Beyond Respectability*, 5.
92. T. Harris, "No Disrespect."
93. Katznelson, *When Affirmative Action Was White*; Lam, "White Students' Unfair Advantage in Admissions."
94. McKee and Marra, "Open Letter."
95. Hobbs, *Chosen Exile*; A. Johnson, *Privilege, Power, and Difference*.
96. Khanna and Johnson, "Passing as Black," 381; Carbado and Gulati, *Acting White?*
97. Dawkins, *Clearly Visible*.
98. Lopez Bunyasi and Rigueur, "'Breaking Bad' in Black and White."

99. Kennedy, *Sellout.*
100. Gaines, *Black for a Day.*
101. DiAngelo, "White Fragility," 54; DiAngelo, *White Fragility.*
102. McIntosh, "White Privilege and Male Privilege."
103. A. Johnson, *Privilege, Power, and Difference,* 38.
104. M. Johnson, "6 Ways Well-Intentioned People Whitesplain Racism."
105. Lavelle, *Whitewashing the South,* 48.
106. Feagin, *Systemic Racism.*
107. Bonilla-Silva, Goar, and Embrick, "When Whites Flock Together."
108. Murray, "Historical Development of Race Laws."

3. THE POLITICS OF RACIAL PROGRESS

1. In 2016, Colin Kaepernick began to protest racial injustice by kneeling during the US national anthem, and later several players joined in solidarity. In response to the exasperation of many viewers as well as the Trump's Twitter storm on this matter, the commissioner and team owners agreed to implement a policy that required all personnel on the sidelines to stand during the national anthem or to remain in the locker room.
2. Theoharis, *More Beautiful and Terrible History.*
3. Anderson, *White Rage.*
4. Theoharis, *More Beautiful and Terrible History.*
5. The Fifteenth Amendment made it illegal to deny people the vote explicitly on the basis of race, so states used new tactics like grandfather clauses, poll taxes, and literacy tests to keep Blacks from voting.
6. Dray, *Capitol Men.*
7. Phillips, *Daily Life during African American Migrations,* 6.
8. Glenn, "Constructing Citizenship," 8–9.
9. Holston, *Insurgent Citizenship.*
10. David Blight, interview in Facing History and Ourselves, "Part Five: Violence and Backlash."
11. Dray, *Capitol Men,* 180–82.
12. Lemann, *Redemption,* 76; Dray, *Capitol Men,* 193–95.
13. Dray, *Capitol Men,* 195–97.
14. Curtin, *Black Prisoners and Their World,* 55–56.
15. Prather, "We Have Taken a City"; LaFrance and Newkirk, "Lost History of an American Coup D'État."
16. Washington, "Freedman's Savings and Trust Company."
17. Senator Charles Sumner of Massachusetts described the federal government in this way upon the ratification of the Fourteenth Amendment.
18. Omi and Winant, *Racial Formation.*
19. "Harvard Students Attempt."

20. Daniel Gitterman in *Calling the Shots* explains that because the federal government is the country's largest employer, purchaser of goods, and health insurance customer, any executive order that the president makes concerning how the business of the federal government is run not only affects a vast array of individuals but oftentimes makes it difficult for the private sector not to follow its lead.
21. Bodroghkozy, *Equal Time.*
22. López, *Dog Whistle Politics.*
23. Kendi, "Racial Progress," SR4.
24. In Justice William O. Douglass's dissenting opinion, he wrote, "Michigan by one device or another has over the years created black school districts and white school districts, the task of equity is to provide a unitary system or the affected area where, as here, the State washes its hands of its own creations." *Milliken v. Bradley* 418 U.S. 717, 762 (1974).
25. Astor, "Rights Groups Report Rise."
26. Smith, "Black Immigrants in the U.S. Face Big Challenges."
27. Theoharis, *More Beautiful and Terrible History*, xiii.
28. Theoharis, *More Beautiful and Terrible History.*
29. Kelley, *Hammer and Hoe.*
30. Lebron, *Making of Black Lives Matter*, xx.
31. FBI Counterterrorism Division, *Black Identity Extremist (BIE) Intelligence Assessment*, 2.
32. Winter and Weinberger, "FBI's New U.S. Terrorist Threat."
33. The remainder of his October 29, 1966, speech on the University of California, Berkeley, campus went on to explain his political viewpoints as the chairman of the Student Nonviolent Coordinating Committee, as well as to expound on his newly coined phrase "Black Power." The transcript and audio recording of this speech can be found at the American Public Media website, in its "Say It Plain" feature: http://americanradioworks.publicradio.org.
34. For a treatise on the tensions between hope and loss and the ethical possibilities of engaging melancholy, see Joseph R. Winters's *Hope Draped in Black.*

4. ARE YOU UPHOLDING WHITE SUPREMACY?

1. In *Arizona v. United States* (2012), the Supreme Court invalidated several parts of Arizona's SB1070 policy, which aimed to expand the scope of local/state enforcement of immigration law, which is in the realm of the federal government. However, parts of the law that remained intact include a provision that allows police to inquire about a person's immigration status, which many people predicted would result in racial profiling.

In *Shelby v. Holder* (2013), the majority opinion dismissed a mountain of evidence of what Justice Ruth Bader Ginsberg referred to as second-generation barriers to voting to dismantle a major provision of the Voting Rights Act.

2. Carter et al., "You Can't Fix What You Don't Look At."

3. Chapman, Kaatz, and Carnes, "Physicians and Implicit Bias"; Samuel Cykert et al., "Factors Associated with Decisions to Undergo Surgery."

4. Sides, Tesler, and Vavreck, "2016 US Election."

5. Baker, "Color-Blind Bind"; Bonilla-Silva, *Racism without Racists*; Bonilla-Silva, Lewis, and Embrick, "I Did Not Get That Job"; Carr, *"Color-Blind" Racism*; Forman, "Color-Blind Racism and Racial Indifference"; Frankenberg, *White Women, Race Matters*; Golash-Boza, "Critical and Comprehensive Sociological Theory."

6. Frankenberg, *White Women, Race Matters*, 142.

7. Mosse, "Racism and Nationalism," 164.

8. K. Taylor, introduction to *How We Get Free*, 8, 7.

9. Useem and Downie, "Third-Culture Kids."

10. Andersen and Junn, "Deracializing Obama."

11. See Price's *The Race Whisperer* as well as Bonilla-Silva and Ray, "When Whites Love a Black Leader."

12. Darity, "How Barack Obama Failed Black Americans."

13. Hillary Clinton, campaign speech, September 9, 2016.

14. Centers for Disease Control and Prevention, "Understanding the Epidemic."

15. Cramer, *Politics of Resentment*; López, *White by Law*.

16. K. Taylor, *From #BlackLivesMatter to Black Liberation*, 5.

17. See Lewis, "There Is No 'Race' in the Schoolyard"; Hagerman, *White Kids*.

18. Apfelbaum et al., "Learning (Not) to Talk about Race"; Apfelbaum, Sommers, and Norton, "Seeing Race and Seeming Racist?"

19. Yancy, "Clevis Headley," 287.

20. Burch, *Trading Democracy for Justice*; Lerman and Weaver, *Arresting Citizenship*.

21. Owens, *Medical Bondage*; Roberts, *Killing the Black Body*.

22. Geraldo on *Fox and Friends*, March 23, 2012, available on YouTube, www.youtube.com (accessed August 28, 2018).

23. O'Reilly, "President Obama and the Race Problem."

24. Schwartz, "CNN's Don Lemon."

25. Higginbotham, *Righteous Discontent*.

26. Obasogie and Newman, "Black Lives Matter and Respectability Politics," 555.

27. K. Taylor, *From #BlackLivesMatter to Black Liberation*, 13.

28. See Cooper, *Beyond Respectability*.

29. Lopez Bunyasi and Rigueur, "'Breaking Bad' in Black and White."

5. IT DOESN'T HAVE TO BE THIS WAY

1. Khan-Cullors and bandele, *When They Call You a Terrorist.*
2. Cobb, "Matter of Black Lives."
3. Kelley, *Freedom Dreams*, 137.
4. Lopez Bunyasi and Smith, "Get in Formation."
5. Movement for Black Lives, "Platform."
6. Black Lives Matter, "What We Believe."
7. Movement for Black Lives, "Platform."
8. Black Lives Matter, "What We Believe."
9. Cobb, "Matter of Black Lives."
10. White, "Incarcerating Youth with Mental Health Problems"; Alexander, *New Jim Crow.*
11. Turner et al., "Why America's Schools Have a Money Problem."
12. Michener, "Policy Feedback in a Racialized Polity."
13. Hannah-Jones, "Segregation Now."
14. Mai and Subramanian, *Price of Prisons*, 11–13.
15. Qui, "Donald Trump's Baseless Claims."
16. Mayhew, *Congress*, 17.
17. Quandt, "1 in 13 African-American Adults."
18. ProCon.org, "State Felon Voting Laws."
19. Brennan Center for Justice, "Automatic Voter Registration."
20. Barnes and Marimow, "Appeals Court Strikes Down North Carolina's Voter-ID Law."
21. Hajnal, Lajevardi, and Nielson, "Voter Identification Laws."
22. Sobel, *High Cost of "Free" Photo Voter Identification Cards.*
23. Hayduk, "Democracy for All."
24. Lewis et al., "Why Do (Some) City Police Departments Enforce Federal Immigration Law?"
25. Baumgartner et al., "Targeting Young Men of Color," 108.
26. Baumgartner, Epp, and Shoub, *Suspect Citizens.*
27. Tom, "Criminal Punishment and Politics."
28. Wright, "How Prosecutor Elections Fail Us."
29. K. Harris, "Bail Reform."
30. Queram, "Greensboro Police Halt Minor Traffic Stops."
31. Schnacke, Jones, and Wilderman, "Increasing Court-Appearance Rates."

6. TWENTY-ONE AFFIRMATIONS FOR THE TWENTY-FIRST CENTURY

1. Collins, *Black Feminist Thought*, 18.
2. Olson, *Abolition of White Democracy.*

3. Krugman, "Why It Can Happen Here."

4. Douglass, *West India Emancipation Speech.*

5. M. King, "Where Do We Go from Here?" Though King's words have been frequently cited, we should note that King probably borrowed this idea from the Transcendentalist and abolitionist Theodore Parker's *Ten Sermons of Religion*, 84–84.

6. Gould, "Wide Hats and Narrow Minds."

7. Jungkunz, "Dismantling Whiteness," 12.

8. Ibid., 13.

9. When this book was in draft, some people remarked that they're not sure what will take longer for Puerto Rico, getting the electricity grid fully up and running or gaining statehood. It took nearly a year to restore power across Puerto Rico after Hurricane Irma.

10. Martin and Yaquinto, *Redress for Historical Injustices*; Robinson, *Debt.*

11. Aja et al., "From a Tangle of Pathology."

12. Washington, "Freedman's Savings and Trust Company."

13. Balfour, "Unthinking Racial Realism."

14. Consider the 2017 House of Delegates race between Shelly Simonds and David Yancey in Virginia.

CONCLUSION

1. Ransby, *Making All Black Lives Matter*, 160.

2. "Black Lives Matter Founders."

3. NPR, "Black Lives Matter Founders."

4. Jenkins, "Black Lives Matter Co-founder Patrisse Cullors."

5. Ransby, "Black Lives Matter Is Democracy in Action."

6. It is phenomenal to see an entire state eradicate an entire industry, but some people are worried that the system that replaces cash bail may still produce racial inequity, as the new policy seems to default to keeping people in jail rather than releasing them or may rely on racially biased algorithms to assess risk of release.

7. Kaufmann, "Poor People's Campaign Is Just Getting Started."

8. Davis, *Freedom Is a Constant Struggle*, 36 (emphasis added).

9. "Black Lives Matter Founders."

10. K. Taylor, *From #BlackLivesMatter to Black Liberation.*

11. J. King, "How Black Lives Matter Has Changed US Politics"; Ross and Lowery, "Turning Away from Street Protests."

12. Theoharis, *More Beautiful and Terrible History*, 208.

Bibliography

Acevedo-Garcia, Dolores, Theresa L. Osypuk, Nancy McArdle, and David R. Williams. "Toward a Policy-Relevant Analysis of Geographic and Racial/Ethnic Disparities in Child Health." *Health Affairs* 27, no. 2 (2008): 321–33.

Aja, Alan, Daniel Bustillo, William Darity Jr., and Darrick Hamilton. "From a Tangle of Pathology to a Race-Fair America." *Dissent* 61, no. 3 (2014): 39–43.

Alexander, Michelle. *The New Jim Crow: Mass Incarceration in the Age of Colorblindness*. New York: New Press, 2010.

American Civil Liberties Union. "Facts about the Over-incarceration of Women in the United States." Accessed January 1, 2019. www.aclu.org.

Andersen, David J., and Jane Junn. "Deracializing Obama: White Voters and the 2004 Illinois U.S. Senate Race." *American Politics Research* 38, no. 3 (2009): 443–70.

Andersen, Margaret L. "The Fiction of 'Diversity without Oppression': Race, Ethnicity, Identity, and Power." Chap. 1 in *Critical Ethnicity: Countering the Waves of Identity Politics*, edited by Robert H. Tai and Mary L. Kenyatta, 5–20. Lanham, MD: Rowman and Littlefield, 1999.

Anderson, Carol. *White Rage: The Unspoken Truth of Our Racial Divide*. New York: Bloomsbury, 2016.

Apfelbaum, Evan P., Kristin Pauker, Nalini Ambady, Samuel R. Sommers, and Michael I. Norton. "Learning (Not) to Talk about Race: When Older Children Underperform in Social Categorization." *Developmental Psychology* 44, no. 5 (2008): 1513–18.

Apfelbaum, Evan P., Samuel R. Sommers, and Michael I. Norton. "Seeing Race and Seeming Racist? Evaluating Strategic Colorblindness in Social

Interaction." *Journal of Personality and Social Psychology* 95, no. 4 (2008): 918–32.

Aslam, Ali. "The Future of Bad Collectivity." *Law, Culture and the Humanities*, 2017, 1–19.

Astor, Maggie. "Rights Groups Report Rise in Deadly Attacks on Transgender People." *New York Times*, November 10, 2017.

Bailey, Moya. "They Aren't Talking about Me . . ." Crunk Feminist Collective, March 14, 2010. www.crunkfeministcollective.com.

Baker, Lee. "The Color-Blind Bind." In *Cultural Diversity in the United States*, edited by Ida Susser and Thomas C. Patterson, 103–19. Oxford, UK: Blackwell, 2001.

Baldwin, James. "An Open Letter to My Sister, Miss Angela Davis." *New York Review of Books*, January 7, 1970. www.nybooks.com.

Balfour, Lawrie. "Unthinking Racial Realism: A Future for Reparations?" *Du Bois Review: Social Science Research on Race* 11, no. 1 (2014): 43–56.

Baptiste, Nathalie. "Them That's Got Shall Get." *American Prospect*, October 12, 2014.

Barnes, Robert, and Ann E. Marimow. "Appeals Court Strikes Down North Carolina's Voter-ID Law." *Washington Post*, July 29, 2016.

Barnett, Larry D. "Anti-Miscegenation Laws." *Family Life Coordinator* 13, no. 4 (1964): 95–97.

Barton, Paul E., and Richard J. Coley. *The Black-White Achievement Gap: When Progress Stopped*. Princeton, NJ: Policy Information Center, Educational Testing Service, 2010.

Baum, Dan. "Legalize It All." *Harper's Magazine*, April 2016. https://harpers.org.

Baumgartner, Frank R., Leah Chrsitiani, Derek A. Epp, Kevin Roach, and Kelsey Shoub. "Racial Disparities in Traffic Stop Outcomes." *Duke Forum for Law and Social Change* (forthcoming).

Baumgartner, Frank R., and Derek A. Epp. *North Carolina Traffic Stop Statistics Analysis: Final Report to the North Carolina Advocates for Justice Task Force on Racial and Ethnic Bias*. Chapel Hill: University of North Carolina–Chapel Hill, 2012.

Baumgartner, Frank R., Derek A. Epp, and Kelsey Shoub. *Suspect Citizens: What 20 Million Traffic Stops Tell Us about Policing and Race*. New York: Cambridge University Press, 2018.

Baumgartner, Frank R., Derek A. Epp, Kelsey Shoub, and Bayard Love. "Targeting Young Men of Color for Search and Arrest during Traffic Stops: Evidence from North Carolina, 2002–2013." *Politics, Groups, and Identities* 5, no. 1 (2017): 107–31.

Baumgartner, Frank R., Amanda J. Grigg, and Alisa Mastro. "#BlackLivesDon'tMatter: Race-of-Victim Effects in US Executions, 1976–2013." *Politics, Groups, and Identities* 3, no. 2 (2015): 209–21.

Beckles, Gloria L., and Benedict I. Truman. "Education and Income—United States, 2009 and 2011." *Centers for Disease Control and Prevention Morbidity and Mortality Weekly Report* 62, no. 3 (2013): 9–19.

Bell, Joyce M., and Douglas Hartmann. "Diversity in Everyday Discourse: The Cultural Ambiguities and Consequences of 'Happy Talk.'" *American Sociological Review* 72, no. 6 (2007): 895–914.

Bellis, Rich. "Here's Everywhere in the U.S. You Can Still Be Fired for Being Gay or Trans." *Fast Company*, March 3, 2016. www.fastcompany.com.

Berrey, Ellen. "Diversity Is for White People: The Big Lie behind a Well-Intended Word." *Salon*, October 26, 2015. www.salon.com.

———. *The Enigma of Diversity: The Language of Race and the Limits of Racial Justice.* Chicago: University of Chicago Press, 2015.

Bertrand, Marianne, and Sendhil Mullainathan. "Are Emily and Greg More Employable than Lakisha and Jamal? A Field Experiment on Labor Market Discrimination." *American Economic Review* 94, no. 4 (2004): 991–1013.

Billings, Stephen B., David J. Deming, and Jonah Rockoff. "School Segregation, Educational Attainment, and Crime: Evidence from the End of Busing in Charlotte-Mecklenburg." *Quarterly Journal of Economics* 129, no. 1 (2014): 435–76.

Black Lives Matter. "What We Believe." Accessed November 1, 2018. https://blacklivesmatter.com.

"Black Lives Matter Founders Describe 'Paradigm Shift' in the Movement." National Public Radio, July 13, 2016. www.npr.org.

Blay, Yaba. *(1)ne Drop: Shifting the Lens on Race.* Philadelphia: BlackPrint, 2014.

Bodroghkozy, Aniko. *Equal Time: Television and the Civil Rights Movement.* Urbana: University of Illinois Press, 2012.

Boehmer, Tegan K., Stephanie L. Foster, Jeffrey R. Henry, Efomo L. Woghiren-Akinnifesi, and Fuyuen Y. Yip. "Residential Proximity to Major Highways—United States, 2010." *Centers for Disease Control and Prevention Morbidity and Mortality Weekly Report* 62, no. 3 (2013): 46–50.

Bonilla-Silva, Eduardo. *Racism without Racists: Color-Blind Racism and the Persistence of Racial Inequality in the United States.* 5th ed. Lanham, MD: Rowman and Littlefield, 2017.

———. "Rethinking Racism: Toward a Structural Interpretation." *American Sociological Review* 62, no. 3 (1997): 465–80.

Bonilla-Silva, Eduardo, Carla Goar, and David G. Embrick. "When Whites Flock Together: The Social Psychology of White Habitus." *Critical Sociology* 32, nos. 2–3 (2006): 229–53.

Bonilla-Silva, Eduardo, Amanda Lewis, and David G. Embrick. "'I Did Not Get That Job Because of a Black Man . . .': The Story Lines and Testimonies of Color-Blind Racism." *Sociological Forum* 19, no. 4 (2004): 555–81.

Bonilla-Silva, Eduardo, and Victor Ray. "When Whites Love a Black Leader: Race Matters in Obamerica." *Journal of African American Studies* 13 (2009): 176–83.

Brennan Center for Justice. "Automatic Voter Registration." November 7, 2018. www.brennancenter.org.

Bristol, Keir. "On Moya Bailey, Misogynoir, and Why Both Are Important." The Visibility Project, May 27, 2014. www.thevisibilityproject.com.

Brown, Robert A., and Todd C. Shaw. "Separate Nations: Two Attitudinal Dimensions of Black Nationalism." *Journal of Politics* 64, no. 1 (2002): 22–44.

Burch, Traci. *Trading Democracy for Justice: Criminal Convictions and the Decline of Neighborhood Political Participation.* Chicago: University of Chicago Press, 2013.

Carbado, Devon, and Mitu Gulati. *Acting White? Rethinking Race in Post-Racial America.* New York: Oxford University Press, 2013.

Carr, Leslie G. *"Color-Blind" Racism.* Thousand Oaks, CA: Sage, 1997.

Carter, Prudence L., Russell Skiba, Mariella I. Arredondo, and Mica Pollock. "You Can't Fix What You Don't Look At: Acknowledging Race in Addressing Racial Discipline Disparities." *Urban Education* 52, no. 2 (2017): 207–35.

Cecelski, David S., and Timothy B. Tyson. *Democracy Betrayed: The Wilmington Race Riot of 1898 and Its Legacy.* Chapel Hill: University of North Carolina Press, 2000.

Centeno, Miguel A., and Joseph N. Cohen. "The Arc of Neoliberalism." *Annual Review of Sociology* 38, no. 3 (2012): 317–40.

Center on Society and Health. "Mapping Life Expectancy." September 26, 2016. www.societyhealth.vcu.edu.

Centers for Disease Control and Prevention. "Understanding the Epidemic." August 30, 2017. www.cdc.gov.

Chapman, Elizabeth N., Anna Kaatz, and Molly Carnes. "Physicians and Implicit Bias: How Doctors May Unwittingly Perpetuate Health Care Disparities." *Journal of General Internal Medicine* 28, no. 11 (2013): 1504–10.

Chiasson, Dan. "Color Codes: An Poet Examines Race in America." *New Yorker*, October 27, 2014.

Clayton, Janet. "Bradley Has an Idea on How to Motivate Children of Watts." *Los Angeles Times*, August 16, 1985. http://articles.latimes.com.

Coates, Ta-Nehisi. *Between the World and Me.* New York: Spiegel and Grau, 2015.
———. "The Case for Reparations." *Atlantic* 313, no. 5 (2014): 54–71.

Cobb, Jelani. "The Matter of Black Lives." *New Yorker*, March 14, 2016. www.newyorker.com.

Cohen, Cathy J. *Democracy Remixed: Black Youth and the Future of American Politics.* Oxford: Oxford University Press, 2010.

Collins, Patricia Hill. *Black Feminist Thought: Knowledge, Consciousness, and the Politics of Empowerment.* New York: Routledge, 2002.

———. "Intersectionality's Definitional Dilemmas." *Annual Review of Sociology* 41 (2015): 1–20.

Cooper, Brittney C. *Beyond Respectability: The Intellectual Thought of Race Women.* Urbana: University of Illinois Press, 2017.

Cramer, Katherine J. *The Politics of Resentment: Rural Consciousness in Wisconsin and the Rise of Scott Walker.* Chicago: University of Chicago Press, 2016.

Crenshaw, Kimberlé. "Mapping the Margins: Intersectionality, Identity Politics, and Violence against Women of Color." *Stanford Law Review* 43 (1991): 1241–99.

Culp-Ressler, Tara. "The Ugly Racial Undertones in Our Panicked Response to Ebola." *ThinkProgress*, October 16, 2014. https://thinkprogress.org.

Curtin, Mary Ellen. *Black Prisoners and Their World, Alabama, 1865–1900.* Charlottesville: University of Virginia Press, 2000.

Cykert, Samuel, Peggye Dilworth-Anderson, Michael H. Monroe, Paul Walker, Franklin R. McGuire, Giselle Corbie-Smith, Lloyd J. Edwards, and Audrina Jones Bunton. "Factors Associated with Decisions to Undergo Surgery among Patients with Newly Diagnosed Early-Stage Lung Cancer." *JAMA* 303, no. 23 (2010): 2368–76.

Darity, William A., Jr. "How Barack Obama Failed Black Americans." *Atlantic*, December 22, 2016. www.theatlantic.com.

———. "Revisiting the Debate on Race and Culture: The New (Incorrect) Harvard/Washington Consensus." *Du Bois Review: Social Science Research on Race* 8, no. 2 (2011): 467–76.

Davis, Angela Y. *Freedom Is a Constant Struggle: Ferguson, Palestine, and the Foundations of a Movement.* Chicago: Haymarket Books, 2016.

Dawkins, Marcia Alesan. *Clearly Visible: Racial Passing and the Color of Cultural Identity.* Waco, TX: Baylor University Press, 2012.

Dawson, Michael C. *Black Visions: The Roots of Contemporary African-American Political Ideologies.* Chicago: University of Chicago Press, 2001.

DeSante, Christopher D., and Candis Watts Smith. *Racial Stasis: The Millennial Generation and Stagnation of Racial Attitudes in American Politics.* Chicago: University of Chicago Press, forthcoming.

Dhamoon, Rita Kaur. "Considerations on Mainstreaming Intersectionality." *Political Research Quarterly* 64, no. 1 (2010): 230–43.

DiAngelo, Robin. "White Fragility." *International Journal of Critical Pedagogy* 3, no. 3 (2011): 54–70.

———. *White Fragility: Why It's So Hard for White People to Talk about Racism.* Boston: Beacon, 2018.

Douglass, Frederick. *West India Emancipation Speech.* Canandaigua, NY, 1857.

Dray, Philip. *Capitol Men: The Epic Story of Reconstruction through the Lives of the First Black Congressmen.* Boston: Houghton Mifflin Harcourt, 2010.

Editorial Board. "College Does Not Close Racial Pay Gaps." *New York Times*, September 20, 2017.

Edson, Charles L. "Affordable Housing—an Intimate History." *Journal of Affordable Housing and Community Development Law* 20, no. 1 (2010): 193–213.

Educational Finance Branch. *Public Education Finances: 2015*. Washington, DC: US Census Bureau, 2017. www.census.gov.

Facing History and Ourselves. "Part Five: Violence and Backlash." *The Reconstruction Era* video series. Accessed March 8, 2018, www.facinghistory.org.

FBI Counterterrorism Division. *Black Identity Extremist (BIE) Intelligence Assessment*. August 3, 2017. https://vault.fbi.gov.

Feagin, Joe R. *Racist America: Roots, Current Realities, and Future Reparations*. New York: Routledge, 2000.

———. *Systemic Racism: A Theory of Oppression*. New York: Routledge, 2013.

Florido, Adrian. "Why Do Black Infants Die So Much More Often than White Infants." 89.3 KPCC, March 3, 2014. www.scpr.org.

Ford, Matt. "The Leader of the Unfree World." *Atlantic*, July 23, 2014. www.theatlantic.com.

Forman, Tyrone A. "Color-Blind Racism and Racial Indifference: The Role of Racial Apathy in Facilitating Enduring Inequalities." In *Changing Terrain of Race and Ethnicity*, edited by Maria Krysan and Amanda E. Lewis, 43–66. New York: Russell Sage Foundation, 2004.

Frankenberg, Ruth. *White Women, Race Matters: The Social Construction of Whiteness*. Minneapolis: University of Minnesota Press, 1993.

Gaines, Alisha. *Black for a Day: White Fantasies of Race and Empathy*. Chapel Hill: University of North Carolina Press, 2017.

Galtung, Johan. "Cultural Violence." *Journal of Peace Research* 27, no. 3 (1990).

———. "Violence, Peace, and Peace Research." *Journal of Peace Research* 6, no. 3 (1969).

Garza, Alicia. "A Herstory of the #BlackLivesMatter Movement." In *Are All the Women Still White? Rethinking Race, Expanding Feminisms*, edited by Janell Hobson, 23–28. Albany: SUNY Press, 2014.

Gay, Claudine, and Katherine Tate. "Doubly Bound: The Impact of Gender and Race on the Politics of Black Women." *Political Psychology* 19, no. 1 (1998): 169–84.

Gitterman, Daniel P. *Calling the Shots: The President, Executive Orders, and Public Policy*. Washington, DC: Brookings Institution Press, 2017.

Glenn, Evelyn Nakano. "Constructing Citizenship: Exclusion, Subordination, and Resistance." *American Sociological Review* 76, no. 1 (2011): 1–24.

Golash-Boza, Tanya. "A Critical and Comprehensive Sociological Theory of Race and Racism." *Sociology of Race and Ethnicity* 2, no. 2 (2016): 129–41.

Gordon, Cynthia, Marnie Purciel-Hill, Nirupa R. Ghai, Leslie Kaufman,

Regina Graham, and Gretchen Van Wye. "Measuring Food Deserts in New York City's Low-Income Neighborhoods." *Health & Place* 17, no. 2 (2011): 696–700.

Gould, Stephen Jay. "Wide Hats and Narrow Minds." *New Scientist*, March 8, 1979.

Grossman, Cathy Lynn. "Sunday Is Still the Most Segregated Day of the Week." *America*, January 16, 2015. www.americamagazine.org.

Guinier, Lani. *The Tyranny of the Meritocracy: Democratizing Higher Education in America*. Boston: Beacon, 2015.

Hagerman, Margaret A. *White Kids: Growing Up with Privilege in a Racially Divided America*. New York: NYU Press, 2018.

Hajnal, Zoltan, Nazita Lajevardi, and Lindsay Nielson. "Voter Identification Laws and the Suppression of Minority Votes." *Journal of Politics* 79, no. 2 (2017): 363–79.

Hamilton, Darrick, William Darity, Anne Price, Vishnu Sridharan, and Rebecca Tippett. *Umbrellas Don't Make It Rain: Why Studying and Working Hard Isn't Enough for Black Americans*. Oakland, CA: Insight Center for Community Economic Development, 2015.

Hannah-Jones, Nikole. "Choosing a School for My Daughter in a Segregated City." *New York Times Magazine*, July 11, 2016.

———. "Segregation Now: Investigating America's Racial Divide." ProPublica, 2014. www.propublica.org.

Harris, Kamala D. "Bail Reform Is about Criminal and Economic Justice." *Root*, September 18, 2017. www.theroot.com.

Harris, Tamara Winfrey. "No Disrespect: Black Women and the Burden of Respectability." *Bitch Media*, May 22, 2012. www.bitchmedia.org.

"Harvard Students Attempt to Take 1964 Louisiana Literacy Test, Fail." *Grio*, November 7, 2014. https://thegrio.com.

Hayduk, Ronald. "Democracy for All: Restoring Immigrant Voting Rights in the US." *New Political Science* 26, no. 4 (2004): 499–523.

Higginbotham, Evelyn Brooks. *Righteous Discontent: The Women's Movement in the Black Baptist Church, 1880–1920*. Cambridge, MA: Harvard University Press, 1993.

Hill, Jane H. *The Everyday Language of White Racism*. Chichester, UK: Wiley, 2009.

Hobbs, Allyson. *A Chosen Exile: A History of Racial Passing in American Life*. Cambridge, MA: Harvard University Press, 2014.

Hochschild, Jennifer L., and Vesla Weaver. "The Skin Color Paradox and the American Racial Order." *Social Forces* 86, no. 2 (2007): 643–70.

Holston, James. *Insurgent Citizenship: Disjunction of Modernity in Brazil*. Princeton, NJ: Princeton University Press, 2009.

Hudnall, David. "In Durham, Rich Neighborhoods Have Plenty of Trees. Poor Neighborhoods, Not So Much." *Indy Week*, June 8, 2016. www.indyweek.com.

Hunter, Margaret. "The Persistent Problem of Colorism: Skin Tone, Status, and Inequality." *Sociology Compass* 1, no. 1 (2007): 237–54.

Hutchings, Vincent L., and Nicholas A. Valentino. "The Centrality of Race in American Politics." *Annual Review of Political Science* 7 (2004): 383–408.

Ingraham, Christopher. "Three Quarters of Whites Don't Have Non-White Friends." *Washington Post*, August 25, 2014.

Jardina, Ashley, and Spencer Piston. "Dehumanization and the Role of Biological Racism in American Politics." Paper presented at the Midwest Political Science Association Meeting, Chicago, IL, April 7, 2016.

Jenkins, Aric. "Black Lives Matter Co-founder Patrisse Cullors on Her Memoir, Her Life and What's Next for the Movement." *Time*, February 26, 2018. http://time.com.

Johnson, Allan G. *Privilege, Power, and Difference*. Columbus, OH: McGraw-Hill, 2006.

Johnson, Lyndon B. "Commencement Address at Howard University: 'To Fulfill These Rights,' June 4, 1965." Speech, Washington DC, June 4, 1965. LBJ Presidential Library. www.lbjlibrary.net.

Johnson, Maisha. "6 Ways Well-Intentioned People Whitesplain Racism (and Why They Need to Stop)." *Everyday Feminism Magazine*, February 7, 2016. http://everydayfeminism.com.

Johnson, Rucker C. "Long-Run Impacts of School Desegregation & School Quality on Adult Attainments." NBER Working Paper Series 16664, National Bureau of Economic Research, 2011.

Jungkunz, Vincent. "Dismantling Whiteness: Silent Yielding and the Potentiality of Political Suicide." *Contemporary Political Theory* 10, no. 1 (2011): 3–20.

Katznelson, Ira. *When Affirmative Action Was White: An Untold History of Racial Inequality in Twentieth-Century America*. New York: Norton, 2005.

Kaufmann, Greg. "The Poor People's Campaign Is Just Getting Started." *Nation*, June 25, 2018. www.thenation.com.

Kellaway, Kate. "Claudia Rankine: 'Blackness in the White Imagination Has Nothing to Do with Black People.'" *Guardian*, December 27, 2015. www.theguardian.com.

Kelley, Robin D. G. *Freedom Dreams: The Black Radical Imagination*. Boston: Beacon, 2002.

———. *Hammer and Hoe: Alabama Communists during the Great Depression*. Chapel Hill: University of North Carolina Press, 1990.

Kelly, Erin, and Frank Dobbin. "How Affirmative Action Became Diversity Management: Employer Response to Antidiscrimination Law, 1961 to 1996." *American Behavioral Scientist* 41, no. 7 (1998): 960–84.

Kendi, Ibram X. "Racial Progress, Then Racist Progress." *New York Times*, January 22, 2017.

———. *Stamped from the Beginning: The Definitive History of Racist Ideas in America*. New York: Nation Books, 2016.

Kennedy, Randall. "Lifting as We Climb." *Harper's Magazine* 26 (2015). https:// harpers.org.

———. *Sellout: The Politics of Racial Betrayal*. New York: Pantheon, 2008.

Khan-Cullors, Patrisse, and asha bandele. *When They Call You a Terrorist: A Black Lives Matter Memoir*. New York: St. Martin's, 2017.

Khanna, Nikki, and Cathryn Johnson. "Passing as Black: Racial Identity Work among Biracial Americans." *Social Psychology Quarterly* 7, no. 4 (2010): 380–97.

King, Jamilah. "How Black Lives Matter Has Changed US Politics." *New Internationalist*, March 5, 2018. https://newint.org.

King, Martin Luther, Jr. "A Testament of Hope." *Playboy*, January 1969.

———. "Where Do We Go from Here?" Address delivered at the Eleventh Annual SCLC Convention, Atlanta, GA, 1967.

Kreitzer, Rebecca, and Candis Watts Smith. "'Contraception Deserts' Are What You Get When You Cut Off This Little-Known Program." *Monkey Cage* (blog), *Washington Post*, September 26, 2016.

Krugman, Paul. "Why It Can Happen Here." *New York Times*, August 27, 2018. www.nytimes.com.

LaFrance, Adrienne, and Vann R. Newkirk II. "The Lost History of an American Coup D'État." *Atlantic*, August 12, 2017.

Lam, Andrew. "White Students' Unfair Advantage in Admissions." *New York Times*, January 30, 2017. www.nytimes.com.

Lavelle, Kristen M. *Whitewashing the South: White Memories of Segregation and Civil Rights*. Lanham, MD: Rowman and Littlefield, 2014.

Lebron, Christopher J. *The Making of Black Lives Matter: A Brief History of an Idea*. New York: Oxford University Press, 2017.

Lemann, Nicholas. *Redemption: The Last Battle of the Civil War*. New York: Farrar, Straus and Giroux, 2006.

Leong, Nancy. "Racial Capitalism." *Harvard Law Review* 126, no. 8 (2013): 2151–226.

Lerman, Amy E., and Vesla M. Weaver. *Arresting Citizenship: The Democratic Consequences of American Crime Control*. Chicago: University of Chicago Press, 2014.

Lewis, Amanda E. "There Is No 'Race' in the Schoolyard: Color-Blind Ideology in an (Almost) All-White School." *American Educational Research Journal* 38, no. 4 (2001): 781–811.

Lewis, Paul G., Doris Marie Provine, Monica W. Varsanyi, and Scott H. Decker. "Why Do (Some) City Police Departments Enforce Federal Immigration

Law? Political, Demographic, and Organizational Influences on Local Choices." *Journal of Public Administration Research and Theory* 23, no. 1 (2012): 1–25.

López, Ian Haney. *Dog Whistle Politics: How Coded Racial Appeals Have Reinvented Racism and Wrecked the Middle Class*. New York: Oxford University Press, 2015.

———. *White by Law: The Legal Construction of Race*. New York: NYU Press, 2006.

Lopez Bunyasi, Tehama, and Candis Watts Smith. "Get in Formation: Black Women's Participation in the Women's March on Washington as an Act of Pragmatic Utopianism." *Black Scholar* 48, no. 3 (2018): 4–16.

Lopez Bunyasi, Tehama, and Leah Wright Rigueur. "'Breaking Bad' in Black and White: What Ideological Deviance Can Tell Us about the Construction of 'Authentic' Racial Identities." *Polity* 47, no. 2 (2015): 175–98.

Mai, Chris, and Ram Subramanian. *The Price of Prisons: Examining State Spending Trends, 2010–2015*. New York: Vera Institute of Justice, 2017.

Marable, Manning. *How Capitalism Underdeveloped Black America: Problems in Race, Political Economy, and Society*. Updated ed. Cambridge, MA: South End, 2000.

Martin, Michael T., and Marilyn Yaquinto, eds. *Redress for Historical Injustices in the United States*. Durham, NC: Duke University Press, 2007.

Massey, Douglas S., Jacob S. Rugh, Justin P. Steil, and Len Albright. "Riding the Stagecoach to Hell: A Qualitative Analysis of Racial Discrimination in Mortgage Lending." *City & Community* 15, no. 2 (2016): 118–36.

Masuoka, Natalie, and Jane Junn. *The Politics of Belonging: Race, Public Opinion, and Immigration*. Chicago: University of Chicago Press, 2013.

Mayhew, David R. *Congress: The Electoral Connection*. New Haven, CT: Yale University Press, 1974.

Mayorga-Gallo, Sarah. *Behind the White Picket Fence: Power and Privilege in a Multiethnic Neighborhood*. Chapel Hill: University of North Carolina Press, 2014.

McClain, Dani. "The Rev. William Barber Is Bringing MLK'S Poor People's Campaign Back to Life." *Nation*, May 19, 2017. www.thenation.com.

McDaniel, Eric L., Irfan Nooruddin, and Allyson F. Shortle. "Proud to Be an American? The Changing Relationship of National Pride and Identity." *Journal of Race, Ethnicity and Politics* 1 (2016): 145–76.

McIntosh, Peggy. 1997. "White Privilege and Male Privilege: A Personal Account of Coming to See Correspondences through Work in Women's Studies." In *Critical White Studies: Looking behind the Mirror*, edited by Richard Delgado and Jean Stefancic, 291–99. Philadelphia: Temple University Press. First published 1988, Wellesley College Center for Research on Women Working Paper No. 189.

McKee, Kimberly, and Andy Marra. "An Open Letter: Why Co-opting 'Transracial' in the Case of Rachel Dolezal Is Problematic." *Medium*, June 16, 2015. https://medium.com.

Michener, Jamila. "Policy Feedback in a Racialized Polity." *Policy Studies Journal* (forthcoming).

Mills, Charles W. *The Racial Contract*. Ithaca, NY: Cornell University Press, 1997.

———. "White Ignorance." In *Race and Epistemologies of Ignorance*, edited by Shannon Sullivan and Nancy Tuana, 11–38. Albany: SUNY Press, 2007.

Mosse, George L. "Racism and Nationalism." *Nations and Nationalism* 1, no. 2 (1995): 163–73.

Movement for Black Lives. "Platform." Accessed January 1, 2018. https://policy.m4bl.org.

Mueller, Jennifer C. "Producing Colorblindness: Everyday Mechanisms of White Ignorance." *Social Problems* 64, no. 2 (2017): 219–38.

Murphy, Raymond. *Social Closure: The Theory of Monopolization and Exclusion*. New York: Oxford University Press, 1988.

Murray, Pauli. "The Historical Development of Race Laws in the United States." *Journal of Negro Education* 22, no. 1 (1953): 4–15.

Nelson, Robert K., et al. "Redlining Richmond." Digital Scholarship Lab, University of Richmond. Accessed July 27, 2018. http://dsl.richmond.edu.

New York Civil Liberties Union. "Stop and Frisk Facts." Accessed January 1, 2018. www.nyclu.org.

Nobles, Melissa. *Shades of Citizenship: Race and the Census in Modern Politics*. Stanford, CA: Stanford University Press, 2000.

NPR. "Black Lives Matter Founders Describe 'Paradigm Shift' in the Movement." July 13, 2016. www.npr.org.

Obasogie, Osagie K., and Zachary Newman. "Black Lives Matter and Respectability Politics in Local News Accounts of Officer-Involved Civilian Deaths: An Early Empirical Assessment." *Wisconsin Law Review* 2016, no. 3 (2016): 541–71.

Oliver, Melvin, and Thomas Shapiro. *Black Wealth / White Wealth: A New Perspective on Racial Inequality*. New York: Routledge, 1995.

Olson, Joel. *The Abolition of White Democracy*. Minneapolis: University of Minnesota Press, 2004.

Omi, Michael, and Howard Winant. *Racial Formation in the United States*. 3rd ed. New York: Routledge, 2014.

O'Reilly, Bill. "President Obama and the Race Problem." *Fox News*, July 23, 2013. www.foxnews.com.

Orfield, Gary, and Erica Frankenberg, with Jongyeon Ee and John Kuscera. "Brown at 60: Great Progress, a Long Retreat and an Uncertain Future." The Civil Rights Project, May 15, 2014. https://civilrightsproject.ucla.edu.

Owens, Deirdre Cooper. *Medical Bondage: Race, Gender, and the Origins of American Gynecology.* Athens: University of Georgia Press, 2017.

Pager, Devah. *Marked: Race, Crime, and Finding Work in an Era of Mass Incarceration.* Chicago: University of Chicago Press, 2007.

Pager, Devah, and Hana Shepherd. "The Sociology of Discrimination: Racial Discrimination in Employment, Housing, Credit, and Consumer Markets." *Annual Review of Sociology* 34 (2008): 181–209.

Parker, Theodore. *Ten Sermons of Religion.* Boston: Ticknor and Fields, 1861.

Patten, Eileen. "Racial, Gender Wage Gap Persist in U.S. Despite Some Progress." Pew Research Center, July 1, 2016. www.pewresearch.org.

Payne, Keith. "Weapon Bias: Split-Second Decisions and Unintended Stereotyping." *Current Directions in Psychological Science* 15, no. 6 (2006): 287–91.

Pérez, Efrén O. *Unspoken Politics: Implicit Attitudes and Political Thinking.* New York: Cambridge University Press, 2016.

Phillips, Kimberley L. *Daily Life during African American Migrations.* Santa Barbara, CA: Greenwood, 2012.

Prather, H. Leon. "We Have Taken a City: A Centennial Essay." In *Democracy Betrayed: The Wilmington Race Riot and Its Legacy,* edited by David S. Cecelski and Timothy B. Tyson, 15–42. Chapel Hill: University of North Carolina Press, 1998.

Price, Melanye T. *The Race Whisperer: Barack Obama and the Political Uses of Race.* New York: NYU Press, 2016.

ProCon.org. "State Felon Voting Laws." Accessed November 1, 2018. https://felonvoting.procon.org.

Purdie-Vaughns, Valerie, and David R. Williams. "Stand-Your-Ground Is Losing Ground for Racial Minorities' Health." *Social Science & Medicine* 147, no. 34 (2015): 341–43.

Quandt, Katie Rose. "1 in 13 African-American Adults Prohibited from Voting in the United States." BillMoyers.com, March 24, 2015. http://billmoyers.com.

Queram, Kate Elizabeth. "Greensboro Police Halt Minor Traffic Stops in Response to Racial Disparity Concerns." *News & Record,* November 10, 2015. www.greensboro.com.

Qui, Linda. "Donald Trump's Baseless Claims about the Election Being 'Rigged.'" *PolitiFact,* August 15, 2016. www.politifact.com.

Race 2012. Directed by Phillip Rodriguez. PBS. 323 Projects, 2012. DVD.

Rankine, Claudia. *Citizen: An American Lyric.* Minneapolis: Graywolf, 2014.

———. "The Condition of Black Life Is One of Mourning." In *The Fire This Time: A New Generation Speaks about Race,* edited by Jesmyn Ward, 145–56. New York: Scribner, 2015.

Ransby, Barbara. "Black Lives Matter Is Democracy in Action." *New York Times,* October 22, 2017.

——. *Making All Black Lives Matter: Reimagining Freedom in the Twenty-First Century*. Oakland: University of California Press, 2018.

Reardon, Sean F., and Ann Owens. "60 Years after *Brown*: Trends and Consequences of School Segregation." *Annual Review of Sociology* 40 (2014): 199–218.

Reeves, Richard V. "Stop Pretending You're Not Rich." *New York Times*, June 10, 2017. www.nytimes.com.

Rickford, Russell. "Black Lives Matter toward a Modern Practice of Mass Struggle." *New Labor Forum* 25, no. 1 (2016): 34–42.

Roberts, Dorothy E. *Killing the Black Body: Race, Reproduction, and the Meaning of Liberty*. New York: Vintage Books, 1999.

Robinson, Randall. *The Debt: What America Owes Blacks*. New York: Dutton, 1999.

Ross, Janell, and Wesley Lowery. "Turning Away from Street Protests, Black Lives Matter Tries a New Tactic in the Age of Trump." *Washington Post*, May 4, 2017. www.washingtonpost.com.

Rothstein, Richard. *The Color of Law: A Forgotten History of How Our Government Segregated America*. New York: Liveright, 2017.

Rugh, Jacob S., Len Albright, and Douglas S. Massey. "Race, Space, and Cumulative Disadvantage: A Case Study of the Subprime Lending Collapse." *Social Problems* 62, no. 2 (2015): 186–218.

Satcher, David, George E. Fryer, Jessica McCann, Adewale Troutman, Steven H. Woolf, and George Rust. "What If We Were Equal? A Comparison of the Black-White Mortality Gap in 1960 and 2000." *Health Affairs* 24, no. 2 (2005): 459–64.

Schnacke, Timothy R., Michael R. Jones, and Dorian M. Wilderman. "Increasing Court-Appearance Rates and Other Benefits of Live-Caller Telephone Court-Date Reminders: The Jefferson County, Colorado, FTA Pilot Project and Resulting Court Date Notification Program." *Court Review* 48 (2012): 86–95.

Schneider, Anne, and Helen Ingram. "Social Construction of Target Populations: Implications for Politics and Policy." *American Political Science Review* 87, no. 2 (1993): 334–47.

Schram, Sanford F., Joe Brian Soss, and Richard Carl Fording, eds. *Race and the Politics of Welfare Reform*. Ann Arbor: University of Michigan Press, 2010.

Schwartz, Ian. "CNN's Don Lemon: Bill O'Reilly's Criticism of Black Community 'Doesn't Go Far Enough.'" *Real Clear Politics*, July 27, 2013. www.realclearpolitics.com.

Sentencing Project. "Criminal Justice Facts." Accessed November 1, 2018. www.sentencingproject.org.

Shelby, Tommie. "Two Conceptions of Black Nationalism: Martin Delany on the Meaning of Black Political Solidarity." *Political Theory* 31, no. 5 (2003): 664–92.

Sides, John, Michael Tesler, and Lynn Vavreck. "The 2016 US Election: How Trump Lost and Won." *Journal of Democracy* 28, no. 2 (2017): 34–44.

Smith, Candis Watts. "Black Immigrants in the U.S. Face Big Challenges. Will African Americans Rally to Their Side?" *Monkey Cage* (blog), *Washington Post*, September 18, 2017. www.washingtonpost.com.

Smith, Candis Watts, and Sarah Mayorga-Gallo. "The New Principle-Policy Gap: How Diversity Ideology Subverts Diversity Initiatives." *Sociological Perspectives* 60, no. 5 (2017): 889–911.

Smith, Chery, and Lois W. Morton. "Rural Food Deserts: Low-Income Perspectives on Food Access in Minnesota and Iowa." *Journal of Nutrition Education and Behavior* 41, no. 3 (2009): 176–87.

Smith, Kelly, and John Weis. "Dividing Durham: HOLC's Survey of the Bull City." Main Street, Carolina, University of North Carolina Libraries. Accessed June 2, 2017. http://mainstreet.lib.unc.edu.

Sobel, Richard. *The High Cost of "Free" Photo Voter Identification Cards.* Cambridge, MA: Charles Hamilton Houston Institute for Race & Justice, Harvard Law School, 2014.

Sue, Derald Wing. *Microaggressions in Everyday Life: Race, Gender, and Sexual Orientation.* Hoboken, NJ: Wiley, 2010.

Taylor, James Lance. *Black Nationalism in the United States: From Malcolm X to Barack Obama.* Boulder, CO: Lynne Rienner, 2010.

Taylor, Keeanga-Yamahtta. *From #BlackLivesMatter to Black Liberation.* Chicago: Haymarket Books, 2016.

———. Introduction to *How We Get Free: Black Feminism and the Combahee River Collective*, edited by Keeanga-Yamahtta Taylor, 1–14. Chicago: Haymarket Books, 2017.

Telles, Edward. *Pigmentocracies: Ethnicity, Race, and Color in Latin America.* Chapel Hill: University of North Carolina Press, 2014.

Theoharis, Jeanne. *A More Beautiful and Terrible History: The Uses and Misuses of Civil Rights History.* Boston: Beacon, 2018.

Thomas, Dexter. "Why Everyone's Saying 'Black Girls Are Magic.'" *Los Angeles Times*, September 9, 2015. www.latimes.com.

Tom, Pamela. "Criminal Punishment and Politics: Elected Judges Take Tougher Stance Prior to Elections." *Haas Newsroom* (Haas School of Business, University of California, Berkeley), October 18, 2012. http://newsroom.haas .berkeley.edu.

Trounstine, Jessica. *Segregation by Design: Local Politics and Inequality in American Cities.* New York: Cambridge University Press, 2018.

Turner, Cory, Reema Khrais, Tim Lloyd, Alexandra Olgin, Laura Isensee, Becky Vevea, and Dan Carsen. "Why America's Schools Have a Money Problem." National Public Radio, April 18, 2016. www.npr.org.

Upkins, Dennis R. "Denying Racism and Other Forms of Gaslighting." Mental Health Matters, August 24, 2016. http://mental-health-matters.com.

Urahn, Susan K., Erin Currier, Dana Elliott, Lauren Wechsler, Denise Wilson, and Daniel Colbert. *Pursuing the American Dream: Economic Mobility across Generations.* Washington, DC: Pew Charitable Trusts, 2012.

US Department of Justice. *Investigation of the Baltimore City Police Department.* Washington, DC: US Department of Justice, 2016.

——. *Investigation of the Ferguson Police Department.* Washington, DC: US Department of Justice, 2015.

US Department of Justice and United States Attorney's Office, Northern District of Illinois. *Investigation of the Chicago Police Department.* Washington, DC: US Department of Justice, 2017.

Useem, Ruth Hill, and Richard D. Downie. "Third-Culture Kids." *Today's Education* 65, no. 3 (1976): 103–5.

Vedantam, Shankar. "The 'Thumbprint of the Culture': Implicit Bias and Police Shootings." *Hidden Brain: A Conversation about Life's Unseen Pattern* (podcast), NPR, June 5, 2017. www.npr.org.

Warikoo, Natasha K. *The Diversity Bargain: And Other Dilemmas of Race, Admissions, and Meritocracy at Elite Universities.* Chicago: University of Chicago Press, 2016.

Washington, Reginald. "The Freedman's Savings and Trust Company and African American Genealogical Research." *Federal Records and African American History* 29, no. 2 (1997). www.archives.gov.

White, Clair. "Incarcerating Youth with Mental Health Problems: A Focus on the Intersection of Race, Ethnicity, and Mental Illness." *Youth Violence and Juvenile Justice* 14, no. 4 (2016): 426–47.

Whiteis, David G. "Hospital and Community Characteristics in Closures of Urban Hospitals, 1980–87." *Public Health Reports* 107, no. 4 (1992): 409–16.

Wilkerson, Isabel. "Where Do We Go from Here?" In *The Fire This Time*, edited by Jesmyn Ward, 59–62. New York: Simon and Schuster, 2016.

Williams, Sheneka M., and Eric A. Houck. "The Life and Death of Desegregation Policy in Wake County Public School System and Charlotte-Mecklenburg Schools." *Education and Urban Society* 45, no. 5 (2013): 571–88.

Wilson, Darren. Testimony to grand jury in *State of Missouri v. Darren Wilson.* November 2014. www.documentcloud.org.

Wilson, Valerie, and William M. Rodgers III. *Black-White Wage Gaps Expand with Rising Wage Inequality.* Washington, DC: Economic Policy Institute, 2016.

Winter, Jana, and Sharon Weinberger. "The FBI's New U.S. Terrorist Threat: 'Black Identity Extremists.'" *Foreign Policy*, October 6, 2017. https://foreign policy.com.

Winters, Joseph R. *Hope Draped in Black: Race, Melancholy, and the Agony of Progress*. Durham, NC: Duke University Press, 2016.

Wright, Ronald F. "How Prosecutor Elections Fail Us." *Ohio State Journal of Criminal Law* 6 (2008): 581–610.

Yancy, George. "Clevis Headley." In *On Race: 34 Conversations in a Time of Crisis*, edited by George Yancy, 279–91. New York: Oxford University Press, 2017.

Young, Vernetta. "Demythologizing the 'Criminalblackman': The Carnival Mirror." In *The Many Colors of Crime: Inequalities in Race, Ethnicity, and Crime in America*, edited by Ruth D. Peterson, Lauren J. Krivo, and John Hagan, 54–66. New York: NYU Press, 2006.

Index

Abele, Julian, 141

Abrams, Stacey, 223

active listening, 203

activism. *See* commitment to action

affirmations. *See* commitment to action

affirmative action, 40, 49–51, 70–71, 133, 148–49, 230n2. *See also* common sense revisited (definitions); discrimination; diversity; reverse discrimination

All Lives Matter, 7–10, 160–62, 163. *See also* epistemology of ignorance; gaslighting

alt-right movement, 4–5, 96, 219. *See also* racial euphemisms

American dream: use of term, 51–52; culture of poverty and, 66–67; economic mobility and, 28–29, 51–52, 66–67, 110; housing and, 25–29; immigrants and, 59; meritocracy and, 11; ubiquity of, 11–12; "un-American" activism and, 137–41; white privilege and, 110. *See also* American mythology (definitions); capitalism; common sense revisited (definitions); meritocracy

American Indians, 8, 20, 92, 93, 94

American mythology (definitions): use of term, 48; American dream and, 51–52;

meritocracy and, 82–83. *See also under specific terms*

André (mini person), 158

anecdotes: use of term, 14

anti-Black racism: use of term, 12–13, 44; Black women and, 87–88; capitalism and, 55–56; dehumanization and, 10–12, 68–69; economic mobility and, 44, 55–56; felon disenfranchisement and, 178; gender and, 87–88, 136–37; hate crimes and, 135–37; health care system and, 44; intersectionality and, 56, 81; misogynoir, 87–88; Movement for Black Lives and, 10–13, 43–44, 167–69, 218; patriotism and, 117, 140, 167–69; sexuality and, 136–37; staying woke and, 117, 140, 167–69. *See also* racism

antiracism: use of term, 53, 69, 145–48, 164; affirmative action and, 50–51; being woke and, 12, 71, 80, 95, 100, 115, 145–48, 164, 167–69; children and, 157–59; colorblindness and, 148–50, 156, 157–59; electoral politics and, 150–57, 223; epistemology of ignorance and, 74–75, 160–62; history of antiracist social movements, 137–40, 220–24; how to use this book and, 3–6, 11–12,

ABOUT THE AUTHORS

Tehama Lopez Bunyasi is Assistant Professor of Conflict Analysis and Resolution at George Mason University.

Candis Watts Smith is Associate Professor of Political Science and African American Studies at The Pennsylvania State University. She is the author of *Black Mosaic: The Politics of Black Pan-Ethnic Diversity* (also available from NYU Press) and coeditor of *Black Politics in Transition: Immigration, Suburbanization, and Gentrification.*